NEW DIRECTIONS

AN INTEGRATED APPROACH
TO READING, WRITING,
AND CRITICAL THINKING

NEW DIRECTIONS

AN INTEGRATED APPROACH TO READING, WRITING, AND CRITICAL THINKING

Peter S. Gardner
Berklee College of Music

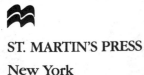

ST. MARTIN'S PRESS
New York

Sponsoring editor: Darcy Meeker
Managing editor: Patricia Mansfield Phelan
Project editor: Diane Schadoff
Production supervisor: Scott Lavelle
Art director: Lucy Krikorian
Text design: Lee Goldstein
Graphics: Huron Valley Graphics, Inc.
Cover design: Lucy Krikorian

Library of Congress Catalog Number: 94-80104

Manufactured in the United States of America.

0 9 8 7 6
f e d c b a

For information, write:
St. Martin's Press, Inc.
175 Fifth Avenue
New York, NY 10010

ISBN: 0-312-11216-5

Acknowledgments

Page 4, Gary Althen, "American Values and Assumptions" from *American Ways: A Guide for
Foreigners in the United States.* Copyright © 1988 by Gary Althen. Reprinted with the permission of Intercultural Press, Inc.

Page 24, Lisa Davis, "Where Do We Stand?," *In Health* (September/October 1990). Copyright ©
1990 by Hippocrates Partners. Reprinted with the permission of the publishers.

Page 34, Premchand, "A Coward" from *Deliverance and Other Stories,* translated by David Rubin
(Penguin Books India Pvt., Ltd., 1988). Reprinted with the permission of the publishers and
translator.

Page 43, Deborah Tannen, "Sex, Sighs, and Conversation" from *You Just Don't Understand.*
Originally appeared in *The Boston Globe,* August 5, 1990. Copyright © 1990 by Deborah
Tannen. Reprinted with the permission of William Morrow & Company, Inc., Virago Press, Ltd.
and International Creative Management.

Acknowledgments and copyrights are continued at the back of the book on pages
279–280, which constitute an extension of the copyright page.

To my mother and father,
who've taught me how to listen

CONTENTS

Preface   xxi

CHAPTER ONE
CROSS-CULTURAL COMMUNICATION   1
Reading Skill: Identifying Main Ideas and Supporting Details

    Brief Quotes   2

    Prereading Activities   3

GARY ALTHEN, American Values and Assumptions   4

    A foreign student adviser analyzes major cultural patterns in the United States.

    Reading Journal   14

    Meaning and Technique   14

        Main Ideas   14

        Well-Written Paragraphs   15

        Supporting Details   16

    Drawing Inferences   17

    Vocabulary: Negative Prefixes   18

    Vocabulary: In Context   19

    Discussion and Debate   20

        Preconceptions and Stereotypes   20

    Writing Activities   22

        Objective Description vs. Value Judgment   22

    Prereading Activities   23

LISA DAVIS, Where Do We Stand?   24

    A journalist describes cross-cultural differences in the use of personal space.

    Reading Journal   28

Meaning and Technique 28

Drawing Inferences 29

Vocabulary: Idioms 30

Vocabulary: In Context 30

Discussion and Debate 31

Writing Activities 32

  Compare-and-Contrast Signals 32

Prereading Activities 33

PREMCHAND, A Coward 34

In this short story, an Indian writer focuses on the lives of two university students from different castes who fall in love.

Reading Journal 41

Vocabulary: Figures of Speech 41

Additional Readings 43

DEBORAH TANNEN, Sex, Sighs, and Conversation: Why Men and Women Can't Communicate 43

A linguistics professor explores differences in the ways females and males use language.

JOHN GODFREY SAXE, The Blind Men and the Elephant: A Hindu Fable 46

Six blind men argue about what an elephant most resembles.

The Adjustment Process in a New Culture 47

A graph illustrates the five common stages of cultural adjustment.

Making Connections 48

CHAPTER TWO

STEREOTYPING AND DISCRIMINATION 50

Reading Skill: Identifying a Writer's Purpose and Tone

Brief Quotes 51

Prereading Activities 52

MARTIN LUTHER KING, JR., I Have a Dream 53

In this famous speech, a prominent civil rights activist passionately argues the need for racial equality in the United States.

Reading Journal 56

Meaning and Technique   57
   Audience   57
   Purpose   57
Drawing Inferences   58
   Tone   58
Vocabulary: Figures of Speech   61
Vocabulary: In Context   62
Discussion and Debate   63
Writing Activities   63

Prereading Activities   64

Barbara Kantrowitz, Striking a Nerve   65

A journalist discusses sexual harassment in the United States.
Reading Journal   73
Meaning and Technique   74
   Tone   74
Drawing Inferences   75
Vocabulary: Verb and Noun Forms   75
Vocabulary: In Context   77
Discussion and Debate   77
Writing Activities   79

Prereading Activities   79

Jeanne Wakatsuki Houston and James D. Houston, It Cannot Be Helped   80

A Japanese American family is placed in a California internment camp during World War II.
Reading Journal   87
Vocabulary: Phrasal Verbs   87

Additional Readings   89

Jonathan Kaufman, Eleven Words That Cast the Power of Bigotry on Honeymoon Couple   89

A Jewish writer describes a personal encounter with anti-Semitism.

Maya Angelou, Caged Bird   92

A poet vividly portrays the lives of two birds: one that is kept in a cage and one that is free to do what it wants.

Jules Feiffer, Cartoon　93

　A cartoonist sheds light on the nature of prejudice.

　Making Connections　93

CHAPTER THREE

GENDER ROLES　95

Reading Skills: Summarizing and Paraphrasing

　Brief Quotes　96

　Prereading Activities　97

Hamilton McCubbin and Barbara Blum Dahl, Sex Roles　98

　*Two sociologists analyze the reasons females and males think and
　act in different ways.*

　Reading Journal　105

　Meaning and Technique　105

　　Summarizing　106

　　Paraphrasing　107

　Drawing Inferences　108

　Vocabulary: Word Parts　109

　Vocabulary: In Context　111

　Discussion and Debate　112

　Writing Activities　113

　Prereading Activities　113

Susan Chira, New Realities Fight Old Images of Mother　114

　*A journalist examines the changing roles of mothers in the United
　States.*

　Reading Journal　122

　Meaning and Technique　122

　Drawing Inferences　124

　Vocabulary: By Theme　125

　Vocabulary: In Context　126

　Discussion and Debate　126

　Writing Activities　127

　Prereading Activities　128

Noel Perrin, The Androgynous Male　129

　*A professor of English discusses "masculine" stereotypes and the
　ways he has cultivated "feminine" qualities in his life.*

Reading Journal   132

Vocabulary: Parts of Speech   132

Additional Readings   133

CHARLES PERRAULT, Cinderella   133

> *A young woman escapes a life of drudgery by marrying a handsome prince.*

CAROL BARKALOW, Women Have What It Takes   138

> *An army officer argues that women should be allowed to engage in military combat.*

WARREN FARRELL,

Men Have the Power—Why Would They Want to Change?   140

> *A psychologist tells the story of a male lawyer who, in devoting his life to his career, becomes a stranger to his wife, his children, and himself.*

CATHY GUISEWITE, Cartoon   145

> *A cartoonist asks whether it is possible to live in a society without gender stereotypes.*

Making Connections   145

CHAPTER FOUR

WORK   147

Reading Skill: Appreciating Figurative Language

Brief Quotes   148

Prereading Activities   148

RUTH SIDEL, The New American Dreamers   149

> *A sociologist examines the career goals of young women in the United States.*

Reading Journal   154

Meaning and Technique   154

   Figures of Speech   154

Drawing Inferences   156

Vocabulary: Connotations   157

Vocabulary: In Context   158

Discussion and Debate   159

Writing Activities   160

Prereading Activities　161

PATRICK FENTON, Confessions of a Working Stiff　162

A cargo loader for an international airline describes one day at his job.

Reading Journal　168

Meaning and Technique　168

Figures of Speech　169

Drawing Inferences　170

Tone　170

Vocabulary: Figures of Speech　171

Vocabulary: In Context　172

Discussion and Debate　173

Writing Activities　174

Prereading Activities　175

TOM MASHBERG,

Worker Poll Shows Family, Fringes Gain Favor　177

A journalist discusses what Americans like and dislike about their jobs.

Reading Journal　181

Vocabulary: Idioms　181

Additional Readings　182

WILLIAM E. BARRETT, Señor Payroll　182

In this short story, an American author humorously portrays the relationship between the management and employees of a Spanish gas company.

MARGE PIERCY, To Be of Use　185

A poet describes the type of work she likes best.

P. STEINER, Cartoon　186

A cartoonist pokes fun at workaholics.

Making Connections　187

CHAPTER FIVE

EDUCATION　188

Reading Skill: Guessing the Meaning of Unfamiliar Words and Expressions from Their Context

Brief Quotes　189

Prereading Activities   190

JOHN HOLT, School Is Bad for Children   191

A teacher discusses the problems with American schools and his suggestions for improvement.

Reading Journal   196

Meaning and Technique   196

Drawing Inferences   196

Vocabulary: Synonyms   197

Vocabulary: In Context   198

Discussion and Debate   199

Writing Activities   200

Prereading Activities   201

CAROL SIMONS,

They Get by with a Lot of Help from Their Kyoiku Mamas   202

An American journalist analyzes the effects of competition on Japanese students and the roles Japanese mothers play in educating their children.

Reading Journal   210

Meaning and Technique   210

Drawing Inferences   211

   Tone   211

Vocabulary: Definitions of Terms   211

Vocabulary: In Context   212

Discussion and Debate   213

Writing Activities   214

Prereading Activities   215

NICHOLAS GAGE, The Teacher Who Changed My Life   217

A writer describes the teacher who inspired him to pursue a career in journalism.

Reading Journal   221

Vocabulary: Guessing Meaning from Context   221

Additional Readings   224

KATE STONE LOMBARDI, Reading, Writing, and Arithmetic and, Now, Right and Wrong   224

A journalist explores a current educational debate in the United States: whether or not moral values should be taught in public schools.

Coyote and the Crying Song   228
In this Hopi folktale, a coyote tries to learn a song from a dove.
CHARLES M. SCHULZ, **Cartoon**   230
A cartoonist jokes about a student's notion of a good essay.
Making Connections   231

Appendix A
THE WRITING PROCESS   233

Appendix B
OUTLINING   250

Appendix C
SUMMARIZING   254

Appendix D
PARAPHRASING   257

Appendix E
TRANSITIONAL WORDS AND PHRASES   260

Appendix F
CONTEXT CLUES   262

Appendix G
EVALUATING A PIECE OF WRITING   268

Glossary   269
Index   281

RHETORICAL CONTENTS

The first part of this table of contents arranges the nonfiction selections according to their dominant rhetorical modes. The second part arranges the selections by genre (autobiography, fiction, and poetry).

RHETORICAL MODES

Narration

JEANNE WAKATSUKI HOUSTON AND JAMES D. HOUSTON,
It Cannot Be Helped   80

WARREN FARRELL,
Men Have the Power—Why Would They Want to Change?   140

PATRICK FENTON, Confessions of a Working Stiff   162

NICHOLAS GAGE, The Teacher Who Changed My Life   217

Description

LISA DAVIS, Where Do We Stand?   24

JEANNE WAKATSUKI HOUSTON AND JAMES D. HOUSTON,
It Cannot Be Helped   80

HAMILTON MCCUBBIN AND BARBARA BLUM DAHL, Sex Roles   98

SUSAN CHIRA, New Realities Fight Old Images of Mother   114

PATRICK FENTON, Confessions of a Working Stiff   162

JOHN HOLT, School Is Bad for Children   191

CAROL SIMONS,
They Get by with a Lot of Help from Their Kyoiku Mamas   202

NICHOLAS GAGE, The Teacher Who Changed My Life   217

Illustration

GARY ALTHEN, American Values and Assumptions   4

LISA DAVIS, Where Do We Stand?   24

DEBORAH TANNEN, Sex, Sighs, and Conversation   43

BARBARA KANTROWITZ, Striking a Nerve   65

HAMILTON MCCUBBIN AND BARBARA BLUM DAHL, Sex Roles   98

SUSAN CHIRA, New Realities Fight Old Images of Mother   114

RUTH SIDEL, The New American Dreamers   149

PATRICK FENTON, Confessions of a Working Stiff   162

TOM MASHBERG, Worker Poll Shows Family, Fringes Gain Favor   177

JOHN HOLT, School Is Bad for Children   191

CAROL SIMONS,
They Get by with a Lot of Help from Their Kyoiku Mamas   202

Division and Classification

GARY ALTHEN, American Values and Assumptions   4

DEBORAH TANNEN, Sex, Sighs, and Conversation   43

BARBARA KANTROWITZ, Striking a Nerve   65

HAMILTON MCCUBBIN AND BARBARA BLUM DAHL, Sex Roles   98

SUSAN CHIRA, New Realities Fight Old Images of Mother   114

Comparison and Contrast

GARY ALTHEN, American Values and Assumptions   4

LISA DAVIS, Where Do We Stand?   24

DEBORAH TANNEN, Sex, Sighs, and Conversation 43

HAMILTON MCCUBBIN AND BARBARA BLUM DAHL, Sex Roles 98

NOEL PERRIN, The Androgynous Male 129

SUSAN CHIRA, New Realities Fight Old Images of Mother 114

CAROL BARKALOW, Women Have What It Takes 138

WARREN FARRELL,
Men Have the Power—Why Would They Want to Change? 140

RUTH SIDEL, The New American Dreamers 149

TOM MASHBERG,
Worker Poll Shows Family, Fringes Gain Favor 177

CAROL SIMONS,
They Get by with a Lot of Help from Their Kyoiku Mamas 202

KATE STONE LOMBARDI, Reading, Writing, and Arithmetic and,
    Now, Right and Wrong 224

Cause and Effect

DEBORAH TANNEN, Sex, Sighs, and Conversation 43

MARTIN LUTHER KING, JR., I Have a Dream 53

JONATHAN KAUFMAN, Eleven Words That Cast the Power of
    Bigotry on Honeymoon Couple 89

BARBARA KANTROWITZ, Striking a Nerve 65

NOEL PERRIN, The Androgynous Male 129

WARREN FARRELL,
Men Have the Power—Why Would They Want to Change? 140

PATRICK FENTON, Confessions of a Working Stiff 162

JOHN HOLT, School Is Bad for Children 191

CAROL SIMONS,
They Get by with a Lot of Help from Their Kyoiku Mamas 202

NICHOLAS GAGE,
The Teacher Who Changed My Life 217

Process Analysis

NOEL PERRIN, The Androgynous Male 129

WARREN FARRELL,
Men Have the Power—Why Would They Want to Change? 140

PATRICK FENTON, Confessions of a Working Stiff 162

JOHN HOLT, School Is Bad for Children 191

NICHOLAS GAGE, The Teacher Who Changed My Life 217

Definition

GARY ALTHEN, American Values and Assumptions 4

MARTIN LUTHER KING, JR., I Have a Dream 53

BARBARA KANTROWITZ, Striking a Nerve 65

SUSAN CHIRA, New Realities Fight Old Images of Mother 114

NOEL PERRIN, The Androgynous Male 129

WARREN FARRELL,
Men Have the Power—Why Would They Want to Change? 140

RUTH SIDEL, The New American Dreamers 149

CAROL SIMONS,
They Get by with a Lot of Help from Their Kyoiku Mamas 202

KATE STONE LOMBARDI, Reading, Writing, and Arithmetic and,
Now, Right and Wrong 224

Argument and Persuasion

DEBORAH TANNEN, Sex, Sighs, and Conversation 43

MARTIN LUTHER KING, JR., I Have a Dream 53

NOEL PERRIN, The Androgynous Male 129

CAROL BARKALOW, Women Have What It Takes 138

JOHN HOLT, School Is Bad for Children 191

KATE STONE LOMBARDI, Reading, Writing, and Arithmetic and,
Now, Right and Wrong 224

GENRES

Autobiography

JEANNE WAKATSUKI HOUSTON AND JAMES D. HOUSTON,
It Cannot Be Helped   80

JONATHAN KAUFMAN, Eleven Words That Cast the Power of
Bigotry on Honeymoon Couple   89

NOEL PERRIN, The Androgynous Male   129

CAROL BARKALOW, Women Have What It Takes   138

PATRICK FENTON, Confessions of a Working Stiff   162

NICHOLAS GAGE, The Teacher Who Changed My Life   217

Fiction

PREMCHAND, A Coward   34

CHARLES PERRAULT, Cinderella   133

WILLIAM E. BARRETT, Señor Payroll   182

Coyote and the Crying Song   228

Poetry

JOHN GODFREY SAXE,
The Blind Men and the Elephant: A Hindu Fable   46

MAYA ANGELOU, Caged Bird   92

MARGE PIERCY, To Be of Use   185

PREFACE

AUDIENCE

New Directions: An Integrated Approach to Reading, Writing, and Critical Thinking is designed for advanced ESL/EFL students who are preparing for study at an English-speaking college or university. The book can also be used by those wishing to improve their English for personal and/or professional purposes. An interactive, content-based reader, *New Directions* is geared toward helping nonnative speakers of English meet the demands of reading and writing assignments in undergraduate courses. It is intended to serve as the primary text in a preuniversity ESL/EFL class that focuses on reading and writing, and it can be used in both intensive and nonintensive settings. The book is also appropriate for ESL students and native speakers of English in college courses that stress the connection between reading and writing.

OVERVIEW

New Directions is a thematically based, integrated skills reader designed to bridge the gap between ESL and college content courses by providing reading and writing assignments representative of *real* college courses. Many nonnative speakers of English experience a large leap when moving from the relatively short readings in most ESL/EFL texts to the long selections in college texts for native English speakers. To help prepare students for the large amount of complex reading they will be doing in college courses, *New Directions* provides a number of long, challenging college-level readings and activities that encourage holistic and synthetic reading strategies. The book focuses on the higher-order cognitive skills of inference, interpretation, evaluation, synthesis, and application that students will need in order to think and write critically about the substance, meaning, and purpose of readings in their college courses.

Rather than emphasizing "skill areas" in isolation, *New Directions* stresses the critical reading strategies that will help students interact with texts and construct meanings. Although the book is content-based, it does introduce one key reading strategy per chapter—practiced within the context of the chapter readings. (The strategies in the first four chapters might better be called "reading/writing" strategies, as they apply equally to both processes.) *New Directions* thus provides an alternative to the large number of tightly controlled, skill-focused texts. Through extended, integrated reading, writing, speaking, and listening activities, students learn to generate hypotheses, argue, analyze critically, distinguish between different types of writing and purposes for reading, identify a writer's point of view and tone, interpret a writer's meaning inferentially as well as literally, discriminate between opinion and fact, detect fallacies in reasoning, reach conclusions and judgments based on supportable criteria, and propose new ideas.

As the title suggests, *New Directions* challenges students to expand their horizons—to question their own cultural preconceptions and to reinterpret old habits, views, and biases (their own as well as those of others). Through its multicultural readings and stress on the social and cultural forces shaping human experience, students gain an appreciation of cultural diversity. Thinking about old things in new ways and new things in new ways, students learn about themselves and the world around them.

IMPORTANT FEATURES OF THE BOOK

- Thematically organized chapters with multiple readings, allowing students to explore subjects in depth from a variety of perspectives
- Development of advanced thinking skills—inference, interpretation, evaluation, synthesis, and application
- Acquisition of reading and writing strategies in interrelated and realistic contexts
- Focus on reading skills within the context of chapter selections—identifying main ideas and supporting details, identifying a writer's purpose and tone, summarizing and paraphrasing, appreciating figurative language, and guessing the meaning of unknown words and expressions from their context
- Large number of authentic multicultural readings, including textbook excerpts, articles, essays, short stories, and poems
- Questions that encourage critical thinking and student interaction with the content of readings
- Variety of writing activities, including journal entries; short, structured exercises; and essay assignments

- In-depth vocabulary development in realistic contexts
- Collaborative tasks, including interviews, debates, role plays, and group presentations
- Appendices that explore the writing process, outlining, summarizing, paraphrasing, transitional words and phrases, context clues, and evaluating a piece of writing
- A glossary explaining the literary, rhetorical, and grammatical terms used in the book
- An Instructor's Manual providing detailed information

READINGS

New Directions contains twenty-five authentic college-level readings of varying length. The selections are interdisciplinary—from such fields as sociology, linguistics, psychology, and international relations—and include excerpts from college texts, newspaper and magazine articles, personal essays, short stories, folktales, and poems. In addition, there are four cartoons. Provocative and challenging, the readings are diverse in subject matter, aim, voice, style, tone, rhetorical technique, and degree of complexity/abstraction and represent a balance of descriptive, narrative, expository, and argumentative writing. Most of the pieces are written by contemporary American authors of different ethnic backgrounds, including African, Asian, Greek, and Jewish, and three are by writers from India, France, and England. (For lack of a more precise term, the word *American* is used throughout the book to refer to someone from the United States.) A conscious effort has been made to include an equal number of female and male writers. Although most of the selections focus on cultural patterns in the United States, several explore prominent values, beliefs, and practices of other countries. Throughout the book, students are encouraged to compare the cultural patterns discussed in the readings with those of their native country. All of the readings have biographical headnotes and footnotes. (Footnotes include words and phrases that would be difficult for students to understand from the context or find in a dictionary. Footnotes also explain cultural/historical references they would unlikely be familiar with.)

ORGANIZATION

New Directions is divided into five thematically based chapters, each introducing one important reading skill. The chapter topics were selected because of their relevance and interest to most students. The skills were chosen because of their stress on the comprehension of both literal and nonliteral (inferential) meaning.

The chapters are based on the following topics and reading skills:

- Chapter One: "Cross-Cultural Communication" (skill: identifying main ideas and supporting details)
- Chapter Two: "Stereotyping and Discrimination" (skill: identifying a writer's purpose and tone)
- Chapter Three: "Gender Roles" (skills: summarizing and paraphrasing)
- Chapter Four: "Work" (skill: appreciating figurative language)
- Chapter Five: "Education" (skill: guessing the meaning of unfamiliar words and expressions from their context)

Each chapter begins with a brief introduction describing the major theme of the chapter, the central questions raised in the readings, and the content of each selection. There is also a list of short quotations relating to major issues raised in the chapter.

Each chapter has three core readings of various length (with a balance of academic pieces, personal essays, and short stories) and three or four additional short selections (in most cases, an article, poem, and cartoon). The first two core readings in each chapter have a full selection of pre- and postreading activities. The third core reading has only prereading activities, a reading journal entry, and a vocabulary exercise. The additional readings have no activities. These extra selections—which can be read in or out of class—allow students to explore issues in greater depth and apply the skill learned earlier in the chapter.

The pedagogical apparatus for the first two readings in each chapter includes the following sections: "Prereading Activities," "Reading Journal," "Meaning and Technique," "Drawing Inferences," "Vocabulary," "Discussion and Debate," and "Writing Activities." The section "Making Connections" appears at the end of each chapter.

- Prereading Activities

    In this section, students write journal entries about topics relating to the readings, make predictions about the content of the selections, respond to brief quotations, agree and disagree with statements, and discuss issues in small groups. These activities encourage students to examine their own views, helping them better understand, analyze, and take issue with perspectives reflected in the readings.

- Reading Journal

    After reading a selection, students write an entry in their reading journal. These entries include discussions of specific topics relating to the readings, interpretations, points of agreement and disagreement with the authors, likes and dislikes, and personal experiences and observations.

- Meaning and Technique

    These activities help students understand the main ideas in the readings and the manner in which they were written. In this section, students learn to think critically about such aspects of writing as purpose, audience, point of view, tone, style, and rhetorical strategy. The reading skill introduced in each chapter is taught and practiced in this and the following section.

- Drawing Inferences

    Whereas the previous section focuses on understanding meaning literally, this section helps students interpret meaning inferentially. The activities in this part encourage students to read between the lines—to use the hints and suggestions a writer provides to understand the unstated meaning of a passage. By focusing on the author's ideas and their own responses and experiences, students are drawn into the fabric of the text.

- Vocabulary

    This section helps students develop their vocabulary by using words and expressions in realistic contexts. Rather than just filling in blanks and matching words with definitions, students actively use vocabulary in formal and informal contexts. The vocabulary exercises include work with phrasal verbs, other types of idioms, parts of speech, synonyms, context clues, word parts (prefixes, roots, suffixes), paraphrasing, figures of speech, and denotations and connotations.

- Discussion and Debate

    These activities help expand the critical context of the readings by encouraging students to search for connections between the ideas in the selections and their own lives, to take issue with the opinions expressed by the authors (and by classmates), and to interact with sources of knowledge outside the classroom. The activities in this section focus on cross-cultural similarities and differences and include group discussions, debates, role plays, oral reports, interviews, library research, and community-related projects, such as trips to stores, museums, and schools.

- Writing Activities

    These activities consist of two short writing exercises, such as summaries, case studies, letters, and paragraphs written in different tones, and longer assignments, including essays, narratives, speeches, and research papers. One of the short exercises is always collaborative. Although the focus of the activities in this section is on expository and argumentative writing, students have ample opportunity to write in descriptive and narrative modes. The writing assignments engage various rhetorical strategies, and most are based on personal experience and observation.

- Making Connections

    This section, appearing at the end of each chapter, includes activities that can be used for both writing assignments and class discussions. The activi-

ties help students to synthesize the information presented in the chapter—
to combine facts, ideas, and beliefs to form their own opinions and judgments about issues. In this section, students compare and contrast chapter
readings and their own experiences and observations. In addition to review-
ing the main ideas of the chapter selections, students practice the reading
skill learned in the chapter by applying it to the additional readings.

A Note to the Teacher

Because the subjects and skills in this book are not presented in any
particular sequence, the chapters can be read in *any* order.

ACKNOWLEDGMENTS

New Directions would not have been possible without the help and support
of many people. I would like to thank the editorial and production staff at St.
Martin's Press: Naomi Silverman for her faith in the project; Diane Schadoff,
project editor, for her endless patience; Patricia Mansfield Phelan, managing
editor; Janice Wiggins, marketing manager; and especially Carl Whithaus for
his encouragement and wise counsel. I would also like to thank Fred
Courtright and Beth Mullen for their efforts to secure the permissions for the
book.

I am particularly indebted to my colleagues Sally Blazar, Walter Harp,
Joseph Coroniti, David Loewus, and Melissa Monroe for their comradeship
and many helpful comments and suggestions. My thanks also go to the follow-
ing reviewers for their thoughtful criticism: Helen Fragiadakis, Contra Costa
College; Sally Gearhart, Santa Rosa Junior College; Joan Gregg, New York City
Technical College, CUNY; Denis Hall, New Hampshire College; George
Krikorian, Boston University; John N. Miller, Normandale Community Col-
lege; and Holly Zaitchik, Boston University.

I would like to thank Berklee College of Music for providing me with the
time necessary to undertake such a project; Charles Combs, chair of the
General Education Department at Berklee, for his continued support; and my
many students, whose insightful responses to the readings and exercises
helped shape the final form of the book. I am also very grateful to my mother
for her encouragement and to my father, whose insights into human nature
inform every aspect of my teaching.

Finally, my special thanks to Clotilde Raemy-Gardner, my wife, for her
valuable feedback, support, and patience. Without her help, this book would
not have been completed.

PETER S. GARDNER

New Directions

AN INTEGRATED APPROACH
TO READING, WRITING,
AND CRITICAL THINKING

CHAPTER ONE

CROSS-CULTURAL COMMUNICATION

Reading Skill:
Identifying Main Ideas and
Supporting Details

"The thing a fish is least likely to understand," someone once said, "is the water in which it swims." The water in which people swim is their *culture*—the values, beliefs, and practices they grow up with in a particular country. Most of us do not appreciate the enormous role culture plays in shaping our lives and choices; we are unaware of the cultural currents in which we swim.

The readings and activities in this chapter explore the unwritten rules of culture—the values and assumptions that lead people from different countries (and from different cultures within a country) to think and act in contrasting ways. The chapter also focuses on beliefs and customs that seem normal in one culture but strange in another and on the problems resulting from these *cross-cultural* variations. Finally, the chapter examines the nature of successful interaction between people from different cultures.

Following are some of the questions you will be considering in this chapter:

- What are the unconscious values and expectations of different cultures?
- What are the major obstacles to cross-cultural communication, and how can they be avoided?
- How can one best adjust to a new culture?

- What are the most important social and cultural factors shaping your own values, beliefs, and behaviors?
- What experiences have you personally had living in a new culture?

In the first reading of this chapter, "American Values and Assumptions," Gary Althen discusses prominent values, expectations, and beliefs in the United States. Next, in "Where Do We Stand?" Lisa Davis explores cross-cultural variations in the use of personal space and problems resulting from these nonverbal differences. After that, the short story "A Coward," by the Indian writer Premchand, focuses on the challenges faced by two university students from different castes who have fallen in love. Then, in "Sex, Sighs, and Conversation," Deborah Tannen analyzes the different ways women and men use language and the misunderstandings caused by these cross-cultural variations. Following this, the Hindu fable "The Blind Men and the Elephant" sheds light on the nature of cross-cultural conflict and resolution. Finally, a graph outlines the five common stages in adjusting to a new culture.

BRIEF QUOTES

The following quotations will help introduce you to the topic of cross-cultural communication. Think about these statements as you read the selections in this chapter.

"Culture regulates our lives at every turn. From the time we are born until we die there is, whether we are conscious of it or not, constant pressure upon us to follow certain types of behavior that other men have created for us."

—CLYDE KLUCKHOHN

"When in Rome, do as the Romans do."

—ENGLISH PROVERB

"What sets us against one another is not our aims—they all come to the same thing—but our methods."

—ANTOINE DE SAINT-EXUPÉRY

"I consider myself a Hindu, Christian, Moslem, Jew, Buddhist, and Confucian."

—MOHANDAS GANDHI

"It does me no injury for my neighbor to say there are twenty gods, or no God."

—THOMAS JEFFERSON

"All people are the same. It's only their habits that are different."

—CONFUCIUS

"It is within the families themselves where peace can begin. If families can learn to respect their members and deal with conflict resolution, that would be the first step to keeping peace on a global level."

—SUSAN PARTNOW

READING

PREREADING ACTIVITIES

1. In your reading journal, spend ten to fifteen minutes writing about any cultural differences you've noticed while living in a foreign country (or in part of your native country that is culturally different from where you grew up).

2. Read the first paragraph of "American Values and Assumptions," in which the author discusses the concept of values. Then write a list of three or four major values in your native culture. Share your list with several classmates.

3. Indicate the extent to which you agree with the following statements by filling in each blank with *SA* (strongly agree), *A* (agree), *U* (undecided), *D* (disagree), or *SD* (strongly disagree). Then compare your responses in a small group.

   a. _____   History doesn't matter; it's the future that counts.

   b. _____   With enough determination and hard work, a person can accomplish almost anything.

   c. _____   Nature should be controlled and used in the service of human beings.

   d. _____   The mass media shape people's values and behaviors more than any other cultural institution.

   e. _____   Any person's opinion is as valid and worthy of consideration as anyone else's.

   f. _____   Children should be encouraged to move away from home when they are around eighteen years old.

   g. _____   People do not have control over their own destinies.

   h. _____   Don't worry about tomorrow; enjoy today.

i. _____ People should be doing something most of the time instead of sitting around for hours talking to other people.

j. _____ It's better to help yourself than to accept help from other people.

American Values and Assumptions
GARY ALTHEN

Gary Althen has been the foreign student adviser at the University of Iowa for many years. Based on his experiences living in Peru and Malaysia, as well as extensive work with students, immigrants, and other visitors to the United States, he has written two books: The Handbook of Foreign Student Advising *(1983) and* American Ways: A Guide for Foreigners in the United States *(1988). This latter book, from which the excerpt below is taken, explores prominent values, beliefs, and cultural patterns in the United States.*

As people grow up, they learn certain values and assumptions from their 1
parents and other relatives, their teachers, their books, newspapers, and television programs. "Values" are ideas about what is right and wrong, desirable and undesirable, normal and abnormal, proper and improper. In some cultures, for example, people are taught that men and women should inhabit separate social worlds, with some activities clearly in the men's domain and others clearly in the women's. In other cultures that value is not taught, or at least not widely. Men and women are considered to have more or less equal access to most roles in the society.

"Assumptions," as the term is used here, are the postulates, the unques- 2
tioned givens, about people, life, and "the way things are." . . . People in some societies assume, for example, that education takes place most efficiently when respectful young people absorb all they can of what older, wiser people already know. The young people do not challenge or even discuss what they are taught. The assumption is that learners are seeking *wisdom,* which comes with age. Young and inexperienced people are not wise enough to know what is worth discussing.

People in other societies assume that education requires learners to ques- 3
tion and challenge the older "expert" when the expert's ideas disagree with the learner's. The assumption is that learners are seeking *knowledge,* which a person can obtain regardless of age or social standing.

People who grow up in a particular culture share certain values and as- 4
sumptions. That does not mean they all share exactly the same values to exactly the same extent; it does mean that most of them, most of the time, agree with each other's ideas about what is right and wrong, desirable and

undesirable, and so on. They also agree, mostly, with each other's assumptions about human nature, social relationships, and so on. . . .

INDIVIDUALISM AND PRIVACY

The most important thing to understand about Americans is probably their 5 devotion to "individualism." They have been trained since very early in their lives to consider themselves as separate individuals who are responsible for their own situations in life and their own destinies. They have not been trained to see themselves as members of a close-knit, tightly interdependent family, religious group, tribe, nation, or other collectivity.

You can see it in the way Americans treat their children. Even very young 6 children are given opportunities to make their own choices and express their opinions. A parent will ask a one-year-old child what color balloon she wants, which candy bar she would prefer, or whether she wants to sit next to mommy or daddy. The child's preference will normally be accommodated.

Through this process, Americans come to see themselves as separate hu- 7 man beings who have their own opinions and who are responsible for their own decisions.

Indeed, American child-rearing manuals (such as Dr. Benjamin Spock's 8 famous *Child and Baby Care*) state that the parents' objective in raising a child is to create a responsible, self-reliant individual who, by the age of 18 or so, is ready to move out of the parents' house and make his or her own way in life. Americans take this advice very seriously, so much so that a person beyond the age of about 20 who is still living at home with his or her parents may be thought to be "immature," "tied to the mother's apron strings," or otherwise unable to lead a normal independent life. . . .

Americans are trained to conceive of themselves as separate individuals, 9 and they assume everyone else in the world is too. When they encounter a person from abroad who seems to them excessively concerned with the opinions of parents, with following traditions, or with fulfilling obligations to others, they assume that the person feels trapped or is weak, indecisive, or "overly dependent." They assume all people must resent being in situations where they are not "free to make up their own minds." They assume, further- more, that after living for a time in the United States people will come to feel liberated from constraints arising outside themselves and will be grateful for the opportunity to "do their own thing" and "have it their own way."

It is this concept of themselves as individual decision-makers that blinds at 10 least some Americans to the fact that they share a culture with each other. They have the idea, as mentioned above, that they have independently made up their own minds about the values and assumptions they hold. The notion that social factors outside themselves have made them "just like everyone else" in important ways offends their sense of dignity.

Americans, then, consider the ideal person to be an individualistic, self- 11 reliant, independent person. They assume, incorrectly, that people from else-where share this value and this self-concept. In the degree to which they glorify "the individual" who stands alone and makes his or her own decisions, Americans are quite distinctive.

The individual that Americans idealize prefers an atmosphere of *freedom,*   12 where neither the government nor any other external force or agency dic-tates what the individual does. For Americans, the idea of individual freedom has strong, positive connotations.

By contrast, people from many other cultures regard some of the behavior   13 Americans legitimize by the label "individual freedom" to be self-centered and lacking in consideration for others. Mr. Wilson and his mother are good American individualists, living their own lives and interfering as little as possi-ble with others. Mohammad Abdullah found their behavior almost immoral.

Foreigners who understand the degree to which Americans are imbued   14 with the notion that the free, self-reliant individual is the ideal kind of human being will be able to understand many aspects of American behavior and thinking that otherwise might not make sense. A very few of the many possi-ble examples:

Americans see as heroes those individuals who "stand out from the crowd"   15 by doing something first, longest, most often, or otherwise "best." Exam-ples are aviators Charles Lindbergh[1] and Amelia Earhart.[2]

Americans admire people who have overcome adverse circumstances (for   16 example, poverty or a physical handicap) and "succeeded" in life. Black educator Booker T. Washington[3] is one example; the blind and deaf author and lecturer Helen Keller[4] is another.

Many Americans do not display the degree of respect for their parents that   17 people in more traditional or family-oriented societies commonly display. They have the conception that it was a sort of historical or biological accident that put them in the hands of particular parents, that the parents fulfilled their responsibilities to the children while the children were young, and now that the children have reached "the age of independence" the close child-parent tie is loosened, if not broken.

It is not unusual for Americans who are beyond the age of about 22 and   18 who are still living with their parents to pay their parents for room and board.

---

[1] *Charles Lindbergh* (1902–1974): American aviator who, in 1927, made the first solo, nonstop transatlantic flight.

[2] *Amelia Earhart* (1897–1937): The first woman to fly across the Atlantic Ocean (in 1928) and to fly across it alone (in 1932).

[3] *Booker T. Washington* (1856–1915): Son of a slave, he went from working in coal mines to founding the Tuskegee Institute and becoming one of the leading educators of his day.

[4] *Helen Keller* (1880–1968): Graduating from Radcliffe College with honors, she went on to write and lecture extensively about social causes.

Elderly parents living with their grown children may do likewise. Paying for room and board is a way of showing independence, self-reliance, and responsibility for oneself.

Certain phrases one commonly hears among Americans capture their devotion to individualism: "Do your own thing." "I did it my way." "You'll have to decide that for yourself." "You made your bed, now lie in it."[5] "If you don't look out for yourself, no one else will." "Look out for number one."   19

Closely associated with the value they place on individualism is the importance Americans assign to *privacy*. Americans assume that people "need some time to themselves" or "some time alone" to think about things or recover their spent psychological energy. Americans have great difficulty understanding foreigners who always want to be with another person, who dislike being alone.   20

If the parents can afford it, each child will have his or her own bedroom. Having one's own bedroom, even as an infant, inculcates in a person the notion that she is entitled to a place of her own where she can be by herself and—notice—keep her possessions. She will have *her* clothes, *her* toys, *her* books, and so on. These things will be hers and no one else's.   21

Americans assume that people have their "private thoughts" that might never be shared with anyone. Doctors, lawyers, psychiatrists, and others have rules governing "confidentiality" that are intended to prevent information about their clients' personal situations from becoming known to others.   22

Americans' attitudes about privacy can be difficult for foreigners to understand. Americans' houses, yards, and even their offices can seem open and inviting, yet, in the Americans' minds, there are boundaries that other people are simply not supposed to cross. When the boundaries are crossed, the Americans' bodies will visibly stiffen and their manner will become cool and aloof.   23

EQUALITY

Americans are also distinctive in the degree to which they believe in the ideal, as stated in their Declaration of Independence,[6] that "all men are created equal." Although they sometimes violate the ideal in their daily lives, particularly in matters of interracial relationships, Americans have a deep faith that in some fundamental way all people (at least all American people) are of equal value, that no one is born superior to anyone else. "One man, one vote," they say, conveying the idea that any person's opinion is as valid and worthy of attention as any other person's opinion.   24

Americans are generally quite uncomfortable when someone treats them   25

---

[5] *to make one's bed and lie in it:* To be responsible for one's actions and to accept the results.

[6] *Declaration of Independence:* Document announcing the creation of the United States and its separation from Great Britain (1776).

with obvious deference. They dislike being the subjects of open displays of respect—being bowed to, being deferred to, being treated as though they could do no wrong or make no unreasonable requests.

It is not just males who are created equal, in the American conception, but 26
females too. While Americans often violate the idea in practice, they do generally assume that women are the equal of men, deserving of the same level of respect. Women, according to the viewpoint of the feminists who since the 1970s have been struggling to get what they consider a "fair shake" for females in the society, may be different from men but are in no way inferior to them.

This is not to say that Americans make no distinctions among themselves as a 27
result of such factors as sex, age, wealth, or social position. They do. But the distinctions are acknowledged in subtle ways. Tone of voice, order of speaking, choice of words, seating arrangements—such are the means by which Americans acknowledge status differences among themselves. People of higher status are more likely to speak first, louder, and longer. They sit at the head of the table, or in the most comfortable chair. They feel free to interrupt other speakers more than others feel free to interrupt them. The higher status person may put a hand on the shoulder of the lower status person; if there is touching between the people involved, the higher status person will touch first.

Foreigners who are accustomed to more obvious displays of respect (such 28
as bowing, averting eyes from the face of the higher status person, or using honorific titles[7]) often overlook the ways in which Americans show respect for people of higher status. They think, incorrectly, that Americans are generally unaware of status differences and disrespectful of other people. What is distinctive about the American outlook on the matter of equality are the underlying assumptions that no matter what his or her initial station in life, any individual has the potential to achieve high standing and that everyone, no matter how unfortunate, deserves some basic level of respectful treatment.

INFORMALITY

Their notions of equality lead Americans to be quite *informal* in their general 29
behavior and in their relationships with other people. Store clerks and waiters, for example, may introduce themselves by their first (given) names and treat customers in a casual, friendly manner. American clerks, like other Americans, have been trained to believe that they are as valuable as any other people, even if they happen to be engaged at a given time in an occupation that others might consider lowly. This informal behavior can outrage foreign visitors who hold high stations in countries where it is not assumed that "all men are created equal."

People from societies where general behavior is more formal than it is in 30

---

[7] *honorific titles:* Titles of honor or respect.

America are struck by the informality of American speech, dress, and pos-
tures. Idiomatic speech (commonly called "slang") is heavily used on most
occasions, with formal speech reserved for public events and fairly formal
situations. People of almost any station in life can be seen in public wearing
jeans, sandals, or other informal attire. People slouch down in chairs or lean
on walls or furniture when they talk, rather than maintaining an erect bearing.

A brochure advertising a highly-regarded liberal-arts college contains a   31
photograph showing the college's president, dressed in shorts and an old T-
shirt, jogging past one of the classroom buildings on his campus. Americans
are likely to find the photograph appealing: "Here is a college president who's
just like anyone else. He doesn't think he's too good for us."

The superficial *friendliness* for which Americans are so well known is re-   32
lated to their informal, egalitarian approach to other people. "Hi!" they will say
to just about anyone. "Howya doin?" (That is, "How are you doing?" or "How
are you?") This behavior reflects less a special interest in the person addressed
than a concern (not conscious) for showing that one is a "regular guy," part of a
group of normal, pleasant people—like the college president. . . .

THE FUTURE, CHANGE, AND PROGRESS

Americans are generally less concerned about history and traditions than are   33
people from older societies. "History doesn't matter," many of them will say.
"It's the future that counts." They look ahead. They have the idea that what
happens in the future is within their control, or at least subject to their
influence. They believe that the mature, sensible person sets goals for the
future and works systematically toward them. They believe that people, as
individuals or working cooperatively together, can change most aspects of
the physical and social environment if they decide to do so, make appropriate
plans, and get to work. Changes will presumably produce improvements.
New things are better than old ones.

The long-time slogans of two major American corporations capture the   34
Americans' assumptions about the future and about change. A maker of electri-
cal appliances ended its radio and television commercials with the slogan,
"Progress is our most important product." A huge chemical company that
manufactured, among many other things, various plastics and synthetic fab-
rics, had this slogan: "Better things for better living through chemistry."

Closely associated with their assumption that they can bring about desir-   35
able changes in the future is the Americans' assumption that their physical
and social environments are subject to human domination or control. Early
Americans cleared forests, drained swamps, and altered the course of rivers in
order to "build" the country. Contemporary Americans have gone to the
moon in part just to prove they could do so.

This fundamental American belief in progress and a better future contrasts   36
sharply with the fatalistic (Americans are likely to use that term with a nega-

tive or critical connotation) attitude that characterizes people from many other cultures, notably Latin, Asian, and Arab, where there is a pronounced reverence for the past. In those cultures the future is considered to be in the hands of "fate," "God," or at least the few powerful people or families that dominate the society. The idea that they could somehow shape their own futures seems naive or even arrogant.

Americans are generally impatient with people they see as passively accept- 37 ing conditions that are less than desirable. "Why don't they do something about it?" Americans will ask. Americans don't realize that a large portion of the world's population sees the world around them as something they cannot change, but rather as something to which they must submit, or at least something with which they must seek to live in harmony. . . .

TIME

For Americans, time is a "resource" that, like water or coal, can be used well 38 or poorly. "Time is money," they say. "You only get so much time in this life; you'd best use it wisely." The future will not be better than the past or the present, as Americans are trained to see things, unless people use their time for constructive, future-oriented activities. Thus, Americans admire a "well-organized" person, one who has a written list of things to do and a schedule for doing them. The ideal person is punctual (that is, arrives at the scheduled time for a meeting or event) and is considerate of other people's time (that is, does not "waste people's time" with conversation or other activity that has no visible, beneficial outcome).

The American attitude toward time is not necessarily shared by others, 39 especially non-Europeans. They are more likely to conceive of time as something that is simply there around them, not something they can "use." One of the more difficult things many foreign businessmen and students must adjust to in the States is the notion that time must be saved whenever possible and used wisely every day.

In their efforts to use their time wisely, Americans are sometimes seen by 40 foreign visitors as automatons, unhuman creatures who are so tied to their clocks and their schedules that they cannot participate in or enjoy the human interactions that are the truly important things in life. "They are like little machines running around," one foreign visitor said.

The premium Americans place on *efficiency* is closely related to their 41 concepts of the future, change, and time. To do something efficiently is to do it in the way that is quickest and requires the smallest expenditure of resources. American businesses sometimes hire "efficiency experts" to review their operations and suggest ways in which they could accomplish more than they are currently accomplishing with the resources they are investing. Popular periodicals carry suggestions for more efficient ways to shop, cook, clean house, do errands, raise children, tend the yard, and on and on.

In this context the "fast-food industry" can be seen as a clear example of an 42

American cultural product. McDonald's, Kentucky Fried Chicken, Pizza Hut, and other fast-food establishments prosper in a country where many people want to minimize the amount of time they spend preparing and eating meals. The millions of Americans who take their meals at fast-food restaurants cannot have much interest in lingering over their food while conversing with friends, as millions of Europeans do. As McDonald's restaurants have spread around the world, they have been viewed as symbols of American society and culture, bringing not just hamburgers but an emphasis on speed, efficiency, and shiny cleanliness. The typical American food, some observers argue, is fast food.

ACHIEVEMENT, ACTION, WORK, AND MATERIALISM

"He's a hard worker," one American might say in praise of another. Or, "She gets the job done." These expressions convey the typical American's admiration for a person who approaches a task conscientiously and persistently, seeing it through to a successful conclusion. More than that, these expressions convey an admiration for *achievers,* people whose lives are centered around efforts to accomplish some physical, measurable thing. Social psychologists use the term "achievement motivation" to describe what appears to be the intention underlying Americans' behavior. "Affiliation" is another kind of motivation, shown by people whose main intent seems to be to establish and retain a set of relationships with other people. The achievement motivation predominates in America.   43

Foreign visitors commonly remark that "Americans work harder than I expected them to." (Perhaps these visitors have been excessively influenced by American movies and television programs, which are less likely to show people working than to show them driving around in fast cars or pursuing members of the opposite sex.) While the so-called "Protestant work ethic"[8] may have lost some of its hold on Americans, there is still a strong belief that the ideal person is a "hard worker." A hard worker is one who "gets right to work" on a task without delay, works efficiently, and completes the task in a way that meets reasonably high standards of quality.   44

Hard workers are admired not just on the job, but in other aspects of life as well. Housewives, students, and people volunteering their services to charitable organizations can also be "hard workers" who make "significant achievements."   45

More generally, Americans like *action.* They do indeed believe it is important to devote significant energy to their jobs or to other daily responsibilities. Beyond that, they tend to believe they should be *doing* something most of the time. They are usually not content, as people from many countries are,   46

---

[8] *Protestant work ethic:* Belief that with hard work and self-discipline, one will eventually succeed.

to sit for hours and talk with other people. They get restless and impatient. They believe they should be doing something, or at least making plans and arrangements for doing something later.

People without the Americans' action orientation often see Americans as 47 frenzied, always "on the go," never satisfied, compulsively active. They may, beyond that, evaluate Americans negatively for being unable to relax and enjoy life's pleasures. Even recreation, for Americans, is often a matter of acquiring lavish equipment, making elaborate plans, then going somewhere to *do* something.

Americans tend to define people by the jobs they have. ("Who is he?" "He's 48 the vice president in charge of personal loans at the bank.") Their family backgrounds, educational attainments, and other characteristics are considered less important in identifying people than the jobs they have.

There is usually a close relationship between the job a person has and the 49 level of the person's income. Americans tend to measure a person's "success" in life by referring to the amount of money he has acquired. Being a bank vice president is quite respectable, but being a bank president is more so. The president gets a higher salary. So the president can buy more things—a bigger house and car, a boat, more neckties and shoes, and so on.

Americans are often criticized for being so "materialistic," so concerned 50 with acquiring possessions. For Americans, though, this materialism is natural and proper. They have been taught that it is a good thing to achieve—to work hard, acquire more material badges of their success, and in the process assure a better future for themselves and their immediate families. And, like people from elsewhere, they do what they are taught.

DIRECTNESS AND ASSERTIVENESS

Americans, as has been said before, generally consider themselves to be frank, 51 open, and direct in their dealings with other people. "Let's lay our cards on the table,"9 they say. Or, "Let's stop playing games and get to the point." These and many other common phrases convey the Americans' idea that people should explicitly state what they think and what they want from other people.

Americans tend to assume that conflicts or disagreements are best settled 52 by means of forthright discussions among the people involved. If I dislike something you are doing, I should tell you about it directly so you will know, clearly and from me personally, how I feel about it. Bringing in other people to mediate a dispute is considered somewhat cowardly, the act of a person without enough courage to speak directly to someone else.

The word "assertive" is the adjective Americans commonly use to describe 53 the person who plainly and directly expresses feelings and requests. People who are inadequately assertive can take "assertiveness training classes."

---

9 *to lay one's cards on the table:* To honestly state one's opinion.

Americans will often speak openly and directly to others about things they dislike. They will try to do so in a manner they call "constructive," that is, a manner which the other person will not find offensive or unacceptable. If they do not speak openly about what is on their minds, they will often convey their reactions in nonverbal ways (without words, but through facial expressions, body positions, and gestures). Americans are not taught, as people in many Asian countries are, that they should mask their emotional responses. Their words, the tone of their voices, or their facial expressions will usually reveal when they are feeling angry, unhappy, confused, or happy and content. They do not think it improper to display these feelings, at least within limits. Many Asians feel embarrassed around Americans who are exhibiting a strong emotional response to something. (On the other hand . . . Latins and Arabs are generally inclined to display their emotions more openly than Americans do, and to view Americans as unemotional and "cold.") 54

But Americans are often less direct and open than they realize. There are in fact many restrictions on their willingness to discuss things openly. It is difficult to categorize those restrictions, and the restrictions are often not "logical" in the sense of being consistent with each other. Generally, though, Americans are reluctant to speak openly when: 55

the topic is in an area they consider excessively personal, such as unpleasant body or mouth odors, sexual functioning, or personal inadequacies;

they want to say "no" to a request that has been made of them but do not want to offend or "hurt the feelings of" the person who made the request;

they are not well enough acquainted with the other person to be confident that direct discussion will be accepted in the constructive way that is intended; and, paradoxically,

they know the other person very well (it might be a spouse or close friend) and they do not wish to risk giving offense and creating negative feelings by talking about some delicate problem. . . .

Americans might feel especially reluctant to say "no" directly to a foreigner, for fear of making the person feel unwelcome or discriminated against. They will often try to convey the "no" indirectly, by saying such things as "it's not convenient now" or by repeatedly postponing an agreed-upon time for doing something. 56

Despite these limitations, Americans are generally more direct and open than people from many other countries. They will not try to mask their emotions, as Scandinavians tend to do. They are much less concerned with "face" (that is, avoiding embarrassment to themselves or others) than most Asians are. To them, being "honest" is usually more important than preserving harmony in interpersonal relationships. 57

Americans use the words "pushy" or "aggressive" to describe a person who 58
is excessively assertive in expressing opinions or making requests. The line
between acceptable assertiveness and unacceptable aggressiveness is difficult
to draw. Iranians and people from other countries where forceful arguing and
negotiating are common forms of interaction risk being seen as aggressive or
pushy when they treat Americans in the way they treat people at home.

READING JOURNAL

In your reading journal, discuss one of the following:

1. What a foreign visitor to your country should know about its values and
   assumptions in order to avoid cross-cultural misunderstandings

2. A cross-cultural misunderstanding you personally experienced

3. A topic of your own choice related to "American Values and Assumptions"

MEANING AND TECHNIQUE

The following questions and activities will help you understand the main
ideas in "American Values and Assumptions" and the manner in which it was
written.

MAIN IDEAS

One of the most important skills you can develop as a good reader is the
ability to recognize the *main idea* (sometimes called the author's "point")
in a piece of writing. When you read something, you should ask yourself
the following questions:

- What is the main idea the writer is trying to convey?

- What does the writer want me to remember about this subject?

- How does the writer develop his or her main point?

---

1. In one or two sentences, write down the main idea you think Althen is
   trying to convey in "American Values and Assumptions." Use your own
   words.

2. According to the reading, what is the most important thing to understand
   about American culture? Why?

WELL-WRITTEN PARAGRAPHS

A paragraph is a group of sentences developing a main idea. A well-written paragraph in an informative or argumentative essay should be:

- *unified:* All of the sentences should clearly relate to the main idea of the paragraph.
- *coherent:* All of the sentences should be logically connected to each other. (For a list of devices that can help writers achieve coherence, see **transition** in the glossary.)
- *fully developed:* The paragraph should provide sufficient detail to explain or support the main idea: examples, facts, statistics, reasons, anecdotes, quotations, definitions, and so on.
- *appropriately organized:* The paragraph should have a clear and logical pattern of organization, such as *chronological order, spatial order, emphatic order, illustration, comparison and contrast,* or *cause and effect.* (For a discussion of these and other types of paragraph arrangement, see **organization** in the glossary.)

Topic Sentence

Most paragraphs have a sentence that clearly states the main idea of the paragraph. This sentence is called the *topic sentence.* It usually appears at the beginning of the paragraph but can also be in the middle or at the end. Some paragraphs lack a topic sentence, with the main idea being implied, or suggested, through details.

3. With a partner, read through paragraphs 9, 18, 21, 31, 37, and 44 in the essay. Underline the topic sentence in each paragraph. At what point does this sentence appear? Do any of the paragraphs have an implied topic sentence?

Example:

"There is usually a close relationship between the job a person has and the level of the person's income. Americans tend to measure a person's 'success' in life by referring to the amount of money he has acquired. Being a bank vice president is quite respectable, but being a bank president is more so. The president gets a higher salary. So the president can buy more things—a bigger house and car, a boat, more neckties and shoes, and so on." (par. 49)

Topic Sentence

> **SUPPORTING DETAILS**
>
> Good writers provide sufficient details (examples, facts, statistics, reasons, personal experiences, quotations, and so on) to back up, or support, their main ideas. Without these *supporting details,* a writer's ideas remain abstract and unconvincing. Experienced writers try, whenever possible, to *show* rather than simply *tell* their readers what they mean.

4. In "American Values and Assumptions," Althen provides a number of concrete details to support his points.

Locate the following specific statements in the reading. Using your own words, write a general sentence that describes the main idea the statement is supporting or illustrating.

Example:

"A brochure... contains a photograph showing the college's president, dressed in shorts and an old T-shirt, jogging past one of the classroom buildings on his campus." (par. 31)

MAIN IDEA: Americans value informality and equality in their everyday lives.

a. "A parent [in the United States] will ask a one-year-old child what color balloon she wants, which candy bar she would prefer, or whether she wants to sit next to mommy or daddy." (par. 6)

Main idea: _____

_____

b. "Doctors, lawyers, psychiatrists, and others have rules governing 'confidentiality' that are intended to prevent information about their clients' personal situations from becoming known to others." (par. 22)

Main idea: _____

_____

c. "People of higher status are more likely to speak first, louder, and longer. They sit at the head of the table, or in the most comfortable chair." (par. 27)

Main idea: _____

_____

d. "Early Americans cleared forests, drained swamps, and altered the course of rivers in order to 'build' the country." (par. 35)

Main idea: _____

_____

e. "Even recreation, for Americans, is often a matter of acquiring lavish equipment, making elaborate plans, then going somewhere to *do* something." (par. 47)

Main idea: _____

_____

DRAWING INFERENCES

In addition to recognizing main ideas, another important reading skill is the ability to *draw inferences*. Often a writer will state an idea not explicitly, or directly, but rather implicitly, or indirectly. For example, in "American Values and Assumptions," Althen never directly states that people from certain cultures will probably not like the photograph of the college president in shorts and an old T-shirt (par. 31), but this can be *inferred* from the context.

In order to fully understand a piece of writing, you need to "read between the lines." By using hints provided by the author, as well as your own knowledge and experience, you will be able to discover ideas in writing that are not stated directly.

The following activities will help develop your ability to understand unstated meanings—that is, to draw inferences.

1. At one point in the original essay not included in your book, Althen writes: "Notice that these values and assumptions [the major ones discussed in the reading] overlap with and support each other. In general, they agree with each other. They fit together."

   What do you think he means by this? Give one or two examples.

2. In discussing Americans, Althen says: "The notion that social factors outside themselves have made them 'just like everyone else' in important ways offends their sense of dignity" (par. 10).

   Fill in the following blanks with four or five social factors that you think foster, or encourage, similarities among people in a particular culture.

Important Social Factors

1. _____

2. _____

3. _____

4. _____

5. _____

3. Some pieces of writing are quite *subjective;* that is, they reflect the author's personal feelings and interpretations. Others are more *objective,* stressing facts rather than personal feelings and judgments.

   Do you have any sense of how Althen feels about the issues he discusses? How objective do you consider his writing? Be as specific as possible.

4. Think of a question of your own to ask your classmates about an issue raised in the reading.

VOCABULARY: NEGATIVE PREFIXES

Often in English, a word is formed by adding a group of letters to the beginning or end of the *word root*—the basic part of the word. Groups of letters attached to the beginning of a word root are called *prefixes.* Those attached to the end of a word root are called *suffixes.* In general, prefixes change the meaning of a word and suffixes change its *part of speech* (noun, verb, adjective, adverb, and so on).

Look at the following examples of roots, prefixes, and suffixes:

Root	operate (verb)	conscious (adjective)
Prefix	*co*operate (verb)	*un*conscious (adjective)
Suffix	operat*ion* (noun)	unconscious*ly* (adverb)

In English, there are many prefixes that indicate something *negative* (that is, meaning "not," "the opposite of," or "lacking in"):

un- in- im- il- ir- a- non- dis-

1. Following are twelve words from the reading, each with the negative prefix removed. Fill in each of the following blanks with the proper negative prefix. (In some cases, there might be more than one possibility.) Then find the words in the text and check your answers.

a. _____ normal (par. 1)

b. _____ questioned (par. 2)

c. _____ experienced (par. 2)

d. _____ mature (par. 8)

e. _____ decisive (par. 9)

f. _____ respectful (par. 28)

g. _____ patient (par. 37)

h. _____ Europeans (par. 39)

i. _____ human (par. 40)

j. _____ adequately (par. 53)

k. _____ emotional (par. 54)

l. _____ directly (par. 56)

2. The following words appear in the reading without negative prefixes. Make these words negative by filling in the blanks with the proper prefix (or prefixes). Then compare your answers with those of several classmates.

a. _____ social (par. 1)

b. _____ distinctive (par. 11)

c. _____ traditional (par. 17)

d. _____ biological (par. 17)

e. _____ associated (par. 20)

f. _____ subtle (par. 27)

g. _____ appealing (par. 31)

h. _____ reverence (par. 36)

i. _____ considerate (par. 38)

j. _____ typical (par. 43)

k. _____ proper (par. 50)

l. _____ assertive (par. 53)

m. _____ inclined (par. 54)

n. _____ logical (par. 55)

VOCABULARY: IN CONTEXT

In this exercise, you will develop your vocabulary by using words and idioms in a realistic context.

- If you don't know the meaning of one of the following italicized vocabulary items, first find it in the essay and see if you can determine its meaning from the context. (Review the major types of context clues on pp. 263–267.)
- If the meaning is still unclear, look up the item in a dictionary or consult with a native speaker of English.
- Then, in a few sentences, describe or explain each of the following situations, ideas, and things. **Do not** just define the italicized words and expressions. Discuss personal experiences and opinions and give examples.

1. Something to which most people in your native culture *have* (or do not have) *access* (par. 1)

2. Several characteristics of a *close-knit* family (par. 5)

3. Someone you think *stands out from the crowd,* and why (par. 15)

4. One or two values you would like to have *inculcated* in your children, and why (par. 21)

5. Why someone might behave in an *aloof* manner (par. 23)

6. What it means if someone dresses in a *subtle* manner (par. 27)

7. How status differences are *acknowledged* in your native culture (par. 27)

8. A time when you *saw something through* to a successful conclusion (par. 43)

9. A time when someone was not *forthright* in telling you something (par. 52)

10. The extent to which you are *inclined* to display your emotions (par. 54)

DISCUSSION AND DEBATE

1. In a small group, discuss a time when you lived in another culture. What differences in values and assumptions were you aware of? Think about beliefs, behaviors, customs, and other cultural patterns. How did these differences make you feel? Did you experience any problems or misunderstandings?

PRECONCEPTIONS AND STEREOTYPES

A major stumbling block to cross-cultural communication is the existence of *preconceptions* and *stereotypes.* A *preconception* is a belief about a person, place, or thing that is not based on actual knowledge or experience. An example of a preconception might be the belief that the people in a certain country are unfriendly.

When a preconception becomes oversimplified and exaggerated and is held in common by a whole group of people, it is called a *stereotype.* An example of a stereotype is the belief mentioned in paragraph 40 of Althen's essay that Americans are "automatons" who cannot enjoy human interactions. (For another definition of a stereotype, see activity 3 on p. 63.)

2. Write a list of the preconceptions (ideas, images, and expectations) you had of another country before visiting it. Consider both positive and negative aspects of the culture. Then share your list with several classmates. Discuss the following questions:

- What is the origin of the preconceptions?
- Did any of them turn out to be stereotypes?
- If so, did this cause any problems?

3. One way to get a sense of the values and assumptions of a culture is to look at its proverbs and sayings.

Following are ten common proverbs in English. With several classmates, discuss as many of the proverbs as time allows. Consider (1) the meaning of each proverb, (2) a situation in which it might be used, (3) the value(s) it reflects, and (4) whether or not an equivalent exists in your native language.

Example:

PROVERB: "The early bird catches the worm."

MEANING: The person who starts early on something has the best chance of success.

SITUATION: Claire began looking for a summer job in December. She knew that "the early bird catches the worm."

VALUE(S): diligence, action, punctuality

NATIVE LANGUAGE: The German equivalent translates as, "The morning hour has gold in its mouth."

a. "Don't cry over spilt milk."

b. "God helps those who help themselves."

c. "Too many cooks spoil the broth."

d. "You can lead a horse to water but you can't make it drink."

e. "The squeaky wheel gets the grease."

f. "A penny saved is a penny earned."

g. "Don't count your chickens before they're hatched."

h. "Strike while the iron is hot."

i. "A man's home is his castle."

j. "A bird in the hand is worth two in the bush."

WRITING ACTIVITIES

OBJECTIVE DESCRIPTION VS. VALUE JUDGMENT

In order to avoid problems when in another country, it is important to observe things as *objectively* as possible. Objective observation involves the ability to simply describe what one sees rather than interpreting it according to the values and assumptions of one's own culture—that is, making *value judgments.* The following activity will help you distinguish between descriptive and evaluative (judgmental) observation.

---

1. In a small group, write five statements about different cultures that contain value judgments, either positive or negative. Consider such aspects of the cultures as family, education, national character, and climate. Then reword the statements to make them purely descriptive.

   Example:

   VALUE JUDGMENT: "American parents encourage their children to move out of the home when they are around eighteen years old, and this shows that the parent-child relationship in the United States is quite weak."

   DESCRIPTIVE STATEMENT: "American parents encourage their children to move out of the home when they are around eighteen years old, and this reflects the stress in the United States on independence and self-reliance."

For the following writing assignments, make sure that your paragraphs are unified, coherent, fully developed, and appropriately organized, and that they have a clearly stated or implied topic sentence. (Review these characteristics of well-written paragraphs on p. 15.) To help you plan, draft, and revise the assignment(s), see Appendix A.

---

2. Imagine you are a member of a governmental agency that helps immigrants adapt culturally to your native country. You have been asked to speak to a large group of new arrivals. The topic of your presentation is "How to Better Understand Your New Homeland."

   Write a short speech welcoming the immigrants to your country and discussing the major cultural values and assumptions they should be aware of to adapt more easily and avoid cross-cultural misunderstandings.

   Then read your speech to the class and respond to any questions the "audience" might have.

3. Gary Althen defines values as "ideas about what is right and wrong, desirable and undesirable, normal and abnormal, proper and improper" (par. 1 of "American Values and Assumptions").

Write an essay discussing any differences you noticed in values and assumptions while in a foreign country (or in part of your native country that is culturally different from where you grew up). Did anything seem "wrong," "undesirable," "abnormal," or "improper"? How did the differences in values make you feel? Did they cause any problems?

READING

PREREADING ACTIVITIES

1. In your reading journal, *freewrite* for ten minutes on the topic of body language. Don't worry about spelling, grammar, punctuation, or organization. Just write for ten minutes, without stopping, about whatever comes to mind when you think about body language. (For a discussion of freewriting and other prewriting strategies, see pp. 234–240.)

   When you have finished, share your thoughts with several classmates.

2. Specialists in the field of communication look at three things when trying to determine what people really mean when they say something: (1) the literal meaning of the words (the "verbal" element), (2) the manner of speaking, including tone, volume, pitch, rhythm, and tempo (the "vocal" element), and (3) the body movements, especially facial expressions (the "nonverbal" element).

   Fill in the following blanks with what you consider the percentages constituting the overall meaning of something someone says. Then share your answers with the rest of the class.

Statement = _____% verbal + _____% vocal + _____% nonverbal

3. Indicate the extent to which you agree with the following statements in relation to your native culture by filling in the blanks with "yes" or "no." Then discuss your responses in a small group.

   a. _____   People usually greet each other by bowing.

   b. _____   It is common for students to avoid eye contact when being reprimanded by a teacher.

   c. _____   People often touch each other while conversing.

d. _____   Men frequently hold hands in public.

e. _____   People often smile at each other in public.

f. _____   When people converse, they usually stand very close to each other.

g. _____   People tend to gesture a lot with their hands.

h. _____   People often show a lot of physical affection in public.

Where Do We Stand?
LISA DAVIS

Cross-cultural variations in nonverbal behavior often cause conflicts and misunderstandings. In the following article, originally published in the magazine In Health, Lisa Davis, an American freelance writer, focuses on cultural differences in the use of personal space and on problems arising from these differences.

Call it the dance of the jet set,[1] the diplomat's tango: A man from the Middle East, say, falls into conversation with an American, becomes animated, takes a step forward. The American makes a slight postural adjustment, shifts his feet, edges backward. A little more talk and the Arab advances; a little more talk and the American retreats. "By the end of the cocktail party," says Middle East expert Peter Bechtold, of the State Department's Foreign Service Institute, "you have an American in each corner of the room, because that's as far as they can back up."   1

What do you do when an amiable chat leaves one person feeling vaguely bullied, the other unaccountably chilled? Things would be simpler if these jet-setters were speaking different languages—they'd just get themselves a translator. But the problem's a little tougher, because they're using different languages of space.   2

Everyone who's ever felt cramped in a crowd knows that the skin is not the body's only boundary. We each wear a zone of privacy like a hoop skirt,[2] inviting others in or keeping them out with body language—by how closely we approach, the angle at which we face them, the speed with which we break a gaze. It's a subtle code, but one we use and interpret easily, indeed automatically, having absorbed the vocabulary from infancy.   3

---

[1] *jet set:* Wealthy people who travel around the world from one fashionable place to another.

[2] *hoop skirt:* A long, full skirt supported by a series of connected hoops, or rings (popular in the late 1850s).

At least, we *assume* we're reading it right. But from culture to culture, 4 from group to group within a single country, even between the sexes, the language of space has distinctive accents, confusing umlauts.[3] That leaves a lot of room for misinterpretation, and the stakes have gotten higher as business has become increasingly international and populations multi-cultural. So a new breed of consultants has appeared in the last few years, interpreting for globe-trotters of all nationalities the meaning and use of personal space.

For instance, says international business consultant Sondra Snowdon, Saudi 5 Arabians like to conduct business discussions from within spitting distance— literally. They bathe in each other's breath as part of building the relationship. "Americans back up," says Snowdon, "but they're harming their chances of winning the contracts." In seminars, Snowdon discusses the close quarters common in Middle Eastern conversations, and has her students practice talking with each other at very chummy distances.

Still, her clients had better be careful where they take their shrunken 6 "space bubble," because cultures are idiosyncratic in their spatial needs. Japanese subways bring people about as close together as humanly possible, for instance, yet even a handshake can be offensively physical in a Japanese office. And, says researcher and writer Mildred Reed Hall, Americans can even make their business counterparts in Japan uncomfortable with the kind of direct eye contact that's normal here. "Not only do most Japanese businessmen not look at you, they keep their eyes down," Hall says. "*We* look at people for hours, and they feel like they're under a searchlight."

The study of personal space got under way in the early 1950s, when 7 anthropologist Edward Hall described a sort of cultural continuum of personal space. (Hall has frequently collaborated with his wife, Mildred.) Accord-

---

[3] *umlaut:* Change in a vowel sound, often indicated by the symbol (¨).

ing to Hall, on the "high-contact" side of the continuum—in Mediterranean and South American societies, for instance—social conversations include much eye contact, touching, and smiling, typically while standing at a distance of about a foot. On the other end of the scale, say in Northern European cultures, a lingering gaze may feel invasive, manipulative, or disrespectful; a social chat takes place at a remove of about two and a half feet.

In the middle-of-the-road United States, people usually stand about 18 8 inches apart for this sort of conversation—unless we want to win foreign friends and influence people, in which case, research shows, we'd better adjust our posture. In one study, when British graduate students were trained to adopt Arab patterns of behavior (facing their partners straight on, with lots of eye contact and smiling), Middle Eastern exchange students found them more likable and trustworthy than typical British students. In contrast, the *mis*use of space can call whole personalities into suspicion: When researchers seated pairs of women for conversation, those forced to talk at an uncomfortably large distance were more likely to describe their partners as cold and rejecting.

Don't snuggle up too fast, though. Men in that study were more irritated by 9 their partners when they were forced to talk at close range. Spatially speaking, it seems men and women are subtly foreign to each other. No matter whether a society operates at arm's length or cheek-to-jowl,[4] the women look at each other more and stand a bit closer than do the men.

It just goes to show that you can't take things for granted even within the 10 borders of a single country. Take that unwilling amalgamation of ethnic minorities, the Soviet Union. According to psychologist Robert Sommer, who along with Hall sparked the study of personal space, spatial needs collide in the republics. "The Estonians are a non-contact people," says Sommer, of the University of California at Davis. "I went to a 'Hands Around the Baltic'[5] event, and nobody touched hands. The Russians, on the other hand, are high-contact. The Estonians say the Russians are pushy, and the Russians say the Estonians are cold."

Nor are things easier within the United States. Researchers have found, for 11 instance, that middle-class, Caucasian schoolteachers often jump to mistaken conclusions when dealing with a child from a different background: If a girl from an Asian family averts her eyes out of respect for her teacher's authority, the teacher may well go on alert, convinced that the child is trying to hide some misbehavior. Ethnically diverse workplaces can be similarly booby-trapped.

Such glitches are all the more likely because spatial behavior is automatic— 12 it snaps into focus only when someone doesn't play by the rules. Say an American businessman is alone in a roomy elevator when another man enters. The newcomer fails to perform the national ritual of taking a corner and staring into

---

[4] *cheek-to-jowl:* Cheek-to-cheek (very close).

[5] *Hands Around the Baltic:* Large group of people expressing solidarity by holding hands in a long line.

space; instead, he stands a few inches away, smiling, which is simple politeness in some cultures. "You start to search for a reasonable explanation," says psychologist Eric Knowles, at the University of Arkansas. "In many cases you come up with one without even being aware of it. You say, 'Is this guy a pickpocket? Is he psychotic?' If no explanation seems to fit, you just think, 'This guy's weird, I better get out of here.' "

In fact, such caution is not always unwarranted, because an abnormal use 13 of space *can* indicate that something odd is going on. Research has shown that when people with schizophrenia approach another person, they often either get closer than normal or stay unusually distant. And a small study of prisoners seemed to show that those with a history of violence needed up to three times the space taken by nonviolent inmates. These are reminders that the human need for space is based in an animal reality: The closer you allow a stranger, the more vulnerable you become.

But the spatial differences among cultures point to something beyond self- 14 protection. Anthropologist Edward Hall suggests that a culture's use of space is also evidence of a reliance on one sense over another: Middle Easterners get much of their information through their senses of smell and touch, he says, which require a close approach; Americans rely primarily on visual information, backing up in order to see an intelligible picture.

Conversational distances also tend to reflect the standard greeting distance 15 in each culture, says State Department expert Bechtold. Americans shake hands, and then talk at arm's length. Arabs do a Hollywood-style, cheek-to-cheek social kiss, and their conversation is similarly up close and personal. And, at a distance great enough to keep heads from knocking together— about two feet—the Japanese bow and talk to each other. On the other hand, the need for more or less space may reflect something of a cultural temperament. "There's no word for privacy in Arab cultures," says Bechtold. "They think it means loneliness."

Whatever their origin, spatial styles are very real. In fact, even those who 16 set out to transgress find it uncomfortable to intrude on the space of strangers, says psychologist John R. Aiello, at Rutgers University. "I've had students say, 'Boy, that was the hardest thing I ever had to do—to stand six inches away when I was asking those questions.' "

Luckily, given coaching and time, it seems to get easier to acculturate to 17 foreign habits of contact. Says Bechtold, "You often see men holding hands in the Middle East and walking down the street together. It's just that they're concerned and don't want you to cross the street unescorted, but I've had American pilots come in here and say, 'I don't want some s.o.b.[6] holding my hand.' Then I see them there, holding the hand of a Saudi.

"Personal space isn't so hard for people to learn," Bechtold adds. "What is 18 really much harder is the business of dinner being served at midnight."

---

[6] *s.o.b.*: Son of a bitch; vulgar term referring to an offensive or disagreeable person, usually a male.

READING JOURNAL

In your reading journal, discuss one of the following:

1. Any differences you've noticed in nonverbal behavior while in a foreign country or in various parts of your native country

2. A misunderstanding you've personally experienced due to cultural differences in nonverbal behavior

3. A subject of your own choice related to "Where Do We Stand?"

MEANING AND TECHNIQUE

The following questions and activities will help you understand the main ideas in the reading and the manner in which it was written.

1. In one or two sentences, write down the *main point* you think Davis is trying to make in the article. Use your own words.

2. What is the major cause of the nonverbal misunderstandings described in the article?

3. With a partner, review the discussion of well-written paragraphs on page 15. Then read through paragraphs 1, 3, 4, 6, 9, and 12 from "Where Do We Stand?" and, in each, locate the *topic sentence* (the sentence that expresses the main idea of the paragraph). At what point does the topic sentence appear? Do any of the paragraphs have an implied topic sentence?

Example:

"Nor are things easier within the United States. Researchers have found, for instance, that middle-class, Caucasian schoolteachers often jump to mistaken conclusions when dealing with a child from a different background: If a girl from an Asian family averts her eyes out of respect for her teacher's authority, the teacher may well go on alert, convinced that the child is trying to hide some misbehavior. Ethnically diverse workplaces can be similarly booby-trapped." (par. 11)

IMPLIED TOPIC SENTENCE: Not all ethnic groups in the United States have the same nonverbal behavior, and this often leads to misunderstandings.

4. Good writers provide sufficient *detail* (examples, facts, statistics, quotations, anecdotes, definitions, and so on) to support and develop their ideas.

Following are five general statements that appear in Davis's essay. Find one or two examples that support or illustrate each general idea (the examples do not necessarily have to come from the same paragraph as the general statement). Use your own words to describe the examples.

a. "But from culture to culture, from group to group within a single country, even between the sexes, the language of space has distinctive accents, confusing umlauts." (par. 4)

_____

_____

b. "Spatially speaking, it seems men and women are subtly foreign to each other." (par. 9)

_____

_____

c. "It just goes to show that you can't take things for granted even within the borders of a single country." (par. 10)

_____

_____

d. "Such glitches are all the more likely because spatial behavior is automatic—it snaps into focus only when someone doesn't play by the rules." (par. 12)

_____

_____

DRAWING INFERENCES

The following questions and activities will help develop your ability to draw inferences—an important reading skill.

1. In paragraph 4, Davis refers to "the language of space." In what ways is the use of space like a spoken language? Try to think of at least two similarities.

2. In paragraph 9, Davis says that in most societies, "the women look at each other more and stand a bit closer than do the men." How might you explain this gender difference?

3. How do you think Davis would recommend avoiding cross-cultural misunderstandings due to body language?

4. Think of a question of your own to ask your classmates about an issue raised in the article.

VOCABULARY: IDIOMS

Many idioms in English are based on parts of the body—for example, "to see eye to eye on something" (to agree with someone completely about something) and "to keep one's chin up" (to have courage). Fill in the chart below with five idioms based on parts of the body, the meaning of each idiom, and a sentence using the idiom correctly. Feel free to use a dictionary to help you.

Then share the idioms with several classmates. Consider whether an equivalent for each idiom exists in your native language.

Idiom	Meaning	Sentence
Example: "To cross one's fingers [for someone]"	To wish someone good luck	I'll cross my fingers (for you) when you take the test.

VOCABULARY: IN CONTEXT

In this exercise, you will develop your vocabulary by using words and idioms in a realistic context.

- If you don't know the meaning of one of the following italicized vocabulary items, find it in the reading and see if you can determine its meaning from the context. (Review the major types of context clues on pp. 263–267.)
- If the meaning is still unclear, look up the item in a dictionary or consult with a native speaker of English.

- Then, in a few sentences, describe or explain each of the following situations, ideas, and things. **Do not** just define the italicized words and expressions. Discuss personal experiences and opinions and give examples.

  1. Something you are only *vaguely* aware of (par. 2)

  2. How a person might feel if he or she were constantly being *bullied* (par. 2)

  3. What it means if a writer makes a point in a *subtle* manner (par. 3)

  4. Someone you know who has a *distinctive* personality (par. 4)

  5. An example of *manipulative* behavior (par. 7)

  6. A pattern of behavior you once *adopted* while in a foreign country or in part of your native country that is culturally different from where you grew up (par. 8)

  7. Something you think many people *take for granted,* and why (par. 10)

  8. An example of someone *jumping to a conclusion* (par. 11)

  9. A time when you *came up with* an idea that someone else liked or didn't like (par. 12)

  10. Something people *tend* to do when they drink too much alcohol (par. 15)

DISCUSSION AND DEBATE

1. With several classmates, try to illustrate the following comments and emotions nonverbally:

   "I don't know," "Good luck," "Shame on you," "That person is intelligent/crazy/beautiful," "He committed suicide," and "I feel angry/happy/sad/afraid/surprised/disgusted/ashamed."

   Next, demonstrate common gestures in your native country and discuss any restrictions regarding their appropriate use.

   Finally, show how you would use nonverbal behavior in the following contexts:

   greeting someone, saying good-bye to someone, insulting someone, flirting with someone, getting a waiter's attention, and ending a conversation.

2. In a small group, discuss several of the following aspects of nonverbal expression in your native culture, as well as cross-cultural similarities and differences. Consider variations based on geography, ethnicity, gender, age, status, and formal/informal contexts.

   - Using space during social conversations
   - Establishing and avoiding eye contact (especially during conversation)

- Showing emotions through facial expressions

- Touching and displaying affection in public (female-male, female-female, and male-male interaction)

3. Observe patterns of nonverbal behavior in public places and report back to the class. Focus on body movements, facial expressions, eye contact, posture, gait, touching, and space.

   Discuss any impressions you had, conclusions you reached, and value judgments you made on the basis of the nonverbal behavior you observed. (You can do the same exercise watching a television program with the volume turned off.)

WRITING ACTIVITIES

COMPARE-AND-CONTRAST SIGNALS

A common strategy of writers to develop and organize their ideas is *comparing* and *contrasting* two people, places, things, or ideas. Often writers will use the compare-and-contrast signals listed on page 261 to show similarities and differences.

---

1. Practice using these transitional signals by writing six sentences: three describing similarities and three describing differences in body language between your native culture and another culture.

2. In a small group, write a case study consisting of two paragraphs. In the first paragraph, describe a misunderstanding between two people of different cultures that is based on nonverbal behavior. In the second paragraph, discuss the source of the misunderstanding.

   When you have finished, read the first paragraph of the case study to one of the other groups. After the members of the group have tried to identify the origin of the misunderstanding, read the second paragraph.

3. Write an essay in which you discuss the patterns of nonverbal behavior a foreign visitor to your native country should be aware of to avoid cross-cultural misunderstandings. Make sure that your paragraphs are unified, coherent, fully developed, and appropriately organized, and that they have a clearly stated or implied topic sentence. (Review these characteristics of well-written paragraphs on p. 15.) To help you plan, draft, and revise the essay, see Appendix A.

READING

PREREADING ACTIVITIES

1. In your reading journal, write for ten to fifteen minutes about one of the following:

   a. A time when you did something against your parents' wishes

   b. The extent to which it is important to follow tradition

2. Indicate the extent to which you agree with the following statements by filling in each blank with *SA* (strongly agree), *A* (agree), *U* (undecided), *D* (disagree), or *SD* (strongly disagree). Then compare your responses in a small group.

   a. _____ I would marry someone even if my parents were against the marriage.

   b. _____ I would marry someone of a different nationality, race, religion, or social class.

   c. _____ People should remain in the social class they were born into.

   d. _____ Children should show the utmost respect for their parents.

   e. _____ Most parents and children don't understand each other very well.

   f. _____ Discrimination on the basis of social class is a problem in my native culture.

   g. _____ Fate governs people's lives.

   h. _____ Women are generally more courageous than men.

   i. _____ It is more important to follow tradition than to embrace new ideas.

   j. _____ Arranged marriages are usually stronger than those based on love.

A Coward
PREMCHAND

Premchand, the pseudonym of Dhanpat Rai (1881–1936), is considered one of the greatest writers of modern India. Born in a village near Benares and raised in a poor family, he went on to study Persian, Urdu, and Hindi and wrote a number of novels and short stories in the latter two languages. Premchand is known as the founder of the serious short story in India—a new style of fiction that abandoned the romantic tales of the past in favor of realistic portrayals of social problems, especially those of the vast peasant masses.

The following story, "A Coward," published in 1933, deals with the caste system in India. A caste is one of the social classes in Hinduism (the predominant religion in India) determined by birth and following certain rules, restrictions, and privileges. In traditional Hindu society, there were four major castes: Brahmans, priests and scholars; Kshatriyas, warriors and rulers; Vaishyas, merchants and artisans; and Sudras, servants and slaves. Below the Sudras were the Panchamas—the outcasts, or untouchables. Today there are more than three thousand subcastes in India, ranging in size from one hundred to millions.

The boy's name was Keshav, the girl's Prema. They went to the same 1 college and they were in the same class. Keshav believed in new ways and was opposed to the old caste customs. Prema adhered to the old order and fully accepted the traditions. But all the same there was a strong attachment between them and the whole college was aware of it. Although he was a Brahman[1] Keshav regarded marriage with this Banya[2] girl as the culmination of his life. He didn't care a straw about his father and mother. Caste traditions he considered a fraud. If anything embodied the truth for him it was Prema. But for Prema it was impossible to take one step in opposition to the dictates of caste and family.

One evening the two of them met in a secluded corner of Victoria Park and 2 sat down on the grass facing one another. The strollers had gone off one by one but these two lingered on. They had got into a discussion it was impossible to end.

Keshav said angrily, "All it means is that you don't care about me." 3

Prema tried to calm him down. "You're being unjust to me, Keshav. It's 4 only that I don't know how I can bring it up at home without upsetting them. They're devoted to the old traditions. If they hear anything about a matter like this from me can't you imagine how distressed they'll be?"

"And aren't you a slave of those old traditions too then?" Keshav asked her 5 sharply.

---

[1] *Brahman:* Highest of the Hindu castes, traditionally consisting of priests and scholars.

[2] *Banya:* Hindu subcaste consisting of merchants and traders.

"No, I'm not," Prema said, her eyes tender, "but what my mother and father 6
want is more important to me than anything."

"And you yourself don't count at all?" 7

"If that's how you want to understand it." 8

"I used to think those old ways were just for silly hypocrites but now it 9
seems that educated girls like you knuckle under to them too. Since I'm ready
to give up everything for you I expect the same thing from you."

In silence Prema wondered what authority she had over her own life. She 10
had no right to go in any way against the mother and father who had created
her from their own blood and reared her with love. To Keshav she said
humbly, "Can love be considered only in terms of husband and wife and not
friendship? I think of love as an attachment of the soul."

"You'll drive me crazy with your rationalizations," Keshav said harshly. 11
"Just understand this—if I'm disappointed I can't go on living. I'm a material-
ist and it's not possible for me to be satisfied with some intangible happiness
in the world of the imagination."

He caught Prema's hand and tried to draw her toward him, but she broke 12
away and said, "I told you I'm not free. Don't ask me to do something I have
no right to do."

If she'd spoken harshly he would not have been so hurt. For an instant he 13
restrained himself, then he stood up and said sadly, "Just as you wish," and
slowly walked away. Prema, in tears, continued to sit there.

2

When after supper that night Prema lay down in her mother's room she 14
could not sleep. Keshav had said things to her that shadowed her heart like
reflections in unquiet waters, changing at every moment, and she could not
calm them. How could she talk to her mother about such things? Embarrassment kept her silent. She thought, "If I don't marry Keshav what's left for me
in life?" While she thought about it over and over again her mind was made
up about just one thing—if she did not marry Keshav she would marry no
one.

Her mother said, "Still not sleeping? I've told you so many times you ought 15
to do a little work around the house. But you can never take any time off from
your books. In a little while you'll be going to some strange house and who
knows what sort of place it will be? If you don't get accustomed to doing
housework, how are you going to manage?"

Naïvely Prema asked, "Why will I be going to a strange house?" 16

Smiling, her mother said, "For a girl it's the greatest calamity, daughter. 17
After being sheltered at home, as soon as she's grown up off she goes to live
with others. If she gets a good husband her days pass happily, otherwise she
has to go through life weeping. It all depends on fate. But in our community
there's no family that appeals to me. There's no proper regard for girls any-

where. But we have to stay within our caste. Who knows how long caste marriages are going to go on?"

Frightened Prema said, "But here and there they're beginning to have 18 marriages outside the caste." She'd said it for the sake of talking but she trembled lest her mother might guess something.

Surprised, her mother asked, "You don't mean among Hindus?" Then she 19 answered herself. "If this has happened in a few places, then what's come of it?"

Prema did not reply. She was afraid her mother had understood her mean- 20 ing. She saw her future in that moment before her like a great dark tunnel opening its mouth to swallow her up. It was a long time before she could fall asleep.

3

When she got up early in the morning Prema was aware of a strange new 21 courage. We all make important decisions on the spur of the moment as though some divine power impelled us toward them, and so it was with Prema. Until yesterday she'd considered her parents' ideas as unchallengeable, but facing the problem courage was born in her, much in the way a quiet breeze coming against a mountain sweeps over the summit in a violent gust. Prema thought, "Agreed, this body is my mother's and father's but whatever my own self, my soul, is to get must be got in this body. To hesitate now would not only be unfitting, it would be fatal. Why sacrifice your life for false principle? If a marriage isn't founded on love then it's just a business bargain with the body. Could you give yourself without love?" And she rebelled against the idea that she could be married off to somebody she had never seen.

After breakfast she had started to read when her father called her affection- 22 ately. "Yesterday I went to see your principal and he had a lot of praise for you."

"You're only saying that!" 23

"No, it's true." Then he opened a drawer of his desk and took out a picture 24 set in a velvet frame. He showed it to her and said, "This boy came out first in the Civil Service[3] examinations. You must have heard of him."

He had brought up the subject in such a way as not to give away his 25 intention, but it was clear to Prema, she saw through it at once. Without looking at the picture she said, "No, I don't know who he is."

With feigned surprise her father said, "What? You haven't even heard his 26 name? His picture and an article about him are in today's paper."

"Suppose they are?" Prema said. "The examinations don't mean anything to 27 me. I always assumed that people who took those exams must be terribly conceited. After all, what do they aim for except to lord it over their

---

[3] *civil service:* Public administration.

wretched, penniless brothers?—and pile up a fortune doing it. That's no great career to aspire to."

The objection was spiteful, unjust. Her father had assumed that after his 28 eulogy she would be interested. When he'd listened to her answer he said sharply, "You talk as though money and power mean nothing to you."

"That's right," she said, "they don't mean a thing to me. I look for self- 29 sacrifice in a man. I know some boys who wouldn't accept that kind of position even if you tried to force it on them."

"Well, I've learned something new today!" he said sarcastically. "And still I 30 see people swarming around trying to get the meanest little jobs—I'd just like to see the face of one of these fellows capable of such self-sacrifice. If I did I'd get down on my knees to him."

Perhaps if she'd heard these words on another occasion Prema might have 31 hung her head in shame. But this time, like a soldier with a dark tunnel behind him, there was no way for her to go except forward. Scarcely controlling her anger, her eyes full of indignation, she went to her room and from among several pictures of Keshav picked out the one she considered the worst and brought it back and set it down in front of her father. He wanted to give it no more than a casual glance, but at the first glimpse he was drawn to it. Keshav was tall and even though thin one recognized a strength and discipline about him; he was not particularly handsome but his face reflected such intelligence that one felt confidence in him.

While he looked at it her father said, "Who is he?" 32

Prema, bowing her head, said hesitantly, "He's in my class." 33

"Is he of our community?" 34

Prema's face clouded over: her destiny was to be decided on the answer. 35 She realized that it was useless to have brought out the picture. The firmness she had had for an instant weakened before this simple question. In a low voice she said, "No, he's not, he's a Brahman." And even while she was saying it, agitated she left the room as though the atmosphere there were suffocating her, and on the other side of the wall she began to cry.

Her father's anger was so great at first that he wanted to call her out again 36 and tell her plainly it was impossible. He got as far as the door, but seeing Prema crying his anger softened. He was aware of what Prema felt for this boy and he believed in education for women but he intended to maintain the family traditions. He would have sacrificed all his property for a suitable bridegroom of his own caste. But outside the limits of his community he could not conceive of any bridegroom worthy or noble enough; he could not imagine any disgrace greater than going beyond them.

"From today on you'll stop going to college," he said with a harsh tone. "If 37 education teaches you to disregard our traditions, then education is wicked."

Timidly Prema said, "But it's almost time for the examinations." 38

"Forget about them." 39

Then he went into his room and pondered a long time. 40

4

One day six months later Prema's father came home and called Vriddha, his 41 wife, for a private talk.

"As far as I know," he said, "Keshav's a well-brought-up and brilliant boy. 42 I'm afraid that Prema's grieving to the point where she might take her life. You and I have tried to explain and so have others but nobody has had the slightest effect on her. What are we going to do about it?"

Anxiously his wife said, "Let her, but if she has her way how can you face 43 the dishonour? How could I ever have borne a wicked girl like that!"

He frowned and said with a tone of reproach, "I've heard that a thousand 44 times. But just how long can we moan about this caste tradition business? You're mistaken if you think the bird's going to stay hopping at home once it's spread its wings. I've thought about the problem objectively and I've come to the conclusion that we're obliged to face the emergency. I can't watch Prema die in the name of caste rules. Let people laugh but the time is not far off when all these old restrictions will be broken. Even today there have been hundreds of marriages outside the caste limitations. If the aim of marriage is a happy life for a man and a woman together we can't oppose Prema."

Vriddha was angry. "If that's your intention then why ask me?" she said. 45 "But I say that I won't have anything to do with this marriage, and I'll never look at that girl's face again, I'll consider her as dead as our sons who died."

"Well then, what else can you suggest?" 46

"What if we do let her marry this boy? He'll take his civil service examina- 47 tions in two years and with what he has to offer it will be a great deal if he becomes a clerk in some office."

"But what if Prema should kill herself?" 48

"Then let her—you've encouraged her, haven't you? If she doesn't care 49 about us why should we blacken our name for her? Anyway, suicide's no game—it's only a threat. The heart's like a wild horse—until it's broken and bridled nobody can touch it. If her heart stays like that who's to say that she'll look after Keshav for a whole life-time? The way she's in love with him today, well, she can be in love with somebody else just as much tomorrow. And because of this you're ready to be disgraced?"

Her husband gave her a questioning look. "And if tomorrow she should go 50 and marry Keshav, then what will you do? Then how much of your honour will be left? Out of shyness or consideration for us she may not have done anything yet, but if she decides to be stubborn there's nothing you or I can do."

It had never occurred to Vriddha that the problem could have such a 51 dreadful ending. His meaning struck her with the violence of a bullet. She sat silent for a moment as though the shock had scattered her wits. Then, backing down, she said, "What wild ideas you have! Until today I've never heard of a decent girl marrying according to her own wish."

"You may not have heard of it but I have, I've seen it and it's entirely 52
possible."

"The day it happens will be my last!" 53

"But if it has to be this way isn't it preferable that we make the proper 54
arrangements? If we're to be disgraced we may as well be efficient about it.
Send for Keshav tomorrow and see what he has to say."

5

Keshav's father lived from a government pension. By nature he was ill- 55
tempered and miserly; he found satisfaction only in religious ostentation. He
was totally without imagination and unable to respect the personal feelings of
anybody else. At present he was still living in the same world in which he had
passed his childhood and youth. The rising tide of progress he called ruin-
ation and hoped to save at least his own family from it by any means available
to him. Therefore when one day Prema's father came to him and broached
the prospect of her marrying Keshav, old Panditji could not control himself.
Staring through eyes dim with anger he said, "Are you drunk? Whatever this
relationship may be it's not marriage. It appears that you too have had your
head turned by the new ideas."

"I don't like this sort of connection either," Prema's father said gently. "My 56
ideas about it are just the same as yours. But the thing is that, being helpless, I
had to come to see you. You're aware too of how willful today's youngsters
have become. It's getting hard for us old-timers to defend our theories. I'm
afraid that if these two become desperate they may take their lives."

Old Panditji brought his foot down with a bang and shouted, "What are you 57
saying, Sir! Aren't you ashamed? We're Brahmans and even among Brahmans
we're of high rank. No matter how low a Brahman may fall he can never be so
degraded that he can countenance a marriage with a shop-keeping Banya's
daughter. The day noble Brahmans run out of daughters we can discuss the
problem. I say you have a fantastic nerve even to bring this matter up with
me."

He was every bit as furious as Prema's father was humble, and the latter, 58
unable to bear the humiliation any longer, went off cursing his luck.

Just then Keshav returned from college. Panditji sent for him at once and 59
said severely, "I've heard that you're betrothed to some Banya girl. How far
has this actually gone?"

Pretending ignorance, Keshav said, "Who told you this?" 60

"Somebody. I'm asking you, is it true or not? If it's true and you've decided 61
to go against your caste, then there's no more room for you in this house. You
won't get one pice[4] of my money. Whatever is in this house I've earned, and

---

[4] *pice:* Indian coin in existence before 1955.

it's my right to give it to whomever I want. If you're guilty of this wicked conduct, you won't be permitted to put your foot inside my house."

Keshav was familiar with his father's temper. He loved Prema and he in- 62 tended to marry her in secret. His father wouldn't always be alive and he counted on his mother's affection; sustained by that love he felt that he was ready to suffer any hardships. But Keshav was like a faint-hearted soldier who loses his courage at the sight of a gun and turns back. Like any average young fellow he would argue his theories with a passion and demonstrate his devotion with his tongue. But to suffer for them was beyond his capacity. If he persisted and his father refused to weaken he didn't know where he would turn, his life would be ruined.

In a low voice he said, "Whoever told you that is a complete liar and 63 nothing else."

Staring at him, Panditji said, "So my information is entirely mistaken?" 64

"Yes, entirely mistaken." 65

"Then you'll write a letter to that shopkeeper this very moment and re- 66 member that if there's any more of this gossip he can regard you as his greatest enemy. Enough, go."

Keshav could say no more. He walked away but it seemed to him that his 67 legs were utterly numb.

6

The next day Prema sent this letter to Keshav: 68

> Dearest Keshav,
>
> I was terribly upset when I heard about the rude and callous way your father 69 treated mine. Perhaps he's threatened you too, in which case I wait anxiously to hear what your decision is. I'm ready to undergo any kind of hardship with you. I'm aware of your father's wealth but all I need is your love to content me. Come tonight and have dinner with us. My mother and father are both eager to meet you.
>
> I'm caught up in the dream of when the two of us will be joined by that bond 70 that cannot be broken, that remains strong no matter how great the difficulties.
>
> Your Prema

By evening there had been no reply to this letter. Prema's mother asked 71 over and over again, "Isn't Keshav coming?" and her father kept his eyes glued on the door. By nine o'clock there was still no sign of Keshav nor any letter.

In Prema's mind all sorts of fears and hopes revolved. Perhaps Keshav had 72 had no chance to write a letter, no chance to come today so that tomorrow he would surely come. She read over again the love letters he'd written her earlier. How steeped in love was every word, how much emotion, anxiety and acute desire! Then she remembered the words he'd said a hundred times and often he'd wept before her. It was impossible to despair with so many proofs, but all the same throughout the night she was tormented by anxiety.

Early in the morning Keshav's answer came. Prema took the letter with 73 trembling hands and read it. The letter fell from her hands. It seemed to her that her blood had ceased to flow. He had written:

> I'm in a terrible quandary about how to answer you. I've been desperate trying to figure out what to do and I've come to the conclusion that for the present it would be impossible for me to go against my father's orders. Don't think I'm a coward. I'm not being selfish either. But I don't have the strength to get over the obstacles facing me. Forget what I told you before. At that time I had no idea of how hard it was going to be.

Prema drew a long, painful breath, then she tore up the letter and threw it 74 away. Her eyes filled with tears. She had never had the slightest expectation that the Keshav she had taken into her heart of hearts as her husband could be so cruel. It was as though until now she'd been watching a golden vision but on opening her eyes it had vanished completely. All her hope had disappeared and she was left in darkness.

"What did Keshav write?" her mother asked. 75

Prema looked at the floor and said, "He's not feeling well." What else was 76 there to say? She could not have borne the shame of revealing Keshav's brutal disloyalty.

She spent the whole day working around the house, as though there were 77 nothing wrong. She made dinner for everyone that evening and ate with them, then until quite late she played the harmonium[5] and sang.

In the morning they found her lying dead in her room at a moment when 78 the golden rays of dawn bestowed on her face the illusory splendour of life.

READING JOURNAL

In your reading journal, discuss one of the following:

1. What you consider the central message of "A Coward"
2. Whether or not you would marry someone if your parents were against it
3. A topic of your own choice related to the story

VOCABULARY: FIGURES OF SPEECH

Figures of speech are comparisons between two things that are usually seen as dissimilar. The two most common figures of speech are *similes* and *metaphors*. A *simile* is an explicit comparison between two dissimilar things using *like* or *as* ("My room looks like a pigsty"). A *metaphor* is an

---

[5] *harmonium:* Small keyboard instrument similar to an organ.

implied comparison between two dissimilar things not using *like* or *as* ("My room is a pigsty").

In "A Coward," Premchand uses many figures of speech to convey his ideas and add color to his writing. Show that you understand the meaning of the following similes and metaphors by restating the main idea of each in simple, literal language. Work either by yourself or with a partner. Then compare your restatements with those of several classmates. (At this point, you might want to review the discussion of figures of speech, or figurative language, on pp. 154–155.)

Example:

"She saw her future in that moment before her like a great dark tunnel opening its mouth to swallow her up." (par. 20)

RESTATEMENT: She envisioned a future filled with despair.

1. "Keshav had said things to her that shadowed her heart like reflections in unquiet waters." (par. 14)

   Restatement: _____

   _____

2. "Courage was born in her, much in the way a quiet breeze coming against a mountain sweeps over the summit in a violent gust." (par. 21)

   Restatement: _____

   _____

3. "If a marriage isn't founded on love then it's just a business bargain with the body." (par. 21)

   Restatement: _____

   _____

4. "You're mistaken if you think the bird's going to stay hopping at home once it's spread its wings." (par. 44)

   Restatement: _____

   _____

5. "The heart's like a wild horse—until it's broken and bridled nobody can touch it." (par. 49)

Restatement: _____

_____

ADDITIONAL READINGS

Sex, Sighs, and Conversation
Why Men and Women Can't Communicate
DEBORAH TANNEN

Deborah Tannen, a professor of linguistics at Georgetown University, has written several popular books on the different ways females and males use language: That's Not What I Meant *(1986),* You Just Don't Understand *(1990), and* Talking from 9 to 5 *(1994). The following selection first appeared in the* Boston Globe, *a large daily newspaper, in August 1990.*

A man and a woman were seated in a car that had been circling the same 1 area for a half hour. The woman was saying, "Why don't we just *ask* someone?" The man was saying, not for the first time, "I'm sure it's around here somewhere. I'll just try this street."

Why are so many men reluctant to ask directions? Why aren't women? And 2 why can't women understand why men don't want to ask? The explanation, for this and for countless minor and major frustrations that women and men encounter when they talk to each other, lies in the different ways that they use language—differences that begin with how girls and boys use language as children, growing up in different worlds.

Anthropologists, sociologists and psychologists have found that little girls 3 play in small groups or in pairs; they have a best friend, with whom they spend a lot of time talking. It's the telling of secrets that makes them best friends. They learn to use language to negotiate intimacy—to make connections and feel close to each other.

Boys, on the other hand, tend to play competitive games in larger groups, 4 which are hierarchical. High-status boys give orders, and low-status boys are pushed around. So boys learn to use language to preserve independence and negotiate their status, trying to hold center stage, challenge and resist challenges, display knowledge and verbal skill.

These divergent assumptions about the purpose of language persist into 5 adulthood, where they lie in wait behind cross-gender conversations, ready to leap out and cause puzzlement or grief. In the case of asking for directions, the same interchange is experienced differently by women and men. From a woman's perspective, you ask for help, you get it, and you get to where you're going. A fleeting connection is made with a stranger, which is fundamentally pleasant. But a man is aware that by admitting ignorance and asking for information, he positions himself one-down to someone else. Far from pleasant, this is humiliating. So it makes sense for him to preserve his independence and self-esteem at the cost of a little extra travel time.

Here is another scene from the drama of the differences in men's and 6 women's ways of talking. A woman and a man return home from work. She tells everything that happened during the day: what she did, whom she met, what they said, what that made her think. Then she turns to him and asks, "How was your day?" He says, "Same old rat race." She feels locked out: "You don't tell me anything." He protests, "Nothing happened at work." They have different assumptions about what's "anything" to tell. To her, telling life's daily events and impressions means she's not alone in the world. Such talk is the essence of intimacy—evidence that she and her partner are best friends. Since he never spent time talking in this way with his friends, best or otherwise, he doesn't expect it, doesn't know how to do it, and doesn't miss it when it isn't there.

Another source of mutual frustration is the difference in women's and 7 men's assumptions about "troubles talk." She begins to talk about a problem; he offers a solution; she dismisses it, with pique. He feels frustrated: "She complains, but she doesn't want to do anything to solve her problems." Indeed, what she wants to do about it is talk. She is frustrated because his solution cuts short the discussion, and implies she shouldn't be wasting time talking about it.

The female search for connection and the male concern with hierarchy is 8 evident here, too. When a woman tells another woman about a problem, her friend typically explores the problem ("And then what did he say?" "What do you think you might do?"); expresses understanding ("I know how you feel"); or offers a similar experience ("It's like the time I . . ."). All these responses express support and bring them closer. But offering a solution positions the problem-solver as one-up. This asymmetry is distancing, just the opposite of what she was after in bringing up the discussion.

A similar mismatch of expectations occurs when a woman complains about 9 her boss, and a man tries to be helpful by explaining the boss' point of view. She perceives this as an attack, and a lack of loyalty to her. One man told me, incredulously, "My girl friend just wants to talk about her point of view." He feels that offering opposing views is obviously a more constructive conversational contribution. But conversations among women are usually characterized by mutual support and exploration. Alternative views may be introduced, but they are phrased as suggestions and questions, not as direct challenges. This is one of the many ways that men value oppositional stances, whereas women value harmonious ones.

A woman was hurt when she heard her husband telling the guests at a 10 dinner party about an incident involving his boss that he hadn't told her. She felt this *proved* that he hadn't been honest when he'd said nothing happened at work. But he didn't think of this experience as a story to tell until he needed to come up with material to put himself forward at the dinner party.

Thus, it isn't that women always talk more, while men are taciturn and 11 succinct. Women talk more at home, since talk, for them, is a way of creating intimacy. Since men regard talk as a means to negotiate status, they often see no need to talk at home. But they talk more in "public" situations with people they know less well. At a meeting, when questions are solicited from the floor, it is almost always a man who speaks first. When the phones are opened on a radio talk show, the vast majority of calls are from men, who are more likely to speak at length, giving introductions to their questions (if they have any) and addressing multiple topics.

Generalizing about groups of people makes many of us nervous. We like to 12 think of ourselves as unique individuals, not representatives of stereotypes. But it is more dangerous to ignore patterns than to articulate them.

If women and men have different ways of talking (and my research, and 13 that of others, shows that they do), then expecting us to be the same leads to disappointment and mutual accusation. Unaware of conversational style differences, we fall back on mutual blame: "You go on and on about nothing." "You don't listen to me."

Realizing that a partner's behavior is not his or her individual failing, but a 14 normal expression of gender, lifts this burden of blame and disappointment. Surprisingly, years together can make the mutual frustration worse, rather than better. After 57 years of marriage, my parents are still grappling with the different styles I have described. When my mother read my book,[1] she said, "You mean it isn't just Daddy? I always thought he was the only one."

Understanding gender differences in ways of talking is the first step toward 15 changing. Not knowing that people of the other gender have different ways of talking, and different assumptions about the place of talk in a relationship, people assume they are doing things right and their partners are doing things wrong. Then no one is motivated to change; if your partner is accusing you of wrong behavior, changing would be tantamount to admitting fault. But when they think of the differences as cross-cultural, people find that they and their partners are willing, even eager, to make small adjustments that will please their partners and improve the relationship.

---

[1] *my book: You Just Don't Understand: Women and Men in Conversation* (1990).

The Blind Men and the Elephant
A Hindu Fable
JOHN GODFREY SAXE

> *The following fable, told in poetic form by John Godfrey Saxe, is part of Hindu tradition. (Hinduism is the dominant religion in India.) The poem's final two stanzas, which explain the moral, or lesson, have been deleted. After you have read the fable, write several sentences in the blanks explaining what you consider the moral of the story to be. Feel free to express your ideas in poetic or prose form.*

It was six men of Indostan[1]
    To learning much inclined,
Who went to see the Elephant
    (Though all of them were blind),
That each by observation
    Might satisfy his mind.

The First approached the Elephant,
    And happening to fall
Against his broad and sturdy side,
    At once began to bawl:
"God bless me! but the Elephant
    Is very like a wall!"

The Second feeling of the tusk,
    Cried, "Ho! what have we here
So very round and smooth and sharp?
    To me 'tis mighty clear
This wonder of an Elephant
    Is very like a spear!"

The Third approached the animal,
    And happening to take
The squirming trunk within his hands,
    Thus boldly up and spake:[2]
"I see," quoth[3] he, "the Elephant
    Is very like a snake!"

---

[1] *Indostan:* Present-day India, Pakistan, and Bangladesh.

[2] *boldly up and spake:* Stood up boldly and spoke.

[3] *quoth:* Said.

The Fourth reached out an eager hand,
  And felt about the knee,
"What most this wondrous beast is like
  Is mighty plain," quoth he;
"'Tis clear enough the Elephant
  Is very like a tree!"

The Fifth who chanced to touch the ear,
  Said: "E'en[4] the blindest man
Can tell what this resembles most;
  Deny the fact who can,
This marvel of an Elephant
  Is very like a fan!"

The Sixth no sooner had begun
  About the beast to grope,
Than, seizing on the swinging tail
  That fell within his scope,[5]
"I see," quoth he, "the Elephant
  Is very like a rope!"

The Moral:

_____

_____

_____

_____

The Adjustment Process in a New Culture

The five common stages of adjustment have the following characteristics:

1. *Honeymoon period*: Initially, everything seems new and exciting—a big adventure.
2. *Culture shock*: At this point, people often feel tired, disoriented, irritable, disappointed, and homesick (and sometimes experience physical prob-

---

[4] *e'en:* Even.

[5] *scope:* Reach.

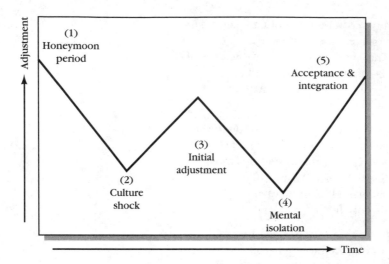

lems, such as stomach upset and insomnia). They also often have difficulty concentrating and working well.

3. *Initial adjustment*: As people get to know the culture and language better, they feel more hopeful, self-confident, and connected. They can also concentrate and work better.

4. *Mental isolation*: During this stage, people often feel angry, frustrated, isolated, and depressed and find fault with the new culture. They frequently avoid contact with people from the new culture and associate with fellow nationals and other "foreigners." (The negative feelings in this stage are usually more intense than in Stage Two.)

5. *Acceptance and integration*: After some time, people become more accustomed to the values, beliefs, and behaviors of the new culture. They know what to expect and feel more at home. They also stop continually glorifying their native culture and criticizing the new culture.

MAKING CONNECTIONS

The following questions and activities can be used for both writing assignments and class discussions. These exercises will help develop your ability to *synthesize* what you read—to combine and integrate information and ideas from different sources.

1. Which of the selections in this chapter did you like best, and why? Which did you like least, and why?

2. All of the readings in this chapter deal with obstacles, or barriers, to effective cross-cultural communication. What do you consider the main obstacles reflected in the six selections?

3. Review the seven major categories of values and assumptions discussed in the first selection in this chapter. To what extent are these values and assumptions reflected in the cultural patterns described in the other readings?

4. Interview someone from another country about any issues raised in this chapter: cultural values, beliefs, and practices; culture shock; cross-cultural conflict; and so on. Then share your findings with the rest of the class.

5. Write an essay or give an oral presentation on a topic of your own choice relating to one or more of the readings in this chapter. Consider research-ing your subject in a university or public library. (*Sample topics:* A custom, myth, art form, or hero in your native culture; differences in body language between females and males; culture shock; cultural differences in attitudes toward time; and a current inter- or intracultural conflict.)

6. Read one of the following selections from another chapter in this book: any of the readings in Chapter 2 or 3, "Señor Payroll" (Chapter 4), or "They Get by with a Lot of Help from Their Kyoiku Mamas" (Chapter 5). Discuss the ways in which the reading reflects issues raised in this chapter. To what extent are the ideas and perspectives similar?

CHAPTER TWO

STEREOTYPING AND DISCRIMINATION

Reading Skill:
Identifying a Writer's Purpose and Tone

"African Americans are good dancers." "Overweight people are lazy." "Moslems are religious fanatics." These three statements are *stereotypes:* overgeneralized and inaccurate beliefs about people, places, and things. The readings and activities in this chapter explore the reasons for such oversimplified beliefs and the negative effect they have on people's lives. All of the readings deal with one of the most severe consequences of stereotyping—*discrimination,* or hostile actions against a particular person or group of people based on such factors as race, ethnicity, gender, social class, nationality, religion, and sexual orientation.

Following are some of the questions you will be considering in this chapter:

- What are the forms and functions of discrimination?
- What are the myths and stereotypes underlying various forms of prejudice?
- How are different ethnic groups portrayed in the mass media?
- What are the best ways to combat stereotyping and discrimination?
- What are your own attitudes toward certain groups of people?
- Have you ever been stereotyped or discriminated against?

All of the readings in this chapter focus on victims of discrimination, especially on the ways negative stereotyping and prejudice have affected their lives. In the first reading, "I Have a Dream," Martin Luther King, Jr., makes an impassioned plea for racial equality in the United States. Next, in

"Striking a Nerve," Barbara Kantrowitz examines sexual harassment in the United States, concentrating on the feelings of women who have been sexually harassed. After that, in "It Cannot Be Helped," Jeanne Wakatsuki Houston describes the incidents leading up to her family's placement in a Japanese American internment camp in California during World War II. Then, in "Eleven Words That Cast the Power of Bigotry on Honeymoon Couple," Jonathan Kaufman discusses a time when he was the victim of anti-Semitism. Following this, the poem "Caged Bird," by Maya Angelou, explores the themes of freedom and oppression. Finally, a cartoon by Jules Feiffer raises questions about the nature of discrimination.

BRIEF QUOTES

The following quotations will help introduce you to the topics of stereotyping and discrimination. Think about these statements as you read the selections in this chapter.

"Prejudices are the props of civilization."

—ANDRÉ GIDE

"Prejudices, it is well known, are most difficult to eradicate from the heart whose soil has never been loosened or fertilized by education; they grow there, firm as weeds among stones."

—CHARLOTTE BRONTË

"Bigotry may be roughly defined as the anger of men who have no opinions."

—G. K. CHESTERTON

"After all, there is but one race—humanity."

—GEORGE MOORE

"What is the difference between making reasonable generalizations about other people and stereotyping? There is no easy answer to this question, and the area between 'well-thought-out generalization' and 'stereotype' is very gray."

—RICHARD BRISLIN

"All of us do not have equal talent, but all of us should have an equal opportunity to develop our talents."

—JOHN F. KENNEDY

"Legislation is not going to change discrimination. That is like trying to legislate morality."

—BEVERLY BUTCHER BYRON

"He who lives with untruth lives in spiritual slavery. Freedom is still the bonus we receive for knowing the truth. 'Ye shall know the truth, and the truth shall set you free.'"

—MARTIN LUTHER KING, JR.

READING

PREREADING ACTIVITIES

1. In your reading journal, write for ten to fifteen minutes about a group of people in your native country that has been the victim of discrimination.

2. With several classmates, discuss the meaning of the following words and phrases. Look up any unfamiliar items in a dictionary or consult with your teacher.

   prejudice, discrimination, stereotype, racism, ghetto, segregation, passive resistance, civil rights, American dream

3. Indicate the extent to which you agree with the following statements by filling in each blank with *SA* (strongly agree), *A* (agree), *U* (undecided), *D* (disagree), or *SD* (strongly disagree). Then compare your responses in a small group.

   a. _____   Certain racial groups are more intelligent than others.

   b. _____   African Americans commit most of the crimes in the United States.

   c. _____   Violence is a more effective means of social change than passive resistance.

   d. _____   Women are by nature more gentle and nurturing than men.

   e. _____   Jews control most of the world's wealth.

   f. _____   Discrimination has existed in every culture throughout history.

   g. _____   Gay men and lesbians can be easily identified in public.

   h. _____   Blacks tend to be better athletes than whites.

   i. _____   Prejudice can be eradicated if people try hard enough.

   j. _____   Women who dress provocatively are responsible for certain types of sexual harassment.

I Have a Dream

MARTIN LUTHER KING, JR.

Born in 1929 in Atlanta, Georgia, Martin Luther King, Jr., attended segregated schools and also preached in his father's Baptist church. After receiving a Ph.D. in theology from Boston University, he was appointed pastor of a Baptist church in Montgomery, Alabama, in 1954 and became known as a moving orator. The next year, he led a twelve-month boycott by blacks of segregated buses in Montgomery. During the 1960s, King gained national prominence as a civil rights leader, advocating passive resistance and other forms of nonviolent protest, including marches, demonstrations, and boycotts. His inspired work in the civil rights movement led to the Nobel Peace Prize in 1964. King was assassinated in Memphis, Tennessee, in 1968.

King delivered the following speech, "I Have a Dream," on August 28, 1963, in Washington, D.C., at a demonstration by 200,000 people for black civil rights.

I am happy to join with you today in what will go down in history as the greatest demonstration for freedom in the history of our nation. 1

Fivescore[1] years ago, a great American,[2] in whose symbolic shadow we stand today, signed the Emancipation Proclamation. This momentous decree came as a great beacon light of hope to millions of Negro[3] slaves who had been seared in the flames of withering injustice. It came as a joyous daybreak to end the long night of their captivity. 2

But one hundred years later, the Negro still is not free; one hundred years later, the life of the Negro is still sadly crippled by the manacles of segregation and the chains of discrimination; one hundred years later, the Negro lives on a lonely island of poverty in the midst of a vast ocean of material prosperity; one hundred years later, the Negro is still languished in the corners of American society and finds himself in exile in his own land. 3

So we've come here today to dramatize a shameful condition. In a sense we've come to our nation's capital to cash a check. When the architects of our republic wrote the magnificent words of the Constitution and the Declaration of Independence, they were signing a promissory note[4] to which every American was to fall heir.[5] This note was the promise that all men, yes, black men as well as white men, would be guaranteed the unalienable rights of life, liberty, and the pursuit of happiness. 4

---

[1] *score:* A group of twenty items (five score is one hundred).

[2] *a great American:* Abraham Lincoln (1809–1865), sixteenth president of the United States. In 1863, he signed the Emancipation Proclamation, abolishing slavery.

[3] *Negro:* Term used until the mid-1960s (since that time, the socially acceptable terms have been *black* and *African American*).

[4] *promissory note:* Written promise to pay someone a certain amount of money at a certain time in the future.

[5] *fall heir:* Inherit.

It is obvious today that America has defaulted on this promissory note in so ⁵ far as her citizens of color are concerned. Instead of honoring this sacred obligation, America has given the Negro people a bad check, a check which has come back marked "insufficient funds." But we refuse to believe that the bank of justice is bankrupt. We refuse to believe that there are insufficient funds in the great vaults of opportunity of this nation. And so we've come to cash this check, a check that will give us upon demand the riches of freedom and the security of justice.

We have also come to this hallowed spot to remind America of the fierce ⁶ urgency of now. This is no time to engage in the luxury of cooling off or to take the tranquilizing drug of gradualism. Now is the time to make real the promises of democracy; now is the time to rise from the dark and desolate valley of segregation to the sunlit path of racial justice; now is the time to lift our nation from the quicksands of racial injustice to the solid rock of brother-hood; now is the time to make justice a reality for all God's children. It would be fatal for the nation to overlook the urgency of the moment. This sweltering summer of the Negro's legitimate discontent will not pass until there is an invigorating autumn of freedom and equality.

Nineteen sixty-three is not an end, but a beginning. And those who hope ⁷ that the Negro needed to blow off steam and will now be content will have a rude awakening if the nation returns to business as usual.

There will be neither rest nor tranquility in America until the Negro is ⁸ granted his citizenship rights. The whirlwinds of revolt will continue to shake the foundations of our nation until the bright day of justice emerges.

But there is something that I must say to my people who stand on the ⁹ warm threshold which leads into the palace of justice. In the process of gaining our rightful place we must not be guilty of wrongful deeds.

Let us not seek to satisfy our thirst for freedom by drinking from the cup of ¹⁰ bitterness and hatred. We must forever conduct our struggle on the high plane of dignity and discipline. We must not allow our creative protest to degenerate into physical violence. Again and again we must rise to the majes-tic heights of meeting physical force with soul force.

The marvelous new militancy which has engulfed the Negro community ¹¹ must not lead us to a distrust of all white people, for many of our white brothers, as evidenced by their presence here today, have come to realize that their destiny is tied up with our destiny, and they have come to realize that their freedom is inextricably bound to our freedom. We cannot walk alone.

And as we walk, we must make the pledge that we shall always march ¹² ahead. We cannot turn back. There are those who are asking the devotees of civil rights,⁶ "When will you be satisfied?" We can never be satisfied as long as the Negro is the victim of the unspeakable horrors of police brutality.

---

⁶ *civil rights:* Rights of personal liberty. In 1964, the U.S. Congress passed the Civil Rights Act, prohibiting discrimination in voting, education, employment, and public facilities on the basis of color, race, religion, or national origin.

We can never be satisfied as long as our bodies, heavy with fatigue of travel, 13 cannot gain lodging in the motels of the highways and the hotels of the cities. We cannot be satisfied as long as the Negro's basic mobility is from a smaller ghetto to a larger one.

We can never be satisfied as long as our children are stripped of their 14 selfhood and robbed of their dignity by signs stating "for whites only." We cannot be satisfied as long as a Negro in Mississippi cannot vote and a Negro in New York believes he has nothing for which to vote. No, we are not satisfied, and we will not be satisfied until justice rolls down like waters and righteousness like a mighty stream.

I am not unmindful that some of you have come here out of excessive trials 15 and tribulation. Some of you have come fresh from narrow jail cells. Some of you have come from areas where your quest for freedom left you battered by the storms of persecution and staggered by the winds of police brutality. You have been the veterans of creative suffering. Continue to work with the faith that unearned suffering is redemptive.

Go back to Mississippi; go back to Alabama; go back to South Carolina; go 16 back to Georgia; go back to Louisiana; go back to the slums and ghettos of the northern cities, knowing that somehow this situation can, and will be changed. Let us not wallow in the valley of despair.

So I say to you, my friends, that even though we must face the difficulties of 17 today and tomorrow, I still have a dream. It is a dream deeply rooted in the American dream that one day this nation will rise up and live out the true meaning of its creed—we hold these truths to be self-evident, that all men are created equal.[7]

I have a dream that one day on the red hills of Georgia, sons of former 18 slaves and sons of former slave-owners will be able to sit down together at the table of brotherhood.

I have a dream that one day, even the state of Mississippi, a state sweltering 19 with the heat of injustice, sweltering with the heat of oppression, will be transformed into an oasis of freedom and justice.

I have a dream my four little children will one day live in a nation where 20 they will not be judged by the color of their skin but by the content of their character. I have a dream today!

I have a dream that one day, down in Alabama, with its vicious racists, with 21 its governor having his lips dripping with the words of interposition and nullification,[8] that one day, right there in Alabama, little black boys and black

---

[7] *we hold these truths . . . :* From the Declaration of Independence (1776), a document announcing the creation of the United States and its separation from Great Britain.

[8] *interposition and nullification: Interposition* means interference; *nullification* means an attempt to prevent the operation of a U.S. law. (King is referring to the governor of Alabama, George Wallace, who tried unsuccessfully to prevent integration of the Alabama public schools in the early 1960s.)

girls will be able to join hands with little white boys and white girls as sisters and brothers. I have a dream today!

I have a dream that one day every valley shall be exalted, every hill and 22 mountain shall be made low, the rough places shall be made plain, and the crooked places shall be made straight and the glory of the Lord will be revealed and all flesh shall see it together.[9]

This is our hope. This is the faith that I go back to the South with. 23

With this faith we will be able to hew out of the mountain of despair a 24 stone of hope. With this faith we will be able to transform the jangling discords of our nation into a beautiful symphony of brotherhood.

With this faith we will be able to work together, to pray together, to 25 struggle together, to go to jail together, to stand up for freedom together, knowing that we will be free one day. This will be the day when all of God's children will be able to sing with new meaning—"my country 'tis of thee; sweet land of liberty; of thee I sing; land where my fathers died, land of the pilgrim's pride; from every mountain side, let freedom ring"[10]—and if America is to be a great nation, this must become true.

So let freedom ring from the prodigious hilltops of New Hampshire. 26

Let freedom ring from the mighty mountains of New York. 27

Let freedom ring from the heightening Alleghenies of Pennsylvania. 28

Let freedom ring from the snow-capped Rockies of Colorado. 29

Let freedom ring from the curvaceous slopes of California. 30

But not only that. 31

Let freedom ring from Stone Mountain of Georgia. 32

Let freedom ring from Lookout Mountain of Tennessee. 33

Let freedom ring from every hill and molehill of Mississippi, from every 34 mountainside, let freedom ring.

And when we allow freedom to ring, when we let it ring from every village 35 and hamlet,[11] from every state and city, we will be able to speed up that day when all of God's children—black men and white men, Jews and Gentiles, Catholics and Protestants—will be able to join hands and to sing in the words of the old Negro spiritual, "Free at last, free at last; thank God Almighty, we are free at last."

READING JOURNAL

In your reading journal, discuss one of the following:

1. A time when you were stereotyped or discriminated against

---

[9] *every valley shall be . . . see it together:* Quotation from the Old Testament, Isaiah 40:4–5.

[10] *"my country, 'tis of thee . . .":* First verse of the traditional song "America."

[11] *hamlet:* Small village.

2. Whether or not it is possible for a society to be free of prejudice

3. A topic of your own choice related to King's speech

MEANING AND TECHNIQUE

The following questions and activities will help you understand the main ideas in the speech and the manner in which it was written.

1. In one or two sentences, write down the *main point* you think King is making in the speech. Use your own words.

AUDIENCE

When writing a speech, most people have a specific *audience* in mind. Knowing whom they are going to be addressing can help writers of speeches formulate and organize their ideas. Similarly, writers of articles and essays usually have an audience in mind (sometimes quite specific and sometimes more general). Keeping an audience in mind can help authors manage the content, organization, tone, and style of their writing.

---

2. What is King's primary *audience?* Is he addressing more than one group of people? Support your answer with examples from the speech.

3. What does King mean when he talks about "meeting physical force with soul force" (par. 10)?

PURPOSE

When authors write a piece of fiction or nonfiction, they have a *reason* for doing so. The same holds true for someone giving a speech. The three most common *purposes* of writing and public speaking are:

- *To inform:* To provide the audience with information about a topic or to explain something

- *To persuade:* To convince the audience to believe something or to take a certain course of action

- *To entertain:* To amuse the audience in some way (often through humor)

Keeping a purpose or goal in mind can help writers and public speakers shape the content, organization, tone, and style of their presentation.

---

4. What do you consider the *main purpose* (or *purposes*) of "I Have a Dream"? What does King want his audience to think or feel after hearing him speak? Back up your answer with examples from the speech.

DRAWING INFERENCES

When you read something, the first thing you should focus on is the *literal,* or factual, meaning—that is, on what is actually said. In order to fully understand a writer's point, however, you will often have to go beyond the literal level to the *inferential* level. At this level, you will be "reading between the lines"— that is, looking at the hints and suggestions a writer provides to understand the unstated (inferred) meaning of a passage.

Writers and speakers often express their ideas *indirectly,* allowing the reader and listener to draw his or her own conclusions. For example, in "I Have a Dream," King says, "And those who hope that the Negro needed to blow off steam and will now be content will have a rude awakening if the nation returns to business as usual" (par. 7). King never directly states that the people hoping for this contentment are white Americans, but this can be *inferred* from the context. (King is careful not to directly attack whites in the speech, but he makes it clear that they are responsible for the plight of black Americans.)

Discovering the implied ideas in a reading passage involves the ability to draw inferences. The following questions and activities will help you develop this reading skill.

1. Explain the metaphor of the "promissory note" and "check" in paragraphs 4 and 5. What point is King trying to make? (A metaphor is an implied comparison between two dissimilar things. See the discussion of figures of speech, or figurative language, on pp. 154–155.)

2. "I still have a dream. It is a dream deeply rooted in the American dream that one day this nation will rise up and live out the true meaning of its creed—we hold these truths to be self-evident, that all men are created equal." (par. 17)

   To what extent do you think King's dream can be achieved in your native country? Does true equality already exist for all people?

TONE

When people speak, their *tone of voice* can reveal a lot about their attitude toward a subject. Similarly, when people write, their "voice" can express a wide range of tones, or feelings, such as anger, amusement, optimism, sorrow, and excitement.

The *tone* of a piece of writing is the author's attitude toward a subject as reflected in the choice of words and details. A writer's tone depends on his or her audience, subject matter, and purpose. Learning to recognize the tone of a piece of writing is essential to understanding and evaluating the ideas an author is trying to convey.

TONE *Continued*

Following is a list of adjectives commonly used to describe the tone of a piece of writing (the meaning of some words is given in parentheses).

objective (factual; keeping the author's feelings and interpretations in the background)

subjective (reflecting the author's personal feelings and judgments)

ironic (saying one thing but meaning the opposite; a situation in which what is expected to happen is different from what actually happens)

sarcastic (ridiculing; mocking; ironic)

ambivalent (uncertain; indecisive)

impassioned (filled with passion, or emotion)

cynical (distrustful and scornful)

outspoken (spoken directly and openly)

optimistic	personal	anxious
pessimistic	impersonal	compassionate
formal	angry	disapproving
informal	excited	concerned
serious	surprised	humorous
playful	regretful	confident
cheerful	critical	apologetic
sorrowful	respectful	arrogant

Look at the following sentences, each of which reflects a different tone, or attitude:

- "I've had a great time living in the United States. It's been one of the best experiences of my life."
  (Tone: enthusiastic, positive)

- "I came to the United States because of all the educational opportunities. After studying in an intensive ESL program for one year, I'm now in my first semester at a liberal arts college."
  (Tone: objective, matter-of-fact)

- "I don't really know if I want to stay in the United States another year. There are certain things I like here, but I miss my family and friends back home."
  (Tone: ambivalent, uncertain)

- "Living in the United States has been a very valuable experience for me. When I return home, I can now tell my friends that I know the difference between a hot dog and a hamburger."
  (Tone: sarcastic, mocking)

3. In the speech "I Have a Dream," King expresses a number of different tones, or attitudes. With a partner, read through the following passages from the speech, each reflecting one of the tones in the box below (if you don't know the meaning of a particular word in the box, look it up in a dictionary or consult with your teacher). Then fill in each blank with the adjective that best describes the predominant tone of the passage.

hopeful	patriotic	impassioned	defiant	urgent

_____ a. "Now is the time to make real the promises of democracy; now is the time to rise from the dark and desolate valley of segregation to the sunlit path of racial justice; . . . now is the time to make justice a reality for all God's children." (par. 6)

_____ b. "We can never be satisfied as long as our children are stripped of their selfhood and robbed of their dignity by signs stating 'for whites only.' We cannot be satisfied as long as a Negro in Mississippi cannot vote and a Negro in New York believes he has nothing for which to vote." (par. 14)

_____ c. "I still have a dream. It is a dream deeply rooted in the American dream that one day this nation will rise up and live out the true meaning of its creed—we hold these truths to be self-evident, that all men are created equal." (par. 17)

_____ d. "My country 'tis of thee; sweet land of liberty; of thee I sing; land where my fathers died, land of the pilgrim's pride; from every mountain side, let freedom ring." (par. 25)

_____ e. "And when we allow freedom to ring, when we let it ring from every village and hamlet, from every state and city, we will be able to speed up that day when all of God's children—black men and white men, Jews and Gentiles, Catholics and Protestants—will be able to join hands and to sing in the words of the old Negro spiritual, 'Free at last, free at last; thank God Almighty, we are free at last.'" (par. 35)

4. Think of a question of your own to ask your classmates about an issue raised in King's speech.

VOCABULARY: FIGURES OF SPEECH

Figures of speech are comparisons between two things that are usually seen as dissimilar. The two most common figures of speech are *similes* and *metaphors.* A *simile* is an explicit comparison between two dissimilar things using *like* or *as* ("Life is like a winding river"). A *metaphor* is an implied comparison between two dissimilar things not using *like* or *as* ("Life is a winding river").

In "I Have a Dream," King uses many figures of speech to convey his ideas in a vivid manner. Show that you understand the meaning of the following similes and metaphors by restating each main idea in simple, literal language. Work either by yourself or with a partner. (At this point, you might want to review the discussion of figures of speech, or figurative language, on pp. 154–155.)

Example:

"Now is the time to rise from the dark and desolate valley of segregation to the sunlit path of racial justice." (par. 6)

RESTATEMENT: If we want to achieve true justice, we must end the oppressive system of racial segregation now.

1. "It [the Emancipation Proclamation] came as a joyous daybreak to end the long night of their captivity." (par. 2)

   Restatement: _____

   _____

2. "America has given the Negro people a bad check, a check which has come back marked 'insufficient funds.' " (par. 5)

   Restatement: _____

   _____

3. "Let us not seek to satisfy our thirst for freedom by drinking from the cup of bitterness and hatred." (par. 10)

   Restatement: _____

   _____

4. "We will not be satisfied until justice rolls down like waters and righteousness like a mighty stream." (par. 14)

Restatement: _____

_____

5. "I have a dream that one day every valley shall be exalted, every hill and mountain shall be made low." (par. 22)

Restatement: _____

_____

VOCABULARY: IN CONTEXT

In this exercise, you will develop your vocabulary by using words and idioms in a realistic context.

- If you don't know the meaning of one of the following italicized vocabulary items, first find it in the reading and see if you can determine its meaning from the context. (Review the major types of context clues on pp. 263–267.)
- If the meaning is still unclear, look up the item in a dictionary or consult with a native speaker of English.
- Then, in a few sentences, describe or explain each of the following situations, ideas, and things. **Do not** just define the italicized words and expressions. Discuss personal experiences and opinions and give examples.

1. Something that might *cripple* the economy of a country (par. 3)
2. How much material *prosperity* there is in your native country (par. 3)
3. An example of *insufficient* evidence at a trial (par. 5)
4. An example of a *fierce* determination to do something (par. 6)
5. An activity you like to *engage in,* and why (par. 6)
6. Something you find *invigorating,* and why (par. 6)
7. An example of a *rude awakening* (par. 7)
8. Something that might help someone achieve spiritual *tranquility* (par. 8)
9. Two things that are *inextricably* bound to each other (par. 11)
10. Something that is *self-evident* (par. 17)

DISCUSSION AND DEBATE

1. In a small group, discuss King's speech "I Have a Dream." First, focus on any passages whose meaning is unclear to you. Then, consider (1) King's purpose and how effective he is in achieving it and (2) the extent to which his dream of racial equality can be realized in today's world.

2. What groups of people are discriminated against in your native culture, and why? Consider discrimination based on such factors as race, ethnicity, gender, socioeconomic class, nationality, sexual orientation, and religion. Do any of these oppressed groups have their own civil rights movement?

3. According to the American educator Christine Bennett, "A *stereotype* is a mental category based on exaggerated and inaccurate generalities used to describe all members of a group. Stereotypes are erroneous beliefs, either favorable or unfavorable, that are applied universally and without exception."

   Fill in the blanks below with at least six stereotypes (positive and/or negative) of different groups of people in your native country: nationalities, ethnic groups, socioeconomic classes, religions, occupations, and so on.

   After you have completed your list, share it with several classmates. Consider the *origins* and *effects* of the stereotypes. Do they contribute to prejudice in any way?

   Stereotypes

   1. _____

   2. _____

   3. _____

   4. _____

   5. _____

   6. _____

   7. _____

   8. _____

WRITING ACTIVITIES

1. Good writers are able to create different *tones,* or moods. Practice this skill with a partner by writing two paragraphs, each describing the same inci-

dent, person, place, thing, or idea in a different tone. For instance, you might change the tone from playful to serious, confident to uncertain, optimistic to pessimistic, or matter-of-fact to ironic. Consider changing the details of the paragraph, the style, or both. (Style includes such aspects of writing as word choice, sentence structure, and figures of speech.)

When you have finished, read your paragraphs to several classmates and see if they can guess the tones you are trying to create.

> To help you plan, draft, and revise the following assignment(s), see Appendix A.

2. Imagine you are going to be giving a speech about an emotional topic: women's rights, gays in the military, abortion, euthanasia, and so on.

    Write a short speech in which you passionately argue a particular point of view. Think carefully about your audience and the tone that will best help you achieve your purpose.

3. Write an essay discussing the extent to which you agree with one of the following statements (or with one of the statements in activity 3 of the "Prereading Activities"). Support your arguments with references to "I Have a Dream" and personal observations and experiences.

    a. It is possible to achieve King's dream of racial equality in the world today.

    b. Stereotypes can seriously affect the way people are treated.

    c. The mass media are largely responsible for perpetuating stereotypes and discrimination.

READING

PREREADING ACTIVITIES

1. In your reading journal, *freewrite* for ten minutes on the topic of sexual harassment. Don't worry about spelling, punctuation, grammar, or organization. Just write for ten minutes, without stopping, about whatever comes to mind when you think about sexual harassment. (For a discussion of freewriting and other prewriting strategies, see pp. 234–240.)

2. Do you consider the following behaviors forms of sexual harassment? Why or why not?

    a. A female supervisor repeatedly asks a male employee for a date, even though he's made it clear he isn't interested in going out with her.

b. A male supervisor tells a female employee she won't get a raise if she doesn't have sex with him.

c. A female employee often tells obscene jokes to her male co-workers.

d. A male employee leers and gawks at a female co-worker.

e. A female professor dates a male student.

f. A man makes an obscene comment to a woman as she passes by on the street.

Striking a Nerve
BARBARA KANTROWITZ

The following article, written by Barbara Kantrowitz, originally appeared in Newsweek *magazine in October 1991 during the Anita Hill–Clarence Thomas controversy. In a weekend of nationally televised hearings, Anita Hill, a law professor at the University of Oklahoma, testified before the Senate Judiciary Committee that Clarence Thomas, a nominee for the Supreme Court, had sexually harassed her while she was working for him in the early 1980s. Thomas also testified before the committee, refuting the charges, and was eventually confirmed as a Supreme Court justice. The Senate hearings sparked a national debate in the United States about what legally constitutes sexual harassment. The following essay appeared as the cover story in* Newsweek *shortly after the Senate hearings and outlines the major issues raised by the debate.*

They may be neurosurgeons or typists, police officers or telephone operators, construction workers or even members of Congress. Last week women around the country who disagree on a hundred other issues listened to Anita Hill's allegations and heard themselves talking. They remembered the boss who threatened them, the co-worker whose lewd remarks echoed for hours. They remembered how angry they felt and how they pushed that anger down deep and how they tried to forget—and how they couldn't forget.

Sexual harassment is a fact of life in the American workplace; 21 percent of women polled by *Newsweek* said they have been harassed at work and 42 percent said they knew someone who had been harassed. Other surveys indicate that more than half of working women have faced the problem at some point in their careers. The situation tends to be worst in male-dominated workplaces; in a 1990 Defense Department study, 64 percent of military women said they had endured such abuse. Although the severity may vary—from a pattern of obscene joking to outright assault—the emotional damage is often profound and long-lasting. Men "don't understand that caged feeling," says University of Texas sociologist Susan Marshall. "But women know what sexual harassment is. It's when your neck hairs stand up, when you feel like you're being stalked."

Defining sexual harassment is one of the law's newest frontiers. While some of the boundaries have been set by recent decisions, there is still considerable debate over just what constitutes actionable behavior.[1] Most people understand that when a supervisor demands that a woman sleep with him in order to keep her job, he's stepped over the legal line. But what about aggressive flirting? Or off-color conversation?[2] Often, it's a matter of perception. Some women may find such activities offensive; others may just shrug. And men and women may see things very differently. University of Arizona professor Barbara Gutek surveyed 1,200 men and women for a study on harassment. She asked her subjects whether they considered a sexual proposition flattering. About 67 percent of the men said they would, while only 17 percent of the women agreed. In contrast, 63 percent of women would be insulted by a proposition, compared with 15 percent of men.

Even when their cases seem clear-cut, women say they feel ashamed—as though they were to blame for what happened to them. "Do we have to talk about the sex?" asks Mitzie Buckelew, as her eyes redden and tears begin to fall. She would like to forget that night with her boss in a suburban Atlanta hotel five years ago. Buckelew has claimed in state and federal lawsuits that Donald Farrar, the DeKalb County assistant police chief, threatened to fire her from her secretarial job if she did not have sex with him. He calls her charges "ludicrous." Buckelew claims that even after she gave in, hoping that would end the abuse, he persisted. "He would sneak up behind me and grab my breasts and my rear end right in the office," she says. "He would feel up and down my legs." Buckelew also claims Farrar gave her herpes; he has refused to give her lawyers his medical records.

Since Buckelew filed a harassment complaint in 1989, her car has been vandalized. Obscene phone calls wake her up in the middle of the night. She's still waiting for a resolution of the state and federal suits she has filed. In the meantime, she's been reassigned: to the county dog pound. Shortly after Buckelew sued, Farrar resigned with a full pension. "You start questioning yourself," Buckelew says. "Maybe I did ask for it. I know I didn't use good judgment . . . I just didn't know what to do."

NO OBJECTIONS

Until just a few years ago, women had no recourse when confronted with unwanted advances or offensive comments by a boss or co-worker. In offices where they were the minority, women thought they had to go along to get

---

[1] *actionable behavior:* A behavior that justifies a lawsuit ("action").

[2] *off-color conversation:* Language (of a sexual nature) that is in bad taste.

along. Palma Formica, a family practitioner[3] in New Jersey, recalls that when she was a medical student more than 30 years ago, it was "standard procedure" for professors to make "male-female jokes, usually genital oriented, with the woman bearing the brunt." Women never objected. "What are you going to do, get up and walk out of class? You want to be a doctor? You want to be in a man's field? Then you swallow hard and pretend you don't hear."

But in the past decade, as women have grown to represent nearly half the 7 work force, the courts have begun to strike down what was once "standard procedure." In 1980, the Equal Employment Opportunity Commission (the federal agency that investigates bias in the workplace) said that making sexual activity a condition of employment or promotion was a violation of the 1964 Civil Rights Act.[4] Also forbidden: the creation of "an intimidating, hostile, or offensive working environment."

The EEOC rules had little effect on most women's lives until 1986, when 8 the Supreme Court agreed that sexual harassment did indeed violate civil rights. In the landmark case of *Meritor Savings Bank v. Vinson,* Washington, D.C., bank employee Mechelle Vinson claimed that her supervisor fondled her in front of other employees, followed her into the ladies' room, exposed himself and, on several occasions, raped her. The supervisor and the bank denied her claims, but the court sided with Vinson.

Two other major federal court decisions in January of this year refined the 9 legal definition. In a Florida case involving a female shipyard worker, the court ruled that nude pinups in the workplace constitute illegal harassment. A week later a three-judge panel in San Francisco stated that in cases where men and women might see a pattern of behavior differently, the deciding factor should be whether a "reasonable woman" might feel threatened. In that case, a female IRS[5] worker turned down a request for a date by a co-worker. He responded by writing unwelcome love letters to her. "Men, who are rarely victims of sexual assault, may view sexual conduct in a vacuum without a full appreciation of the underlying threat of violence that a woman may perceive," wrote Judge Robert R. Beezer.

STATE STANDARDS

States have also been trying to set their own standards. Kent Sezer, general 10 counsel[6] for the Illinois Human Rights Commission, describes one case in that state in which a judge developed what Sezer calls the "stub-your-toe

---

[3] *family practitioner:* Family physician (one who practices "family medicine").

[4] *Civil Rights Act:* Act passed by the U.S. Congress, prohibiting discrimination in voting, education, employment, and public facilities on the basis of color, race, religion, or national origin.

[5] *IRS:* Internal Revenue Service, responsible for the assessment and collection of federal taxes.

[6] *counsel:* Lawyer or group of lawyers.

test." An employer had been using profane language; a female employee claimed he had created a hostile environment. The employer said the words were simply expletives and protected as free speech. The judge disagreed. He said that the expletives should be put to a simple test. If the employer had awakened at night and, as he got out of bed, stubbed his toe, would he have shouted, "Oh, cunt!"?[7] The judge didn't think so, and ruled against the employer.

These decisions and others have spurred hundreds of public and private 11 employers to write sexual-harassment policies telling workers exactly how to behave. "Nowadays, it's basically a legal requirement that you have an anti-harassment policy," says Joan Engstrom, equal-employment-opportunity director for General Mills (109,000 employees), based in Minneapolis. Courts may hold employers liable for maintaining a harassment-free environment; the bill for failure can be steep. Although many cases are settled out of court and then sealed, there have been several multi-million-dollar awards in recent years. Avoiding huge payments isn't the only incentive for companies (many awards are, in fact, under $10,000). The publicity surrounding a harassment charge can damage a company's standing with the public.

But corporate policies are only as good as the supervisors who enforce 12 them. Freada Klein, who heads a Cambridge, Mass., consulting firm that advises companies on harassment, says that one-third of harassers are the victims' immediate supervisors. Another third, she says, are even higher up on the corporate ladder but do not directly supervise their victims. The rest are the victims' peers. Like many companies with well-respected records in this area, General Mills runs regular training sessions for employees, with videos explaining sexual harassment. Engstrom says General Mills tries to give its employees a simple explanation of its policy: "Employees are to be treated with dignity and respect. Unbusinesslike conduct that could be considered offensive or intimidating will not be tolerated."

Other companies have more bureaucratic systems in place. At AT&T,[8] 13 whose national work force is 47 percent female, managers must attend an annual training session that includes a discussion of sexual harassment. Nonmanagers learn about the company policy through a book that explains the company's investigation process. Employees also get a copy of the company's code of conduct and many see training tapes on sexual harassment. Company spokesman Burke Stinson says 95 percent of complaints filed with AT&T's personnel office "turn out to be founded." AT&T officials won't give out exact figures, but they say that some employees have been fired and others transferred or sent to counseling.

---

[7] *cunt:* Vulgar term for vagina, used as a derogatory reference to a woman.

[8] *AT&T:* American Telephone and Telegraph Company, the largest telecommunications company in the United States.

NO REWARDS

Even if they work for a company with a well-established harassment policy, 14 many women still keep their mouths shut. They don't want to be seen as troublemakers—and they worry about the long-term consequences of complaining. "The individual who makes the complaint is immediately subjected to scrutiny, criticism, and blame," says Carolyn Chalmers, a Minneapolis lawyer who handles harassment cases. "You're immediately put on the defensive to justify your existence and your credibility." It's a rather simple risk-and-reward equation that for many women adds up to one big zero. The number of cases of sexual harassment reported to the EEOC and local bias agencies has increased somewhat in the past few years, from 4,380 in 1984 to 5,694 last year. Yet those numbers represent just a tiny fraction of actual incidents, lawyers say. According to Joan Huwiler of the NOW Legal Defense Fund, only about 6 percent of victims file formal complaints to the EEOC, other anti-bias agencies, or their employers.

Frances Conley, a neurosurgeon at Stanford Medical School, endured 15 nearly twenty-five years of insults before she finally quit her job this spring. Her charges of harassment drew national headlines and letters of support from around the country. The university responded by setting up a committee to investigate the charges. Now Conley's back at her job, hoping that

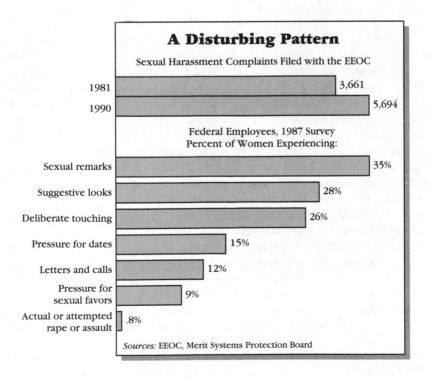

A Disturbing Pattern

Sexual Harassment Complaints Filed with the EEOC

1981	3,661
1990	5,694

Federal Employees, 1987 Survey
Percent of Women Experiencing:

Sexual remarks	35%
Suggestive looks	28%
Deliberate touching	26%
Pressure for dates	15%
Letters and calls	12%
Pressure for sexual favors	9%
Actual or attempted rape or assault	.8%

Sources: EEOC, Merit Systems Protection Board

things will get better. But the four months since her resignation "have been the worst four months in my life," Conley says. "I hate conflict. I hate people disapproving of me. It's very difficult to go around with people not liking you."

Women who take their accusations to court face even more formidable ob- 16 stacles than public disapproval. The legal process is long and cumbersome—it can be years from first complaint to final verdict—and in the interim, the woman is in a legal, professional, and often financial limbo. "A woman will complain and then becomes a pariah," says Judith Vladeck, a New York lawyer who has argued anti-bias cases for twenty years. "If the male is in any way sanctioned, his male cohorts come to his defense, and the woman becomes the wrongdoer, and she's frozen out."

Lawyers, too, say the cases are draining. Women are not entitled to collect 17 damages under the Civil Rights Act—just back pay. Often, that's not enough for a lawyer to spend years in litigation. There are larger judgments in civil suits, but the legal proceedings can be time-consuming. Patricia J. Barry, the Los Angeles lawyer who argued the precedent-setting Vinson case before the Supreme Court in 1986, filed for bankruptcy in 1988 and announced she was giving up civil rights work. Now she's arguing divorce and child-custody cases. "Most judges perceive themselves as identifying with the man no matter how horrible he is," Barry says. "It becomes the woman versus the man."

DARK VICTORY

Even some of those who win harassment cases say they feel they lost. As a 18 public-information officer for the Illinois Department of Corrections,[9] Lynda Savage earned glowing evaluations and two salary increases in the early 1980s. But, according to court records, her supervisor, Nicholas Howell, commonly used obscenities when referring to women, brought in suggestive lingerie catalogs, and asked Savage to pick out something for his wife and even told her she should buy a vibrator for her one-year-old daughter. Howell denies directing obscene comments to Savage. She complained to three different administrators, but nothing happened. For months, she says, Howell's behavior got worse. She was fired just before her second child was born.

Nearly five years later, a state court ruled in her favor and awarded her 19 $137,000, along with an offer of reinstatement to her job. Savage did go back, but says her co-workers shunned her so she quit. She has not received another job offer. "In a lot of ways, I have tested my limits so I know where I'm strong and where I'm not," she says. "Some good has come out of it. But was it worth it?" She thinks about the years of strain on her children and her husband, the lost work opportunities. And she concludes: "No."

Sexual-harassment cases have been particularly controversial on college 20 campuses. A 1986 survey by the Association of American Colleges reported

---

[9] *Department of Corrections:* State agency responsible for the custody and rehabilitation of criminal offenders.

that 32 percent of tenured faculty women at Harvard and 49 percent of untenured women had reported some form of sexual harassment. Consultant Freada Klein says that 40 percent of undergraduate women and 28 percent of female graduate students say they've been harassed. In 1989, the Minnesota legislature passed a law requiring all educational institutions in the state to develop sexual-harassment policies. "Some universities have gone so far as to indicate that for a faculty member to date a student is a prima facie[10] case of sexual harassment," says Margaret Neale, a professor at Northwestern's Kellogg Graduate School of Management. "There is no way to separate the power of the faculty member from the rank of the student."

21 Male-dominated campuses, like male-dominated professions, have the most entrenched problems. In early September a sophomore at Texas A&M University was attacked by three male cadets when she decided to try out for an elite ceremonial unit within the A&M Corps of Cadets.[11] Only three of the unit's fifty members were female. One of the men held her while two others struck her in the breasts and back. One of the attackers threatened her with a knife, dragging the handle against her flesh and warning that he would use the blade on her if she didn't withdraw her application. The university leveled disciplinary charges against twenty cadets, but officials soon found out this was not an isolated incident.

22 Within days A&M president William Mobley met with four women cadets who detailed a pattern of harassment. One woman told Mobley that she had been raped by a senior while his roommate watched. The women got Mobley's attention. He appointed a committee to investigate and named a woman psychologist with no university affiliation to cochair it. "I don't want to destroy the university," says one of the women students who met with Mobley. "But men hide behind the mask of harassment and say it's tradition. That needs to stop."

23 Some experts believe that "hostile environments" extend far beyond the campus and the workplace. Earlier this year, thirteen female tenants won an $800,000 settlement against their San Francisco landlord who continued to employ an apartment manager even after they repeatedly notified the landlord that the manager was harassing the women. According to court records, the manager touched one woman's vaginal area and grabbed her breast. He told another woman he would evict her if she had an overnight visitor. He told women who were behind on their rent they would have to pay immediately or model lingerie for him. The women, all single mothers, were usually financially or emotionally vulnerable to his manipulations.

24 While that situation seems extreme, some feminist legal scholars argue that harassment is part of everyday life for most women and should be regulated. Indiana University professor Carol Brooks Gardner, author of a forthcoming book called *Passing By,* argues that it should be considered illegal harassment

---

[10] *prima facie:* Latin phrase meaning "at first sight" and, in this context, "clear" or "self-evident."

[11] *Corps of Cadets:* Students studying military and naval subjects in preparation for service in the armed forces (army, navy, air force, and marines).

when a man makes an obscene comment to a woman in the street. Of course, not all street comments are threatening. A simple wolf whistle[12] probably wouldn't traumatize most women. "But," says Gardner, "it's not OK for a man to touch me in any way whatsoever or to mutter salacious comments in my ear, or to yell out vulgar verbal evaluations." Any regulations against this type of harassment would be extremely difficult to enforce. For example, who would detain the assailant? Women in such a situation usually just want to get away as quickly as possible.

HONOR ROLL

Whatever happens on the street or in the courts, the publicity surrounding 25 Anita Hill's allegations has brought the issue into the open. "The fact that this claim scuttled the nomination or delayed the nomination helps the cause like nothing else does," says Nancy Gertner, a Boston civil rights attorney. It shows that charges of sexual harassment can be taken seriously—even in an almost all-male institution like the Senate. In fact, Congress[13] could be the first test of how well the public has been educated by the week's proceedings. Congressional employees are not covered by the Civil Rights Act, and therefore have no protection against harassment. To correct this oversight, the Women's Political Caucus[14] sent a written policy in April to all 535 members of Congress. Those who agreed to run harassment-free offices joined the caucus's "Honor Roll."[15] At the start of last week, there were two hundred members. By the end of the week, twelve more had signed up. After listening to Anita Hill, a lot of women voters would like to see Congress put its own House—and Senate—in order.

Have you, or has someone you know personally, ever filed a formal complaint of sexual harassment?		
	Women	*Men*
Yes	13%	11%
No	87%	89%
From the *Newsweek* Poll of Oct. 10–11, 1991		

---

[12] *Wolf whistle:* A whistle consisting of two sliding tones, usually sounded by a male to express admiration for a female's appearance.

[13] *Congress:* Legislative branch of the U.S. government, consisting of two houses: the Senate and the House of Representatives.

[14] *Woman's Political Caucus:* Organization of American women (founded in 1971) seeking equality with men in employment opportunity.

[15] *"Honor Roll":* List of students (usually at a high school) who have achieved grades above a certain average during a semester or school year.

Has someone you know personally been a victim of sexual harassment at work or school, on the street, in a private club you belong to, or in a store or commercial place?		
	Women	*Men*
Yes	42%	37%
No	55%	62%
From the *Newsweek* Poll of Oct. 10–11, 1991		

Do you think it should be considered sexual harassment—or not—when a man (percent saying yes):		
	Women	*Men*
Repeatedly asks a woman who works for him to have sex	96%	94%
Repeatedly asks a woman who works for him to have a date	47%	48%
Makes sexual remarks or jokes to a woman who works for him	75%	64%
Makes sexual remarks or noises at women on the street	72%	75%
From the *Newsweek* Poll of Oct. 10–11, 1991		

READING JOURNAL

In your reading journal, discuss one of the following:

1. Three behaviors mentioned in the essay: one that, in your opinion, is a clear-cut example of sexual harassment; one that is clearly not such an example; and one that might or might not constitute sexual harassment, depending on the context

2. An experience you had where you were treated prejudicially because of your sex. In what way(s) were you treated unfairly? How did this make you feel?

3. A topic of your own choice related to "Striking a Nerve"

MEANING AND TECHNIQUE

The following questions and activities will help you understand the main ideas in the essay and the manner in which it was written.

1. In one or two sentences, write down the *main idea* of the essay. Use your own words.

2. What is the significance of the title of the essay? How does the idiom "to strike a nerve" relate to issues Kantrowitz discusses?

3. What does Margaret Neale mean when she says, "There is no way to separate the power of the faculty member from the rank of the student" (par. 20)?

TONE

The *tone* of a piece of writing is the author's attitude toward his or her subject and audience as expressed in the choice of words and details. Tone can be defined by using such adjectives as *playful, regretful, confident, pessimistic, ironic, formal, disillusioned, compassionate,* and *outspoken.*

Some pieces of writing are quite *subjective;* that is, they reflect the author's personal feelings and interpretations. Others are more *objective,* stressing facts rather than personal feelings and judgments. (For a more complete discussion of tone, see pp. 58–59.)

---

4. With a partner, read through the following passages from "Striking a Nerve," each reflecting one of the tones in the box below. (If you don't know the meaning of a particular word in the box, look it up in a dictionary or consult with your teacher.) Then fill in each blank with the adjective that best describes the speaker's attitude.

---

resigned   determined   anxious   uncertain   objective

_____ a. "Men 'don't understand that caged feeling.... But women know what sexual harassment is. It's when your neck hairs stand up, when you feel like you're being stalked.' " (par. 2)

_____ b. "You start questioning yourself.... Maybe I did ask for it [her boss's sexual advances]. I know I didn't use good judgment ... I just didn't know what to do." (par. 5)

_____ c. "What are you going to do [when a male professor makes a sexual joke about women], get up and walk out of class? You want to be a doctor? You want to be in a man's field? Then you swallow hard and pretend you don't hear." (par. 6)

_____ d. "Men, who are rarely victims of sexual assault, may view sexual conduct in a vacuum without a full appreciation of the underlying threat of violence that a woman may perceive." (par. 9)

_____ e. "I don't want to destroy the university. . . . But men hide behind the mask of harassment and say it's tradition. That needs to stop." (par. 22)

DRAWING INFERENCES

The following questions will help develop your ability to draw inferences—an important reading skill.

1. How do you interpret the survey results that show differences in the way women and men regard sexual propositions (par. 3)?

2. Why do you think only about six percent of sexual-harassment victims file formal complaints? Write a list of the reasons mentioned in the essay and any others you can think of.

3. What do you consider the main *purpose* (or *purposes*) of the essay? Review the three major purposes of writing mentioned on page 57: *to inform, to persuade,* and *to entertain.* What does Kantrowitz want her reader to think or feel after finishing the selection? Support your answer with examples from the essay.

4. Look at the poll results in the charts on pages 72 and 73. Are these results what you would have expected? Did you find anything surprising?

5. Think of a question of your own to ask your classmates about an issue raised in the essay.

VOCABULARY: VERB AND NOUN FORMS

Many verbs and nouns have the same form—for example, *exchange, mistake, answer,* and *control.* Note how *purchase* is used in the following two sentences:

I hope to *purchase* a gift for $20. (verb)
I made a *purchase* of $20. (noun)

Other verbs and nouns have different but related forms—for example:

Verb	Noun
arrange	arrange*ment*
arrive	arriv*al*
manage	manag*er*
defend	defend*ant*

In these cases, a *suffix*—one or more letters attached to the end of a word—has been added to the verb to change it into a noun.

1. For each of the following words, write down the corresponding verb or noun form. If there is no corresponding form, put an asterisk (*) in the blank. Try to do this exercise first without using a dictionary.
2. Then write a list of all the suffixes you have found that can be used to change verbs into nouns.

    The first blank has been filled in for you.

allegations (par. 1) __allege__   enforce (par. 12) _____

survey (par. 2) _____   advise (par. 12) _____

abuse (par. 2) _____   complain (par. 14) _____

persist (par. 4) _____   equation (par. 14) _____

refuse (par. 4) _____   sanction (par. 16) _____

recourse (par. 6) _____   refer (par. 18) _____

professor (par. 6) _____   affiliation (par. 22) _____

effect (par. 8) _____   detain (par. 24) _____

expose (par. 8) _____   proceedings (par. 25) _____

incentive (par. 11) _____   oversight (par. 25) _____

Suffixes to change verbs to nouns: _____

_____

VOCABULARY: IN CONTEXT

In this exercise, you will develop your vocabulary by using words and idioms in a realistic context.

- If you don't know the meaning of one of the following italicized vocabulary items, first find it in the essay and see if you can determine its meaning from the context. (Review the major types of context clues on pp. 263–267.)
- If the meaning is still unclear, look up the item in a dictionary or consult with a native speaker of English.
- Then, in a few sentences, describe or explain each of the following situations, ideas, and things. **Do not** just define the italicized words. Discuss personal experiences and opinions and give examples.

    1. How it might feel to be *stalked* (par. 2)
    2. Why someone might *shrug* his or her shoulders (par. 3)
    3. A *clear-cut* example of sexist behavior (par. 4)
    4. Something that is *ludicrous* (par. 4)
    5. Something you find *intimidating* (par. 7)
    6. Something that might *spur* you to file a legal complaint against someone (par. 11)
    7. A time when someone questioned your *credibility,* or when you questioned someone else's *credibility* (par. 14)
    8. Something you find *cumbersome* (par. 16)
    9. A time when you felt in *limbo* (par. 16)
    10. A behavior or belief in your native country that might result in someone becoming a *pariah* (par. 16)

DISCUSSION AND DEBATE

1. With several classmates, fill in the following chart with all the behaviors you can find in the essay that have been claimed to constitute sexual harassment. Which of these behaviors do you consider clear-cut examples of sexual harassment? Which are not forms of sexual harassment? Which might or might not constitute sexual harassment, depending on the context? (Also feel free to discuss other behaviors not mentioned in the article.)

Clear Harassment
Not Harassment
Might Be Harassment

2. In a small group, discuss cross-cultural similarities and differences in attitudes toward sexual harassment. Do you think sexual harassment is a
problem in your native country? If so, do you know what is being done
about it? How do varying attitudes toward sexual harassment reflect differences in cultural values and expectations?

3. In a small group, research sexual-harassment policies that exist at several
universities and/or companies in your community. (If you are focusing on
universities, you might also want to find out about policies dealing with
date rape and other forms of sexual assault.) What, for example, are the
policies, and how are they enforced? How are they publicized? Do you find
the guidelines too general? Too specific?
   After you have completed your research, share your findings with the
rest of the class.

WRITING ACTIVITIES

1. Imagine you are working at a company that, in your opinion, is doing far too little to discourage sexual harassment. You have seen a number of instances of sexual harassment and been a victim yourself. You have spoken with your supervisor several times about improving the situation, but he or she has not been very responsive.

   Write a letter to your supervisor in which you discuss your concerns and argue the necessity of improving the work environment. Think about the *tone* that will best help you achieve your purpose.

2. An important aspect of good writing is the ability to create different *tones,* or moods. Practice this skill with several classmates by writing three short paragraphs, each describing the same incident, person, place, or thing from a different perspective.

   In the first paragraph, use language that creates a *positive* impression; in the second paragraph, a *negative* impression; and in the third paragraph, a *neutral* impression. You might want to change the details of the paragraph, the style, or both. (Style includes such aspects of writing as word choice, sentence structure, and figures of speech.)

3. In "Striking a Nerve," Kantrowitz cites the view of Carol Brooks Gardner, who argues that "it should be considered illegal harassment when a man makes an obscene comment to a woman in the street" (par. 24).

   Write an essay discussing the extent to which you agree with Gardner's view. Support your arguments with examples from the essay and personal experiences and observations. (You might want to get hold of Gardner's book *Passing By* and learn more about her views.)

4. Write an essay in which you discuss an experience you had where you were treated prejudicially because of your sex. In what ways were you treated unfairly? How did this make you feel? What was your response? (To help you plan, draft, and revise your essay, see Appendix A.)

READING

PREREADING ACTIVITIES

1. In your reading journal, write for ten to fifteen minutes about one of the following:

   a. A time when you were discriminated against or when you discriminated against someone else

   b. A group of people that has traditionally been discriminated against in your native country

2. Write a list of several causes of discrimination. Then share your list in a small group.

3. Indicate the extent to which you agree with the following statements by filling in each blank with *SA* (strongly agree), *A* (agree), *U* (undecided), *D* (disagree), or *SD* (strongly disagree). Then share your responses with several classmates.

a. _____ Sometimes a government is justified in suspending the civil liberties of its citizens.

b. _____ Most people personally experience discrimination at some point in their life.

c. _____ Some people who are discriminated against are responsible for the discrimination.

d. _____ It is impossible to grow up in a racist society and not to be racist.

e. _____ There is little discrimination of any kind in my native culture.

f. _____ Discrimination tends to increase during difficult economic times.

g. _____ The mass media play a large role in perpetuating stereotypes and discrimination.

h. _____ Adults who were neglected or mistreated as children are more likely to be prejudiced than those who had a happy childhood.

i. _____ No individual is free of prejudice.

j. _____ Education is the best way to combat discrimination.

It Cannot Be Helped

JEANNE WAKATSUKI HOUSTON AND JAMES D. HOUSTON

On December 7, 1941, the Japanese attacked Pearl Harbor (the American naval headquarters in Hawaii), leading the United States to enter World War II. Viewing

Japanese Americans on the West Coast as a threat to U.S. security, President Roosevelt signed an order in February 1942 authorizing the removal of all people of Japanese ancestry from important "military areas." During the next five weeks, 110,000 Japanese Americans—more than two-thirds of them native-born U.S. citizens—were removed from the West Coast and placed in ten internment camps in remote inland areas of six states.

Jeanne Wakatsuki Houston, the daughter of Japanese immigrants, was born in California in 1935. When she was seven years old, she and her family were sent to the first internment camp, in Manzanar, California, where they remained for three and a half years. After the war, Houston studied sociology and journalism at San Jose State University, receiving her bachelor's degree in 1956. Together with her husband, the novelist James D. Houston, she wrote Farewell to Manzanar *(1973), a record of her family's life in the camp. The following selection is the second chapter of the book.*

In December of 1941 Papa's disappearance[1] didn't bother me nearly so much as the world I soon found myself in.

He had been a jack-of-all-trades. When I was born he was farming near Inglewood. Later, when he started fishing, we moved to Ocean Park, near Santa Monica, and until they picked him up, that's where we lived, in a big frame house with a brick fireplace, a block back from the beach. We were the only Japanese family in the neighborhood. Papa liked it that way. He didn't want to be labeled or grouped by anyone. But with him gone and no way of knowing what to expect, my mother moved all of us down to Terminal Island.[2] Woody[3] already lived there, and one of my older sisters had married a Terminal Island boy. Mama's first concern now was to keep the family together; and once the war began, she felt safer there than isolated racially in Ocean Park. But for me, at age seven, the island was a country as foreign as India or Arabia would have been. It was the first time I had lived among other Japanese, or gone to school with them, and I was terrified all the time.

This was partly Papa's fault. One of his threats to keep us younger kids in line was "I'm going to sell you to the Chinaman." When I had entered kindergarten two years earlier, I was the only Oriental in the class. They sat me next to a Caucasian girl who happened to have very slanted eyes. I looked at her and began to scream, certain Papa had sold me out at last. My fear of her ran so deep I could not speak of it, even to Mama, couldn't explain why I was screaming. For two weeks I had nightmares about this girl, until the teachers finally moved me to the other side of the room. And it was still with me, this fear of Oriental faces, when we moved to Terminal Island.

---

[1] *Papa's disappearance:* Jeanne's father was arrested by the FBI on the false charge of delivering oil to Japanese submarines.

[2] *Terminal Island:* Island off the coast of southern California; temporary home to around five hundred Japanese families.

[3] *Woody:* One of Jeanne's older brothers; the other is Bill. (Woody's wife is named Chizu; Bill's wife, Tomi. Kiyo is one of Jeanne's cousins.)

In those days it was a company town, a ghetto owned and controlled by 4
the canneries. The men went after fish, and whenever the boats came back—
day or night—the women would be called to process the catch while it was
fresh. One in the afternoon or four in the morning, it made no difference. My
mother had to go to work right after we moved there. I can still hear the
whistle—two toots for French's, three for Van Camp's[4]—and she and Chizu
would be out of bed in the middle of the night, heading for the cannery.

The house we lived in was nothing more than a shack, a barracks with 5
single plank walls and rough wooden floors, like the cheapest kind of migrant
workers' housing. The people around us were hardworking, boisterous, a
little proud of their nickname, *yo-go-re,* which meant literally *uncouth one,*
or roughneck, or dead-end kid. They not only spoke Japanese exclusively,
they spoke a dialect peculiar to Kyushu, where their families had come from
in Japan, a rough, fisherman's language, full of oaths and insults. Instead of
saying *ba-ka-ta-re,* a common insult meaning *stupid,* Terminal Islanders
would say *ba-ka-ya-ro,* a coarser and exclusively masculine use of the word,
which implies gross stupidity. They would swagger and pick on outsiders and
persecute anyone who didn't speak as they did. That was what made my own
time there so hateful. I had never spoken anything but English, and the other
kids in the second grade despised me for it. They were tough and mean, like
ghetto kids anywhere. Each day after school I dreaded their ambush. My
brother Kiyo, three years older, would wait for me at the door, where we
would decide whether to run straight home together, or split up, or try a new
and unexpected route.

None of these kids ever actually attacked. It was the threat that frightened 6
us, their fearful looks, and the noises they would make, like miniature Samurai,[5] in a language we couldn't understand.

At the time it seemed we had been living under this reign of fear for years. 7
In fact, we lived there about two months. Late in February the navy decided
to clear Terminal Island completely. Even though most of us were American-
born, it was dangerous having that many Orientals so close to the Long Beach
Naval Station, on the opposite end of the island. We had known something like
this was coming. But, like Papa's arrest, not much could be done ahead of
time. There were four of us kids still young enough to be living with Mama,
plus Granny, her mother, sixty-five then, speaking no English, and nearly
blind. Mama didn't know where else she could get work, and we had nowhere
else to move *to.* On February 25 the choice was made for us. We were given
forty-eight hours to clear out.

The secondhand dealers had been prowling around for weeks, like wolves, 8
offering humiliating prices for goods and furniture they knew many of us
would have to sell sooner or later. Mama had left all but her most valuable

---

[4] *French's and Van Camp's:* Fish companies.

[5] *samurai:* Japanese warrior class that arose in the twelfth century and was abolished in 1868.

possessions in Ocean Park, simply because she had nowhere to put them. She had brought along her pottery, her silver, heirlooms like the kimonos[6] Granny had brought from Japan, tea sets, lacquered tables, and one fine old set of china, blue and white porcelain, almost translucent. On the day we were leaving, Woody's car was so crammed with boxes and luggage and kids we had just run out of room. Mama had to sell this china.

One of the dealers offered her fifteen dollars for it. She said it was a full   9 setting for twelve and worth at least two hundred. He said fifteen was his top price. Mama started to quiver. Her eyes blazed up at him. She had been packing all night and trying to calm down Granny, who didn't understand why we were moving again and what all the rush was about. Mama's nerves were shot, and now navy jeeps were patrolling the streets. She didn't say another word. She just glared at this man, all the rage and frustration channeled at him through her eyes.

He watched her for a moment and said he was sure he couldn't pay more   10 than seventeen fifty for that china. She reached into the red velvet case, took out a dinner plate and hurled it at the floor right in front of his feet.

The man leaped back shouting, "Hey! Hey, don't do that! Those are valu-   11 able dishes!"

Mama took out another dinner plate and hurled it at the floor, then another   12 and another, never moving, never opening her mouth, just quivering and glaring at the retreating dealer, with tears streaming down her cheeks. He finally turned and scuttled out the door, heading for the next house. When he was gone she stood there smashing cups and bowls and platters until the whole set lay in scattered blue and white fragments across the wooden floor.

The American Friends Service helped us find a small house in Boyle   13 Heights, another minority ghetto, in downtown Los Angeles, now inhabited briefly by a few hundred Terminal Island refugees. Executive Order 9066 had been signed by President Roosevelt, giving the War Department authority to define military areas in the western states and to exclude from them anyone who might threaten the war effort. There was a lot of talk about internment, or moving inland, or something like that in store for all Japanese Americans. I remember my brothers sitting around the table talking very intently about what we were going to do, how we would keep the family together. They had seen how quickly Papa was removed, and they knew now that he would not be back for quite a while. Just before leaving Terminal Island Mama had received her first letter, from Bismarck, North Dakota. He had been imprisoned at Fort Lincoln, in an all-male camp for enemy aliens.

Papa had been the patriarch. He had always decided everything in the   14 family. With him gone, my brothers, like councilors in the absence of a chief, worried about what should be done. The ironic thing is, there wasn't much left to decide. These were mainly days of quiet, desperate waiting for what

---

[6] *kimonos:* Long Japanese robes worn by women.

seemed at the time to be inevitable. There is a phrase the Japanese use in such situations, when something difficult must be endured. You would hear the older heads, the Issei,[7] telling others very quietly, "*Shikata ga nai*" (It cannot be helped). "*Shikata ga nai*" (It must be done).

Mama and Woody went to work packing celery for a Japanese produce **15** dealer. Kiyo and my sister May and I enrolled in the local school, and what sticks in my memory from those few weeks is the teacher—not her looks, her remoteness. In Ocean Park my teacher had been a kind, grandmotherly woman who used to sail with us in Papa's boat from time to time and who wept the day we had to leave. In Boyle Heights the teacher felt cold and distant. I was confused by all the moving and was having trouble with the classwork, but she would never help me out. She would have nothing to do with me.

This was the first time I had felt outright hostility from a Caucasian. Look- **16** ing back, it is easy enough to explain. Public attitudes toward the Japanese in California were shifting rapidly. In the first few months of the Pacific war, America was on the run. Tolerance had turned to distrust and irrational fear. The hundred-year-old tradition of anti-Orientalism on the west coast soon resurfaced, more vicious than ever. Its result became clear about a month later, when we were told to make our third and final move.

The name Manzanar meant nothing to us when we left Boyle Heights. We **17** didn't know where it was or what it was. We went because the government ordered us to. And, in the case of my older brothers and sisters, we went with a certain amount of relief. They had all heard stories of Japanese homes being attacked, of beatings in the streets of California towns. They were as frightened of the Caucasians as Caucasians were of us. Moving, under what appeared to be government protection, to an area less directly threatened by the war seemed not such a bad idea at all. For some it actually sounded like a fine adventure.

Our pickup point was a Buddhist church in Los Angeles. It was very early, **18** and misty, when we got there with our luggage. Mama had bought heavy coats for all of us. She grew up in eastern Washington and knew that anywhere inland in early April would be cold. I was proud of my new coat, and I remember sitting on a duffel bag trying to be friendly with the Greyhound driver. I smiled at him. He didn't smile back. He was befriending no one. Someone tied a numbered tag to my collar and to the duffel bag (each family was given a number, and that became our official designation until the camps were closed), someone else passed out box lunches for the trip, and we climbed aboard.

I had never been outside Los Angeles County, never traveled more than ten **19** miles from the coast, had never even ridden on a bus. I was full of excitement,

---

[7] *Issei:* First generation. Born in Japan, most Issei immigrated to the United States between 1890 and 1915.

the way any kid would be, and wanted to look out the window. But for the first few hours the shades were drawn. Around me other people played cards, read magazines, dozed, waiting. I settled back, waiting too, and finally fell asleep. The bus felt very secure to me. Almost half its passengers were immediate relatives. Mama and my older brothers had succeeded in keeping most of us together, on the same bus, headed for the same camp. I didn't realize until much later what a job that was. The strategy had been, first, to have everyone living in the same district when the evacuation began, and then to get all of us included under the same family number, even though names had been changed by marriage. Many families weren't as lucky as ours and suffered months of anguish while trying to arrange transfers from one camp to another.

We rode all day. By the time we reached our destination, the shades were 20 up. It was late afternoon. The first thing I saw was a yellow swirl across a blurred, reddish setting sun. The bus was being pelted by what sounded like splattering rain. It wasn't rain. This was my first look at something I would soon know very well, a billowing flurry of dust and sand churned up by the wind through Owens Valley.

We drove past a barbed-wire fence, through a gate, and into an open space 21 where trunks and sacks and packages had been dumped from the baggage trucks that drove out ahead of us. I could see a few tents set up, the first rows of black barracks, and beyond them, blurred by sand, rows of barracks that seemed to spread for miles across this plain. People were sitting on cartons or milling around, with their backs to the wind, waiting to see which friends or relatives might be on this bus. As we approached, they turned or stood up, and some moved toward us expectantly. But inside the bus no one stirred. No one waved or spoke. They just stared out the windows, ominously silent. I didn't understand this. Hadn't we finally arrived, our whole family intact? I opened a window, leaned out, and yelled happily. "Hey! This whole bus is full of Wakatsukis!"

Outside, the greeters smiled. Inside there was an explosion of laughter, 22 hysterical, tension-breaking laughter that left my brothers choking and whacking each other across the shoulders.

We had pulled up just in time for dinner. The mess halls[8] weren't com- 23 pleted yet. An outdoor chow[9] line snaked around a half-finished building that broke a good part of the wind. They issued us army mess kits,[10] the round metal kind that fold over, and plopped in scoops of canned Vienna sausage, canned string beans, steamed rice that had been cooked too long, and on top of the rice a serving of canned apricots. The Caucasian servers were thinking that the fruit poured over rice would make a good dessert. Among the Japa-

---

[8] *mess hall:* Military term for a place where food is served to a large group.

[9] *chow:* Food.

[10] *mess kit:* Small set of cooking and eating utensils, used by soldiers and campers.

nese, of course, rice is never eaten with sweet foods, only with salty or savory foods. Few of us could eat such a mixture. But at this point no one dared protest. It would have been impolite. I was horrified when I saw the apricot syrup seeping through my little mound of rice. I opened my mouth to complain. My mother jabbed me in the back to keep quiet. We moved on through the line and joined the others squatting in the lee of half-raised walls, dabbing courteously at what was, for almost everyone there, an inedible concoction.

After dinner we were taken to Block 16, a cluster of fifteen barracks that 24 had just been finished a day or so earlier—although finished was hardly the word for it. The shacks were built of one thickness of pine planking covered with tarpaper. They sat on concrete footings, with about two feet of open space between the floorboards and the ground. Gaps showed between the planks, and as the weeks passed and the green wood dried out, the gaps widened. Knotholes gaped in the uncovered floor.

Each barracks was divided into six units, sixteen by twenty feet, about the 25 size of a living room, with one bare bulb hanging from the ceiling and an oil stove for heat. We were assigned two of these for the twelve people in our family group; and our official family "number" was enlarged by three digits— 16 plus the number of this barracks. We were issued steel army cots, two brown army blankets each, and some mattress covers, which my brothers stuffed with straw.

The first task was to divide up what space we had for sleeping. Bill and 26 Woody contributed a blanket each and partitioned off the first room: one side for Bill and Tomi, one side for Woody and Chizu and their baby girl. Woody also got the stove, for heating formulas.

The people who had it hardest during the first few months were young 27 couples like these, many of whom had married just before the evacuation began, in order not to be separated and sent to different camps. Our two rooms were crowded, but at least it was all in the family. My oldest sister and her husband were shoved into one of those sixteen-by-twenty-foot compartments with six people they had never seen before—two other couples, one recently married like themselves, the other with two teenage boys. Partitioning off a room like that wasn't easy. It was bitter cold when we arrived, and the wind did not abate. All they had to use for room dividers were those army blankets, two of which were barely enough to keep one person warm. They argued over whose blanket should be sacrificed and later argued about noise at night—the parents wanted their boys asleep by 9:00 P.M.—and they continued arguing over matters like that for six months, until my sister and her husband left to harvest sugar beets in Idaho. It was grueling work up there, and wages were pitiful, but when the call came through camp for workers to alleviate the wartime labor shortage, it sounded better than their life at Manzanar. They knew they'd have, if nothing else, a room, perhaps a cabin of their own.

That first night in Block 16, the rest of us squeezed into the second room— 28

Granny, Lillian, age fourteen, Ray, thirteen, May, eleven, Kiyo, ten, Mama, and me. I didn't mind this at all at the time. Being youngest meant I got to sleep with Mama. And before we went to bed I had a great time jumping up and down on the mattress. The boys had stuffed so much straw into hers, we had to flatten it some so we wouldn't slide off. I slept with her every night after that until Papa came back.

READING JOURNAL

In your reading journal, discuss one of the following:

1. Why people discriminate against each other
2. How prejudice and discrimination can be reduced
3. A topic of your own choice related to "It Cannot Be Helped"

VOCABULARY: PHRASAL VERBS

Often in English, a preposition is combined with a verb to form a new vocabulary item—one that functions as an idiom. These verb-preposition combinations are called *phrasal verbs* or *two-word verbs*. (Some verbs are followed by two prepositions and are called *three-word verbs*.) Consider the following examples:

"*Call* me *up* when you have a chance." (To *call up* means to telephone.)
"I hope you *get over* your cold soon." (To *get over* means to recover from.)

Some phrasal verbs are *separable;* that is, the noun may come either between the verb and preposition or after the preposition ("*Call* your mother *up*" or "*Call up* your mother"). Others are *nonseparable,* with the noun always coming after the preposition ("I *got over* my cold" but *not* "I *got* my cold *over*").

"It Cannot Be Helped" contains many phrasal verbs. Fill in the following blanks with the appropriate preposition or prepositions. Also write down the meaning of the phrasal verb and a sentence of your own using it correctly. Then share your sentences with several classmates.

Example:

"We would decide whether to run straight home together, or split up, or try a new and unexpected route." (par. 5)

MEANING: To separate or go in different directions

SENTENCE: My husband and I were having so many problems that we decided to split up.

1. "We moved to Ocean Park, near Santa Monica, and until they picked him
   _____, that's where we lived." (par. 2)

   Meaning:_____

   Sentence:_____

   _____

2. "I looked at her and began to scream, certain Papa had sold me_____ at
   last." (par. 3)

   Meaning:_____

   Sentence:_____

   _____

3. "They would swagger and pick_____ outsiders and persecute anyone
   who didn't speak as they did." (par. 5)

   Meaning:_____

   Sentence:_____

   _____

4. "On February 25 the choice was made for us. We were given forty-eight
   hours to clear_____." (par. 7)

   Meaning:_____

   Sentence:_____

   _____

5. "Woody's car was so crammed with boxes and luggage and kids we had just
   run_____ room." (par. 8)

   Meaning:_____

   Sentence:_____

   _____

6. "She had been packing all night and trying to calm _____ Granny, who didn't understand why we were moving again." (par. 9)

Meaning: _____

Sentence: _____

_____

7. "I was confused by all the moving and was having trouble with the classwork, but she would never help me _____." (par. 15)

Meaning: _____

Sentence: _____

_____

8. "Someone else passed _____ box lunches for the trip, and we climbed aboard." (par. 18)

Meaning: _____

Sentence: _____

_____

ADDITIONAL READINGS

Eleven Words That Cast the Power of Bigotry on Honeymoon Couple

JONATHAN KAUFMAN

The following article by Jonathan Kaufman, a staff writer for the Boston Globe, *originally appeared in this large daily newspaper in August 1989.*

I had not planned to spend the first few days of my honeymoon fighting 1 anti-Semitism in the Adirondacks.[1] Somehow, it turned out that way.

My wife, Barbara Howard, and I had been married on Upper Saranac Lake, 2 on a beautiful day surrounded by our families and friends. The reception was

---

[1] *Adirondacks:* Mountains in the northeastern part of New York State (a popular resort area).

catered by a local hotel, the Hotel Saranac, run by a local college, Paul Smith's College, that trains people in hotel and restaurant management.

The catering went badly. The caterers arrived late and ran out of food. The next day we went in to dispute the bill. 3

We arrived with a friend, a lawyer who is Jewish, and gathered in a meeting room with six members of the hotel's executive staff. We outlined our complaints and said we were prepared to pay half of the total cost. The hotel agreed, providing I would write a letter of apology to the staff for being angry with them. We refused. We felt that if anyone was owed an apology, it was clearly us. 4

At this point, as the meeting broke up, the general manager said, "Now I know why they are fighting you people in Beirut."² 5

For a moment I was stunned, and confused. I am not in the Marines, I thought. Who is fighting us in Beirut? Then I wondered: Perhaps something has happened to the American hostages in Beirut?³ 6

Then, like a flame that catches fire on a pile of dry kindling, it dawned on me what the hotel manager had said and why he had said it. The manager was not yelling at me for what I had done or what I had said. He made that remark because I am Jewish. 7

Our friend turned to me and said, "Yes, Jon, that was an anti-Semitic remark." 8

I am not naive about anti-Semitism and bigotry. I have spent most of my career at the *Globe* writing about racism and discrimination. Barbara works for "Eyes on the Prize," the public television civil rights documentary. I have, on occasion, had people yell "Jew" at me on the street. What the general manager of the Hotel Saranac said is far less than what many blacks endure on a regular basis or what Jews of my parents' generation heard 30 or 40 years ago. 9

But here, stripped of my reporter's notebook, I felt the full power of bigotry. Eleven words—they rang in my head day after day. I spent the next few hours in a fog. Such is the power of prejudice: that it was able to cast a pall over the first weeks of my marriage, crowding out the happiness that had enveloped us before we stepped into that meeting room Monday afternoon. 10

I woke up every morning thinking about those words, filled with a furious but impotent rage. Suddenly, it did not matter that I was a reporter, or a customer, or a husband on his honeymoon. I was, simply, a "Jew," an object, one of "those people." I felt violated, as if someone had broken into my home, rummaged through my things and left them scattered on the floor, broken and covered with mud. 11

---

² *Beirut:* Capital of Lebanon. Israel invaded Lebanon in the summer of 1982, hoping to drive the Palestine Liberation Organization out of Beirut. That same summer, a group of U.S. Marines was sent to Lebanon to help maintain peace.

³ *hostages in Beirut:* Starting in 1983, Islamic militants began taking American hostages in Beirut.

Part of the power of prejudice is that it turns the traditional rules and 12 norms of society upside down. It is the way that untalented people strike out at talented people, ignorant people against those who know more, those who have risen without merit against those with merit who challenge them.

What do you call a black professor with a Ph.D. in astrophysics from 13 Harvard, Malcolm X[4] asked audiences, tauntingly, back in the 1960s.

Answer: Nigger.[5]   14

Worst of all, being the target of a bigoted slur made me feel dirty and 15 suspicious. For several days after the general manager made that remark I found myself doubting the motives of most everyone I came into contact with. The clerk developing our wedding pictures, people on the street, the man in the car up ahead. Perhaps they were anti-Semitic too?

Barbara also felt the sting of the remark. She is not Jewish, but the hotel 16 manager had assumed she was. The remark was aimed at her as well. For 30 years she had vacationed on a nearby lake. For her, the Adirondacks had always been a perfect place, safe and secure, a second home. That was why we had gotten married there. Now she struggled to recapture the innocence of the place.

I was pulled by alternating emotions of anger and, curiously, shame. Part of 17 me wanted to ignore what had happened, to joke about it, to chalk it up to ignorance and stupidity.

Largely at Barbara's prodding, we decided to fight. We met with the presi- 18 dent of Paul Smith's College and filed a complaint with the Anti-Defamation League.[6] In the end, that was not only the right thing to do but also the right thing to do on a honeymoon.

The Jewish marriage ceremony ends with one of the best-known Jewish 19 traditions, the smashing of a glass. Smashing a glass has many meanings. It commemorates the destruction of the temples in ancient Jerusalem and the sufferings Jews have endured through the ages. It reminds us how fragile marriage is, how easily it can be shattered. Smashing a glass also tells us something about the world. Jewish tradition teaches that the world is a broken place, filled with injustice. One of the commandments is, in Hebrew, *tikkun olam,* to "heal the world" by fighting injustice.

This is what I learned on our honeymoon: One never knows where 20 prejudice lies poised, ready to smash in front of your path. And sometimes the shards of glass strike you in the most vulnerable, and unexpected, places.

---

[4] *Malcolm X* (1925–1965): Prominent black civil rights leader in the 1960s.

[5] *Nigger:* Insulting reference to a black person.

[6] *Anti-Defamation League:* Civil rights organization founded in 1913 to secure justice and fair treatment for all Americans.

Caged Bird
Maya Angelou

Maya Angelou, born in 1928, is an author, poet, playwright, actor, and civil rights activist. She is best known for her autobiography I Know Why the Caged Bird Sings *(1970), which describes her experiences growing up in the segregated South. The following poem comes from her collection* Shaker, Why Don't You Sing? *(1983).*

A free bird leaps
on the back of the wind
and floats downstream
till the current ends
and dips his wing
in the orange sun rays
and dares to claim the sky.

But a bird that stalks
down his narrow cage
can seldom see through
his bars of rage
his wings are clipped and
his feet are tied
so he opens his throat to sing.

The caged bird sings
with a fearful trill
of things unknown
but longed for still
and his tune is heard
on the distant hill
for the caged bird
sings of freedom.

The free bird thinks of another breeze
and the trade winds[1] soft through the sighing trees
and the fat worms waiting on a dawn-bright lawn
and he names the sky his own.

But a caged bird stands on the grave of dreams
his shadow shouts on a nightmare scream
his wings are clipped and his feet are tied
so he opens his throat to sing.

---

[1] *trade winds:* Winds that blow almost constantly in the same direction.

The caged bird sings
with a fearful trill
of things unknown
but longed for still
and his tune is heard
on the distant hill
for the caged bird
sings of freedom.

Cartoon
JULES FEIFFER

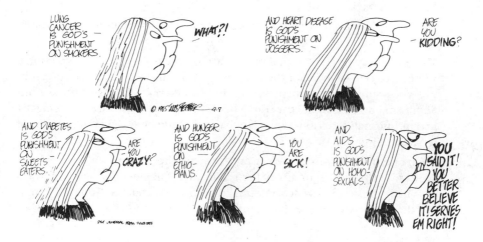

1. What is the main point Feiffer is making in the cartoon?

2. To what extent do you agree with him?

MAKING CONNECTIONS

The following questions and activities can be used for both writing assignments and class discussions. These exercises will help develop your ability to *synthesize* what you read—to combine and integrate information and ideas from different sources.

1. Which of the readings in this chapter did you like best, and why? Which did you like least, and why?

2. The *tone* of a piece of writing is the author's attitude toward his or her subject and audience as expressed in the choice of words and details. Reread the poem "Caged Bird" or the article "Eleven Words That Cast the Power of Bigotry on Honeymoon Couple." What do you consider the major tone (or tones) of the selection? How does this tone relate to the author's purpose?

3. What do the victims of discrimination in "Striking a Nerve," "It Cannot Be Helped," and "Eleven Words That Cast the Power of Bigotry on Honeymoon Couple" have in common emotionally? What similar feelings do they express?

4. Using as evidence material from the readings in this chapter and personal experiences and observations, discuss the extent to which you agree with one of the following statements:

   a. Stereotyping has little effect on people's lives.

   b. No culture is free of prejudice.

   c. The best way to overcome stereotyping and prejudice is through education.

5. Write an essay or give an oral presentation on a topic of your own choice relating to one or more of the readings in this chapter. Consider researching your subject in a university or public library. (*Sample topics:* Anti-Semitism, homophobia, the Ku Klux Klan or other white supremacist group, affirmative action, sexist language, and the civil rights movement of a particular group.)

6. Read one of the following selections from another chapter in this book: "A Coward" (Chapter 1) or any of the readings in Chapter 3. Discuss the ways in which the reading reflects issues raised in this chapter. To what extent are the ideas and perspectives similar?

CHAPTER THREE

GENDER ROLES

Reading Skills:
Summarizing and Paraphrasing

The French author Simone de Beauvoir once said that "one is not born a woman, one becomes one." What she meant is that the roles a female plays in society and her sense of sexual identity are determined not by biology but by the expectations and attitudes of the culture in which she lives (doubtless, de Beauvoir would say the same thing about males).

The readings and activities in this chapter focus on *gender roles:* the culturally defined expectations, assumptions, and rules associated with female and male character and behavior. The chapter also explores the effects of *gender-role stereotyping:* expecting people to behave in a certain way or have certain traits because they are female or male.

Following are some of the questions you will be considering in this chapter:

- How do definitions of gender affect people's lives, choices, and identities?
- How does a society convey its expectations about appropriate female and male character and behavior?
- What are the consequences of behaving in a manner considered inappropriate for one's sex?
- In what ways are females and males portrayed in the mass media?
- What are the traditional gender roles in your native culture, and how have they changed over the last thirty years?
- How have gender roles affected your own life, positively and negatively?

In the first reading of the chapter, "Sex Roles," Hamilton McCubbin and Barbara Blum Dahl explore theories about the biological and cultural origins of gender roles. Next, in "New Realities Fight Old Images of Mother," Susan Chira describes the changing roles of mothers in the United States. After that, in "The Androgynous Male," Noel Perrin discusses masculine stereotypes and his own experience breaking out of traditional male roles. Then the fairy tale "Cinderella" reveals powerful stereotypes about the place of females and males in society. Following this, in "Women Have What It Takes," Carol Barkalow argues that women should be allowed to fight in wars. In the last reading of the chapter—"Men Have All the Power—Why Would They Want to Change?"—Warren Farrell tells the story of a man who pays a high price for rigidly adhering to the masculine stereotype of success. Finally, a cartoon by Cathy Guisewite questions whether it is possible to raise children free from gender stereotypes.

BRIEF QUOTES

The following quotations will help introduce you to the topic of gender roles. Think about these statements as you read the selections in this chapter.

"The word love has by no means the same sense for both sexes, and this is one of the serious misunderstandings that divides them."

—SIMONE DE BEAUVOIR

"The greatest mind must be androgynous."

—SAMUEL TAYLOR COLERIDGE

"What are little girls made of?
Sugar and spice and everything nice,
and that's what little girls are made of.
What are little boys made of?
Snips and snails and puppy dog tails,
and that's what little boys are made of."

—ENGLISH NURSERY RHYME

"I hate housework! You make the beds, you do the dishes—and six months later you have to start all over again."

—JOAN RIVERS

"Wives, submit unto your husbands, as unto the Lord. For the husband is the head of the wife, even as Christ is the head of the church."

—ST. PAUL, FROM EPHESIANS IN THE NEW TESTAMENT

"There is more difference within the sexes than between them."

—IVY COMPTON-BURNETT

"Whatever women do they must do twice as well as men to be thought half as good. Luckily, this is not difficult."

—CHARLOTTE WHITTON

READING

PREREADING ACTIVITIES

1. In your reading journal, write for ten to fifteen minutes about any nonphysical differences you've noticed between females and males.

2. Fill in the following chart with what you consider five or six advantages and disadvantages of being female or male (focus on your own sex).
   When you are finished, share your thoughts with several classmates.

Advantages of Being Female or Male	Disadvantages of Being Female or Male
1.	1.
2.	2.
3.	3.
4.	4.
5.	5.
6.	6.

3. Indicate the extent to which you agree with the following statements by filling in each blank with *SA* (strongly agree), *A* (agree), *U* (undecided), *D* (disagree), or *SD* (strongly disagree). Then share your responses in a small group.

a. _____   Males are innately more aggressive and competitive than females.

b. _____   Most parents treat their daughters and sons differently.

c. _____   There are some jobs that women are better at than men.

d. _____   In most cultures, men occupy and actively exclude women from positions of economic and political power.

e. _____   Females and males are born with different needs, desires, and capabilities.

f. _____ The mass media are very important in shaping a person's sense of gender.

g. _____ In my native culture, male children are generally preferred over female children.

h. _____ The ways females and males learn to behave is the same throughout the world.

i. _____ It is possible to raise girls and boys free from gender differences.

j. _____ In my native culture, there are not enough positive role models for girls.

Sex Roles

HAMILTON MCCUBBIN AND BARBARA BLUM DAHL

The following reading is part of a chapter from the book Marriage and Family: Individuals and Life Cycles *(1985), by Hamilton McCubbin and Barbara Blum Dahl, former professors at the University of Minnesota. Because the authors are reporting research to an academic audience, they are careful to cite their sources. The numbers in brackets ([ ]) refer to the authors' endnotes, grouped at the close of the selection.*

Man for the field and woman for the hearth:[1]
Man for the sword and the needle she:
Man with the head and woman with the heart:
Man to command and woman to obey:
All else confusion.

—ALFRED, LORD TENNYSON[2]

Many, if not all, of the personality traits which we have called masculine or feminine are as lightly linked to sex as are the clothing, the manners, and the form of headdress that a society at any given period assigns to either sex.

—MARGARET MEAD[3]

How is it that this world has always belonged to the men?

—SIMONE DE BEAUVOIR[4]

---

[1]*hearth:* Home (literally, the stone or cement area in front of a fireplace).
[2]*Alfred, Lord Tennyson* (1809–1892): Well-known English poet.
[3]*Margaret Mead* (1901–1978): Prominent American anthropologist.
[4]*Simone de Beauvoir* (1908–1986): Noted French author and feminist.

SEX ROLES AND GENDER IDENTITY

A role in a play is a part for an actor; it includes certain scripted actions, ways [1] of walking, talking, expressing feelings, and so forth. A **sex role**[5] is a part that an individual plays as a social actor—the patterns of feeling and behavior deemed appropriate or inappropriate because of her or his gender. The "script" comes from social expectations about masculine and feminine nature: men should be brave, strong, ambitious, and aggressive, while keeping their feelings under control; women should be gentle, nurturant, passive, dependent, and expressive of their feelings.

Sex roles are based on social **norms**—the agreed-upon standards of acceptable behavior within a society. These norms—such as the norms that men should keep their feelings under control and women should be passive—influence our judgments not only of others but also of ourselves. Thus, if you are male and prone to tears during highly emotional moments or female and likely to dominate classroom discussions and arguments, you may judge yourself harshly because you have internalized traditional sex-role assumptions. Sex roles, then, are part of our concept of ourselves, our **gender identity** [1]. [2]

Sex roles are of great interest to psychologists, sociologists, and other [3] social scientists. Psychologists focus primarily on "inner" personality traits and stereotypes associated with femininity and masculinity, while sociologists emphasize patterns of "outer" behavior or interaction in society. For example, a sociologist studying the paid labor force of the United States would note that most truck drivers are male while most nurses are female. Family sociologists have studied the inclination of judges in child custody cases to assume that mothers are innately better at parenting than fathers.

THE CAUSE OF SEX ROLES: BIOLOGY OR CULTURE?

How do gender differences come about? Do sex roles result from biological [4] differences between the sexes? Or do women and men *learn* to behave differently because of the effects of culture and society?

We know that women as a group score consistently lower than men as a [5] group on mathematics and science achievement tests. (Notice that we said "as a group"; some women score extremely high, while some men score extremely low. But women's average scores are consistently somewhat lower than men's average scores.)

Does this mean that women's brains function differently than men's, that [6] they are not as equipped to do math problems? Does it mean that the male power structure—which for so long prohibited women from receiving any type of formal education—is still inhibiting women in the traditionally

---

[5]*sex role:* Most scholars today prefer the term *gender role* to *sex role.*

male preserves of math and science? Or is it that women lose interest in these subjects because they fear that achievement in math and science will make them less attractive to men?

In short, are traditional sex roles the result of "nature" (biological differ- 7 ences), "nurture" (culture and socialization), or some combination of both?

Genetics: The Biological Evidence

No one disputes that there are biological differences between the sexes. The 8 controversy arises, however, when we try to establish links between these biological differences and the behavior of men and women. Specifically, does biology limit the potential achievements of one or both sexes?

Men and women differ in their genetic structure. Women have two "X" 9 **chromosomes;** men have one "X" and one "Y" chromosome. The complex links between genes and behavior are now being researched; it is impossible to say at this time how differences in chromosome structure may affect women's and men's behavior. We do know that genetic structure determines physical development. The average male is taller, heavier, and more muscular than the average female. Women develop breasts and can bear and nurse children; men cannot.

It is not unreasonable to assume that men did the hunting and heavier 10 physical labor in earlier societies because they were better suited to do so, while women raised the children because they could breast-feed them and food was scarce. Perhaps these differing behavioral patterns for women and men in such societies were the result of **adaptation;** that is, the traits helped them to survive and reproduce at a time when subsistence was a full-time job. But should these differences matter in an industrialized era in which most heavy labor is done by machines and even the fighting of wars relies on sophisticated technology?

Researchers have speculated that certain behavioral differences are due to 11 male and female **hormones.** Both men and women produce the male hormone, androgen, and the female hormone, estrogen, but in differing quantities. The male embryo's "Y" chromosome gives a "command" to release androgen at specific stages of **prenatal** development. The hormone signals the embryo to develop as a male, with male body shape and male sexual organs. Later on, hormones influence bodily changes during puberty; for example, androgen gives signals to the male's body for the growth of facial and body hair and for the deepening of the voice.

Thus, hormones clearly play a role in human physical development. But 12 what effect do they have on emotional development and actual behavior? Again, this question is still being debated and studied. Some research shows that the male hormone testosterone appears to stimulate aggressive behavior in female animals. At the same time, a female hormone, prolactin, seems to stimulate nurturing, motherly activity in male animals [2].

John Money and his colleagues have conducted studies on those rare 13
individuals known as **hermaphrodites** who are a mixture of male and
female biology. The researchers have looked, for example, at girls who
received more androgen at birth than is normal for females. While geneti-
cally they were girls with XX chromosomes, they behaved more like our
society expects boys to act. That is, they enjoyed rough games, were
physically active, and preferred toy trucks to dolls. Money speculates that
early exposure to the male hormone influenced the behavior of these
girls [3].

Hormones may also have an impact on certain differences in brain func- 14
tions. Jerre Levy of the University of Chicago has found differences in the way
male and female brains are organized. In Levy's view, men's brains work in
such a way as to give them superior visual-spatial skills, while women's brains
may give them an advantage in verbal skills [4]. Men are therefore better at
dealing with abstract concepts; women are more effective in picking up
information from the surrounding environment about people, sounds, and so
forth. These brain differences may result from the release of certain hormones at critical periods of prenatal development.

From the point of view of human evolution, such differences make sense. 15
Men were the hunters and needed good visual skills. In addition, they had to
be extremely goal-oriented to succeed in their work. Women lived in groups
and took care of children and the sick; thus, sensitivity to others was a crucial
skill. As noted earlier, the development of these patterns had an adaptive
value in terms of survival and reproduction [5].

Still, we must emphasize that the research on hormonal effects remains at 16
an early and primitive stage. The biological differences between the sexes
which exist serve only as loose boundaries within which culturally learned
differences appear. For example, while prenatal exposure to androgen may
have predisposed the girls in Money's study toward more aggressive, "boyish"
behavior, they also needed a social environment that would encourage (or at
least allow) such behavior.

Estelle Ramey [6] points out that while men and women vary as groups in 17
their respective levels of male and female hormones, there can also be striking hormonal differences between one man and another or one woman and
another. Ramey stresses that these individual differences in levels of testosterone, estrogen, and other hormones are much more significant than any gener-
alized differences between the sexes.

Thus, while the biological basis for sex-related distinctions is important, 18
the role that society and culture play is probably more significant. Our biological nature may be like a rough piece of stone from which society, like a
sculptor, chisels, sharpens, and defines the shapes of male and female behavior. Research in the next decade should begin to clarify the complex interrelationship of genetic and hormonal differences, environmental influences, and
the behavior of women and men.

Culture: The Anthropological Evidence

How, then, does society shape differences between men and women? Cross- 19
cultural studies, generally conducted by anthropologists, have shown that the
typical behavior of males and females in other cultures is quite different from
traditional "masculine" and "feminine" behavior in the United States.

Margaret Mead, in her pioneering anthropological study, *Sex and Tempera- 20
ment in Three Primitive Societies* [7], observed three distinct tribes in New
Guinea. She found that one of them, the Arapesh, expected both women and
men to be warm, cooperative, and nurturing, and generally to exhibit traits
that we have traditionally described as "feminine." By contrast, among the
Mundugumor tribe, both sexes exhibit traits seen as "masculine" in American
society: they were aggressive, competitive, and prone to fighting and controversy. Finally, in the Tchambuli tribe, the character traits seemed the reverse
of those expected under our traditional norms. Women were dominant, controlling, and hardworking, while men were emotionally dependent, irrespon-
sible, and extremely concerned about personal appearance. Mead's famous
study is often cited by those who argue against the view that biology is the
cause of sex differences. If biological distinctions dictate our behavior, they
argue, then how can one explain the vast differences in the lives of the
Arapesh, the Mundugumor, and the Tchambuli—not to mention the difference between these three cultures and our own?

Anthropologists have also noted that a power dynamic is often attached to 21
sex-role distinctions. In early societies, men's role as hunters and warriors gave
them more prestige than women. With that prestige came power: men could
distribute food for the entire community and determine its social structure. By
contrast, women's influence was limited mainly to the domestic sphere. They
were not really participants in the public sphere and gained few rights [8].

In societies where women control their economic well-being, they de- 22
velop more power. Anthropologist Peggy Sanday [9] has illustrated this pattern through her study of the Afikpo Ibo women of Nigeria. Ibo men had
traditionally controlled money and tribal social life because they grew the
yam[6] crop—a main source of food with important religious significance.
When the tribe increased its contact with European cultures, the cassava
plant[7] (used for tapioca) was introduced to them.

The Ibo men disdained the new plant, preferring to continue growing the 23
religiously valued yam. However, they permitted women to cultivate the
cassava and to keep any profits from its sale. Subsequently, the cassava proved
to be extremely lucrative, and the Ibo women became financially independent. With financial independence, the women became less subservient to
their husbands and a more powerful force within tribal culture.

---

[6]*yam:* Edible root of various plants common in the tropics; similar to a sweet potato.
[7]*cassava plant:* Edible root of several plants grown in the tropics; similar to a yam. (Tapioca is a
type of pudding.)

Society: Learning Evidence

How do we learn society's standards about appropriate behavior for each sex? 24
Socialization is the general term used to describe the process of learning
social roles. Most differences between females and males are learned through
family interactions, socialization in schools, and the mass media.

Social learning theory holds that children are rewarded for conforming to 25
their parents' expectations and are punished for behavior that meets with disapproval. Thus, Johnny's parents beam with pride when he shows prowess on
the basketball court, but gasp with horror if he displays an interest in becoming
a dancer. Johnny learns to act "like a boy" in order to please his parents.

The process of differential treatment of girls and boys begins the minute 26
children are born. Adults describe infant girls as "delicate," "sweet," or
"dainty" and hold them more carefully. By contrast, boys are perceived as
more active and are described as "bouncing," "sturdy," or "handsome" [10]. As
toddlers and preschoolers, children learn that baseball and trucks are for boys
while dolls and "dressing up" are for girls.

A study by Judith G. Tudiver [11] demonstrated the differential socializa- 27
tion of preschool-age children. Both mothers and fathers tended to be permissive and supportive with daughters, but did not feel that daughters needed to
achieve or perform. However, parents of sons stressed the importance of
achievement and independence. Fathers, in particular, were extremely concerned about socializing sons into a rather rigid definition of the masculine
role. Tudiver [12] concludes that "a great deal of pressure" is associated with
the socialization of sons, which "probably reflects the high value associated
with being male in our society."

Children and adolescents are influenced by the role models available in a 28
society. If they see that most doctors, police officers, and U.S. Senators are
male, while most nurses, secretaries, and early childhood teachers are female,
they will begin to draw conclusions about which jobs are for them and which
are not. "Real-life" role models affect children's thinking; so, too, do the role
models presented in literature (including comics and children's books), film,
and television.

In a 1979 report [13], the U.S. Commission on Civil Rights was highly critical 29
of television stereotyping of women and minorities. The report concluded:

> Female characters are far more likely than male characters to be portrayed as
> having no identifiable occupation. When they are shown in an occupation, it is
> most frequently as a secretary, nurse, homemaker, household worker, or student.

The commission also noted that women were frequently seen less than fully
clothed in sexually exploitive roles. Actress Kathleen Nolan, former president
of the Screen Actors Guild, has stated: "Women ... are desperately disheart-
ened to be faced ... with the disgraceful trash ... being transmitted in the
guise that this is the American woman" [14].

Feminist Critique: Sex Roles and Social Control

Jessie Bernard, a feminist sociologist, has suggested that theories about sex 30
roles which emphasize the role of socialization tend to let the power structure off the hook too easily. In Bernard's view, power and control are the real
motives behind the division of sex roles. Since the male sex role has higher
status, men attain power over women and gain control of many of society's
valued rewards.

Bernard [15] argues that socialization theorists make this male-dominated 31
power structure seem respectable and reasonable, and are too complacent
about the denial of equal opportunities to women. She believes that these
theorists are saying, in effect, to women:

> Sorry, girls, too bad you haven't got what it takes.... I know it isn't your fault, I
> know it's just the way you were socialized as a child. You'd be just as superior as I
> am if you had played with trucks instead of dolls. But what can I do about it after
> all?

Bernard and other feminists are critical of socialization research because it
fails to challenge the power structure that keeps women and men in unequal
and prescribed roles.

Barbara Bovee Polk [16] has offered a useful summary of the feminist "power 32
analysis" of sex roles and cultural differences between men and women:

1. Men have power and privilege by virtue of their sex.

2. It is in men's interest to maintain that power and privilege.

3. Men occupy and actively exclude women from positions of economic and
   political power in society.

4. Although most males are oppressed by the system under which we live,
   they are not oppressed, as females are, *because* of their sex.

5. Feminine roles and cultural values are the product of oppression. Idealization of them is dysfunctional to change.[8]

Feminists believe that traditional sex roles are used to keep women in their 33
(disadvantaged) place. In the view of Letty Cottin Pogrebin [17], the messages of sex role stereotypes can be condensed into two simple propositions:
boys are better, and girls are meant to be mothers.

ENDNOTES

1. L. Feldman, "Husband-Wife Differences in Marital Problem Identification." Unpub-
   lished data.

---

[8]*dysfunctional to change:* Limiting the emotional growth of females.

2. R. Rose, T. Gordon, and I. Bernstein, "Plasma Testosterone Levels in the Male Rhesus: Influences of Sexual and Social Stimuli," *Science* 178 (1972): 638–643.

3. J. Money, and A. Ehrhardt, *Man and Woman, Boy and Girl* (Baltimore: Johns Hopkins University Press, 1972).

4. J. Durden-Smith, "Male and Female—Why?" *Quest/80* 4(8) (1980): 15–19, 93–97, 99.

5. Durden-Smith: 15–19, 93–97, 99.

6. E. Ramey, "Sex Hormones and Executive Ability," *Annals of the New York Academy of Sciences* 208 (1973): 237–245.

7. M. Mead, *Sex and Temperament in Three Primitive Societies* (New York: Morrow, 1933).

8. M. Rosaldo, and L. Lamphere, *Woman, Culture, and Society* (Stanford: Stanford University Press, 1974).

9. P. Sanday, "Toward a Theory of the Status of Women," *Anthropologist* 75 (1973): 1682–1700.

10. D. Papalia, and S. Olds, *Human Development* (New York: McGraw-Hill, 1979).

11. J. Tudiver, "Parents and the Sex-Role Development of the Pre-School Child," *Sex Roles: Origins, Influences and Implications for Women,* ed. Stark Adamo (Montreal: Eden's Press Women's Publications, 1980).

12. Tudiver: 44.

13. U.S. Commission on Civil Rights, "Window Dressing on the Set: An Update" (Washington, D.C.: U.S. Government Printing Office, 1979).

14. *Broadcasting* (June 5, 1978): 55.

15. J. Bernard, *Women, Wives, Mothers: Values and Options* (Chicago: Aldine Publishing Co., 1975).

16. B. Polk, "Male Power and the Women's Movement," *Journal of Applied Behavioral Science* 10(3) (1974): 415–431.

17. L. Pogrebin, *Growing Up Free: Raising Your Child in the '80's* (New York: McGraw-Hill, 1980).

READING JOURNAL

In your reading journal, discuss one of the following:

1. How your life would be different if you woke up tomorrow and discovered you were the opposite sex

2. Whether you think biology or culture is more important in shaping gender roles

3. A topic of your own choice related to the reading

MEANING AND TECHNIQUE

The following questions and activities will help you understand the main ideas in the reading and the manner in which it was written.

SUMMARIZING

Writing a *summary*—a brief restatement, in your own words, of the main points in a reading passage—is an excellent way to make sure you fully understand what you have read. Summarizing a passage focuses your attention on its content as you separate the main ideas from the supporting details (examples, facts, reasons, anecdotes, and so on). Writing an effective summary also involves analyzing the purpose and organization of a selection. This helps you not only to comprehend a writer's ideas but also to identify their strengths and weaknesses. (At this point, you might want to review the discussion of summarizing in Appendix C.)

1. In one or two sentences, summarize the *main idea* of the section in the reading titled "Genetics: The Biological Evidence." Use your own words.

2. A good way to develop your ability to write a summary of a whole article (a task you will be doing later in this chapter) is to write single-sentence summaries of paragraphs.

   Practice this skill by writing a one-sentence summary of the following paragraphs—that is, a sentence explaining the main idea of each paragraph. Be sure to use your own words.

   Example:

   "Thus, hormones clearly play a role in human physical development. But what effect do they have on emotional development and actual behavior? Again, this question is still being debated and studied. Some research shows that the male hormone testosterone appears to stimulate aggressive behavior in female animals. At the same time, a female hormone, prolactin, seems to stimulate nurturing, motherly activity in male animals." (par. 12)

   SUMMARY OF PARAGRAPH 12: Hormones are shown to influence physical development, but their link to emotions and behavior, though intriguing, is far less certain.

   a. Summary of paragraph 3: _____

   _____

   _____

   b. Summary of paragraph 18: _____

   _____

   _____

c. Summary of paragraph 30: _____

_____

_____

d. Summary of paragraph 31: _____

_____

_____

PARAPHRASING

Writing a *paraphrase* of a passage is similar to writing a summary of it: both involve restating someone else's ideas in your own words. But whereas a summary is a condensed, or shortened, version of the original, a paraphrase is a complete restatement—it retains all of the writer's ideas and key supporting details and is therefore about the same length as the original.

---

3. Show that you understand the meaning of the following sentences from the reading by *paraphrasing,* or restating, the main ideas in your own words. You can use simpler vocabulary and leave out some details as long as you retain the general meaning of the sentences. (See the guidelines for paraphrasing on p. 258.)

Example:

"Feminine roles and cultural values are the product of oppression. Idealization of them is dysfunctional to change." (par. 32)

PARAPHRASE: The roles and values associated with feminine behavior are the result of oppression, and glorifying them hinders emotional growth.

a. "Researchers have speculated that certain behavioral differences are due to male and female hormones." (par. 11)

Paraphrase: _____

_____

_____

b. "Our biological nature may be like a rough piece of stone from which society, like a sculptor, chisels, sharpens, and defines the shapes of male and female behavior." (par. 18)

Paraphrase: _____

_____

_____

c. "Anthropologists have also noted that a power dynamic is often attached to sex-role distinctions." (par. 21)

Paraphrase: _____

_____

_____

d. "Thus, Johnny's parents beam with pride when he shows prowess on the basketball court, but gasp with horror if he displays an interest in becoming a dancer." (par. 25)

Paraphrase: _____

_____

_____

4. What is the difference between a person's "sex role" and "gender identity"?

DRAWING INFERENCES

S. I. Hayakawa, an American linguist and politician, once defined an inference as "a statement about the unknown made on the basis of what is known." Often a writer will state an idea not explicitly, or directly, but implicitly, or indirectly. That is, the writer will provide certain hints or suggestions and allow the reader to draw his or her own conclusions. For example, in paragraph 25 of "Sex Roles," the authors say that "Johnny's parents beam with pride when he shows prowess on the basketball court, but gasp with horror if he displays an interest in becoming a dancer." The authors never directly state that the parents' shock at the thought of their son becoming a dancer is due to the link in their minds between male dancing and homosexuality, but this can be *inferred* from the context.

Learning to make statements about the unknown on the basis of what is known—that is, drawing inferences—is essential to understanding a writer's meaning. The following questions and activities will help you develop this ability.

1. Do you disagree with any statements made by the authors of "Sex Roles" or by any people mentioned in the article? If so, why?

2. Do you think biology or culture is more important in determining gender roles? Why?

3. What is your opinion of the feminist "power analysis" of sex roles described in paragraphs 30–33?

4. Think of a question of your own to ask your classmates about an issue raised in the reading.

VOCABULARY: WORD PARTS

Often in English, a word is formed by adding a group of letters to the beginning or end of the *word root*—the basic part of the word. Groups of letters added to the beginning of a word root are called *prefixes*. Those added to the end of a word root are called *suffixes*. In general, prefixes change the meaning of a word and suffixes change its *part of speech* (noun, verb, adjective, adverb, and so on).

Look at the following examples of roots, prefixes, and suffixes:

Root	national (adjective)	agree (verb)
Prefix	international (adjective)	disagree (verb)
Suffix	internationally (adverb)	disagreement (noun)

If you are reading a passage and come across an unfamiliar word whose meaning you can't figure out from the context, *don't* immediately reach for your dictionary. Often by looking at the prefixes and roots of words (many of which come from ancient Greek and Latin), you can get a good sense of the general meaning of the words. Learning how to analyze key components of words can help you better understand what you are reading and expand your vocabulary.

The following words are all made up of smaller parts (a prefix and root, a root and suffix, or a prefix, root, and suffix).

With a partner, analyze the parts that make up the following words. Then explain the meaning of the word and use it correctly in a sentence. Feel free to use a dictionary to help you.

Example:

psychologist (par. 3)
   Made up of a prefix, root, and suffix: *psych + logia + ist.*

Psych- means "mind or mental processes." *Logia* means "study or science." *-Ist* means "someone who specializes in something."

Psychologist thus means "someone who specializes in the science of the mind."

SENTENCE: Because Clotilde was very interested in children and psychotherapy, she decided to become a child psychologist.

1. *biological* (par. 7): _____

_____

Sentence: _____

_____

2. *prenatal* (par. 11): _____

_____

Sentence: _____

_____

3. *hermaphrodite* (par. 13): _____

_____

Sentence: _____

_____

4. *androgen* (par. 13): _____

_____

Sentence: _____

_____

5. *interrelationship* (par. 18): _____

_____

Sentence: _____

_____

6. *anthropologist* (par. 21): _____

_____

Sentence: _____

_____

7. *television* (par. 28): _____

_____

Sentence: _____

_____

8. *dysfunctional* (par. 32): _____

_____

Sentence: _____

_____

VOCABULARY: IN CONTEXT

In this exercise, you will develop your vocabulary by using words and idioms in a realistic context.

- If you don't know the meaning of one of the following italicized vocabulary items, first find it in the reading and see if you can determine its meaning from the context. (Review the major types of context clues on pp. 263–267.)
- If the meaning is still unclear, look up the item in a dictionary or consult with a native speaker of English.

    Then, in a few sentences, describe or explain each of the following situations, ideas, and things. **Do not** just define the italicized words and expressions. Discuss personal experiences and opinions and give examples.

    1. Something that many people are *prone to* (par. 2)
    2. Something that *inhibits* the learning of a foreign language (par. 6)
    3. Something that might *predispose* someone to antisocial behavior (par. 16)
    4. An example of a *vast* difference between two people, places, or things (par. 20)

5. Something you *disdain,* and why (par. 23)

6. A way to *cultivate* cross-cultural communication (par. 23)

7. A *lucrative* profession in your native culture, and whether you think the financial rewards are justified (par. 23)

8. An example of parents behaving in a *permissive* manner toward their children (par. 27)

9. An example of someone being *let off the hook* (par. 30)

10. Why being *complacent* about something might have a negative result (par. 31)

DISCUSSION AND DEBATE

1. In a small group, discuss whether you think "nature" or "nurture" (biology or culture) is more important in shaping gender roles. Consider evidence presented in the reading, other information you are aware of, and your own experiences and observations.

2. Fill in the following chart with a list of traits and behaviors considered typical of females and males in your native culture (use single words and/or phrases).

   After you have filled in both columns with at least ten items, share your thoughts with several classmates. Consider the extent to which the descriptions reflect *stereotypes* (exaggerated and inaccurate generalities) and reality.

Female	*Male*
Example: domestic	macho

3. In a small group, go to an art museum and examine representations of females and males. (You might want to concentrate on a particular time period or observe changes over time.) Focus on predominant images, roles, values, and ideals. As an experiment, try substituting a female for a male figure in any given picture and vice versa. What is the effect?

 After discussing the various pictures, share your observations and conclusions with the rest of the class.

WRITING ACTIVITIES

1. A common strategy of writers to develop and organize their ideas is *comparing* and *contrasting* two people, places, things, or ideas. Often writers will use the compare-and-contrast signals listed on page 261 to show similarities and differences.

 Practice using these transitional signals by writing six sentences: three describing similarities and three describing differences between females and males.

2. With several classmates, write a one-paragraph summary of the section in the reading titled "The Cause of Sex Roles: Biology or Culture?" Follow the guidelines on page 255. Remember that a summary should be *concise, accurate, objective,* and *coherent.*

3. Write an essay discussing the extent to which you agree with one of the following statements (or with one of the quotations on p. 96). Support your arguments with examples from "Sex Roles" and personal experiences and observations. (To help you plan, draft, and revise the essay, see Appendix A.)

 a. In my native culture, there are more advantages to being female than there are to being male.

 b. The experiences considered necessary for girls to become women and for boys to become men are quite different in my native culture.

READING

PREREADING ACTIVITIES

1. In your reading journal, write for ten to fifteen minutes about the qualities of a good mother.

2. In a small group, discuss several of the quotations on page 96. Do you agree with the views expressed?

3. Indicate the extent to which you agree with the following statements by filling in each blank with *SA* (strongly agree), *A* (agree), *U* (undecided), *D* (disagree), or *SD* (strongly disagree). Then share your responses in a small group.

a. _____ Women are instinctively better than men at nurturing and taking care of children.

b. _____ Changing gender roles are contributing to the breakdown of the family.

c. _____ Working mothers should receive at least four months of paid maternity leave.

d. _____ It is better for young children to be at home with their mothers than in day care.

e. _____ The world would be a better place if more women were in positions of power.

f. _____ Females and males have equal access to educational and employment opportunities in my native country.

g. _____ Women's roles have changed a lot in my native country over the past thirty years.

h. _____ A woman cannot feel totally fulfilled unless she has a child.

i. _____ Women should not work outside the home when they have young children.

j. _____ Family values were stronger in the 1950s than today.

New Realities Fight Old Images of Mother
SUSAN CHIRA

The following article, written by Susan Chira, an American journalist, originally appeared in the New York Times, *a large daily newspaper, in October 1992. The article was the first in "The Good Mother: Searching for an Ideal," a series focusing on the changing roles of mothers in the United States. Written during the 1992 presidential election (with Republican President George Bush running against*

Democratic Governor Bill Clinton), Chira's article also examines the "family values" debate. During the election, this was a controversial issue, with Republicans arguing the need to return to the traditional family values of the 1950s and Democrats maintaining that a changing society requires new definitions of families and "good mothers."

The American mother—that self-sacrificing, self-effacing, cookie-baking 1 icon—has been shoved into the center of a political morality play,[1] one where stick-figure mothers battle in a debate that does not begin to suggest the complexity, diversity and confusion of being a mother in 1992.

Instead of Marilyn Quayle[2] and Hillary Clinton,[3] those emblems of stay-at- 2 home and working mothers, talk to Toni Rumsey, who cried when her first child was born and realized she would have to keep her factory job at Gerber Baby Foods here in Fremont[4] or face living in a trailer.

Or Stacy Murdock, who watches every penny on her farm in Murray, Ky., 3 because her family's income dropped by more than half when she quit teaching, unable to bear leaving her children.

Or Nancy Cassidy, a garment worker in Easton, Pa., who loves to work and 4 believes her children are the better for it.

REDEFINING MOTHERHOOD

These mothers are haunted by the ghost of the mythical 1950's television 5 mother—one that most women today cannot be, even if they want to. Caught between a fictional ideal, changing expectations of women's roles and the reality that many mothers now work because they must, women around the country are groping for a new definition of the good mother.

The old images linger, but they fit fewer people's lives. Motherhood in 6 America has undergone a breathtaking transformation in little more than 30 years, propelled by shrinking wages of husbands and changing social attitudes.

In 1960, 20 percent of mothers with children under 6 years old were in 7 the labor force; by last year the figure had swelled to 58 percent, with most of them working full time. Twenty-nine percent of all American families are now headed by one parent.

Some more affluent women choose to work for self-fulfillment, and some 8 who started out that way found that they could not afford to leave their jobs as the economy soured. Whether or not a conservative backlash movement is

---

[1]*morality play:* Allegorical play in the fifteenth and sixteenth centuries providing moral instruction (the reference is to the debate about "family values" during the 1992 presidential campaign).

[2]*Marilyn Quayle:* Conservative Republican lawyer married to Dan Quayle, former vice-president under George Bush (1988–1992).

[3]*Hillary Clinton:* Liberal Democratic lawyer married to Bill Clinton, forty-second president of the United States.

[4]*Fremont:* A town in Michigan.

trying to shame women into staying at home, more and more mothers see work as a financial and personal necessity.

Small wonder, then, that Republican strategists quickly folded their family 9 values banner[5] when they found the reality of motherhood in this election year at odds with campaign slogans. With politicians in both parties now courting middle America, many of these same working-class women have been forced to take jobs outside the home, often monotonous and regimented ones at low wages that may not allow them to buy help with child care and housecleaning.

As interviews with more than 30 mothers around the country show, politi- 10 cians have waded into one of the most wrenching issues of American life.

"I never feel like I'm a full mom," said Mrs. Rumsey, a 34-year-old mother of 11 two who checks Gerber's baby food for shards of glass and signs of spoilage from 7 A.M. to 3 P.M. "I make the cookies, the homemade costumes for Hallow-een. I volunteer for everything to make up to them for not being here. When I do all that, I make myself so tired that they lose a happy cheerful mom, and then I'm cheating them again. It's hard when you were raised with Donna Reed and the Beav's mom."[6]

In another factory in Easton, Pa., Mrs. Cassidy inspects sportswear, and her 12 life as a working mother, for flaws. "I think you can work and be a good mother," said the 42-year-old mother of two. "We're doing it. When people compliment you that they're nice children, then I think you've been a terrific mother."

THE OLD IDEAL: MYTHIC VERITIES AND APPLE PIE[7]

Some women have found that they could not be good mothers in the old 13 sense because working has become so important to their identities. These women say they know in their hearts that being at home all day does not automatically make a good mother.

"You can be there without being there," said Cheryl Moorefield, a labor 14 nurse in Winston-Salem, N.C., who has two children.

Yet ask most women their image of a good mother, and the old verities 15 come tumbling forth. "A mother doesn't have a right to be tired or sick," said Deborah Gray, a 38-year-old mother of six whose shift can run 12 hours a day during the busy summer season at Heinz's pickling plant in Holland, Mich. "A mother must be available no matter what. A mother is a person that can perform miracles."

---

[5]*folded their family values banner:* Stopped talking about family values and the need for mothers of young children to stay at home.

[6]*Donna Reed/Beav's mom:* Mothers in *The Donna Reed Show* and *Leave It to Beaver,* popular TV shows in the 1950s depicting traditional family values.

[7]*Apple Pie:* Symbol of traditional American values.

In Murray, Ky., which boasts the National Scouting[8] Museum, tobacco and 16
soybean farms, a state university branch and what seems like a church on
every corner, Stacy Murdock comes close to this cherished ideal. Mrs.
Murdock, who gave up her teaching job, is up at 6 A.M., starts breakfast and
then wakes her three children a half-hour later. The whole family eats breakfast at 7 A.M., and then her husband drives the two older children to school.
Her husband, one of a vanishing breed of small farmers who can work close to
home, tends his 600 acres of corn, beans, wheat and cattle while his wife
plays with her 14-month-old daughter, cleans, cooks and pays bills. At noon
he returns for a hot meal with his family.

By 2:30 P.M., Mrs. Murdock is on her way to school to pick up her older 17
daughters. Some afternoons she takes them to dancing school, which she pays
for by keeping the school's books.[9] On Wednesdays the children's grand-
mother drops by to baby-sit so that Mrs. Murdock can volunteer at the older
children's school.

"The most important thing you're going to get in your life is your chil- 18
dren," Mrs. Murdock said, explaining why the family has given up eating out,
planning for a bigger house and having many other extras. "I just can't imagine giving that responsibility to someone else."

It is precisely because convictions about what kind of mother is best run so 19
strong and deep that family values became such an explosive issue. Despite all
the talk about fathers' becoming more involved with children, it is mothers
who remain at the center of this debate, and mothers who shoulder the praise
or blame. Most women interviewed said they were worried about the future
of the family, but many said the debate, at least as conducted by politicians,
seemed irrelevant or insulting.

"Family values is a cheap way out," Mrs. Rumsey said. "We all believe in 20
family morals and values. I'm not going to put down what you're doing and
don't put me down for what I'm trying to do."

For some, the debate intensified their own guilt. "My heart pounds a little 21
bit," said Kris Northrop, the mother of a 4-month-old girl, who has just returned to her job running a candy-wrapping machine at the Life Savers plant
in Holland, Mich. "I think, Is this right? Should I try to not be a working
mother, even though my image is of an independent mother?"

And for others the verdict is clear: working and mothering small children 22
cannot mix. "I had these children and I wanted to raise them," said Celisa
Cunningham, a Baptist minister's wife who returned to work designing and
supervising asphalt mixes once her children started school. "I've given 10
years to my children and I'm going to give 30 to my career, and I'm going to

---

[8]*Scouting* (Girl Scouts and Boy Scouts): Organizations promoting character development and
good citizenship in girls and boys.

[9]*keeping the school's books:* Recording the school's accounts (bookkeeping).

see more from those 10 years in the long run than from the 30. I think many mothers cop out and make a life-style choice."

THE NEW REALITY: HARRIED JUGGLERS ON A TIGHTROPE

But for many working-class women, Mrs. Murdock's life, and the comfortable 23 certainties invoked by the champions of family values, are as remote as the television characters that helped shape their idea of the good mother.

Instead of family breakfasts and school volunteer work, Jan Flint works 24 nights and her husband works days in a Welch's juice and jam plant in Lawton, Mich., so that one of them can always be home with the children.

"That's what God meant for me—to stay at home, cook and sew, and I can't 25 do that," said Mrs. Flint, who had to return to work seven years ago when money got tight. "I used to have a clean house all the time. I always enjoyed being involved in my older two's education. Last night was open house[10] and my children wanted me to go. I bribed them—'I'll let you bring friends over if I don't go.' That's what's happening to the American family. Nobody's there, and children don't have full-time guidance."

Measuring themselves against such an exacting, idealized standard, where 26 good mothering equals how much time is spent with the children rather than how secure or happy the children are, many working women feel they fall short. For the most part, these women struggle without help from society or their employers, who seldom give them long maternity leaves or flexible hours.

And because motherhood itself has been transformed in less than a genera- 27 tion, these mothers have no guides. "What is happening now is that parents are relying on child care who themselves were often raised by their mothers," said Deborah Phillips, a psychologist and expert in child development at the University of Virginia. "So there is incredible anxiety and uncertainty, especially in a society that holds firmly to the belief that mother care is superior."

Sheila Lencki, a mother of four who works as a school secretary in Murray, 28 Ky., says she fears she is failing to meet the standard her own mother set.

"My own mother stayed at home, and that's what I wanted to do," she said. 29 "I respect my mother so much. I think that everything she does is right."

Even more troubling, many women fear they have somehow relinquished 30 their children. "When I put them in day care, I did feel a pull; I'm not the one raising my children," said Mrs. Moorefield, who raised her two children alone for seven years until her remarriage several years ago. "Who's teaching them values?"

That anxiety deepens if mothers suspect their child care is not very good, a 31 suspicion that experts in the field say is often correct. Working-class women

---

[10]*open house*: An evening (usually once or twice a year) during which parents visit their children's school and talk to their teachers.

usually cannot afford to buy one-on-one attention for their children; most of the women interviewed either left their children with relatives or took them to the home of another mother who was looking after several children for pay.

The quality of such care, in both the physical settings and the attention the 32 children receive, varies considerably. The best care is also often the most expensive, and many women said government could help them most by giving them some financial help with child care.

Many women said they felt lucky to have found help from their families or 33 loving baby sitters. But some said they were making compromises that disturbed them, either leaving children as young as 9 at home alone until they returned from work or having to switch baby sitters frequently.

Although she loves her work, Mrs. Moorefield is torn because she believes 34 her recent change to a 12-hour shift may be hurting her children, who are not doing well in school. She is considering sharing a job, but she must first wait to see whether her husband, who works in an airline stockroom, goes on strike.

Generally, though, most women say, with an air of surprise, that they 35 believe their children are actually turning out all right, even if working interferes with their ideal of a good mother.

"For me, looking at my kids tells me I'm doing O.K.," Mrs. Rumsey said. "My 36 kids are excellent students. They are outgoing. They have minds of their own. No matter how much I've never wanted to work, there's never been any drastic indication from my kids that I shouldn't."

BLAZING A NEW PATH: LEAVING THE LAND OF MAKE-BELIEVE

With little chance of living out their ideal of the good mother, many mothers 37 are searching for a new way to think about motherhood.

Elesha Lindsay works days checking references at Forsyth Memorial Hospi- 38 tal in Winston-Salem, N.C., and two nights a week studying for a higher-paying job as a medical stenographer[11] while her husband juggles four jobs as a cook. She leaves her 16-month-old daughter at the hospital's day-care center, where she believes her daughter is happy and well-cared for. Yet she cried all week when she first had to return to work, when her daughter was 9 weeks old. She and a friend filled in for each other so she could add three weeks onto the hospital's normal six-week maternity leave.

Although she would rather work part time when her daughter is small, Mrs. 39 Lindsay sees herself as a good mother, and work as a welcome part of her life.

"Being a good mother depends on what type of person you are and what 40 you instill," she said. "My mother wasn't there the majority of the time, but I was watching her, knowing the type of person she was. We knew what our mother expected from us. That child is spending more time with that day-

---

[11]*stenographer:* Person who writes down what someone else is dictating.

care giver than you, but I still feel like I'm a better person for her, out working, financially helping the family."

Mrs. Cassidy, the garment worker, also believes that too many mothers 41 become obsessed with motherhood's gestures rather than its substance. "It doesn't matter if you bake cookies for them, and don't take them to Cub Scouts[12] every time," she said. "You're not going to be there for their first step. But I never heard mine say, 'You were never there when I needed you.' "

Still, many mothers worry that they may be deluding themselves. "It looks 42 fine to me," Mrs. Lencki said, "but maybe I'm not looking."

While there is debate about the effects of extensive nonmaternal care early 43 in life, experts agree that with conscientious, loving parents and high-quality care the vast majority of children do just fine, by any measurement of intellectual and emotional development. Some studies suggest that mothers' attitudes are crucial; if they are happy, whether staying at home or working, that will have an enormous impact on their relationship with their children.

Employer flexibility clearly makes a difference, said Arlie Hochschild, a 44 sociologist and author of "The Second Shift: Working Parents and the Revolution at Home" (Viking, 1989), who is now studying the workplace and its effects on family life. "We have to acknowledge that the majority of American women will work for the majority of their lives through their childbearing years and we have to adapt the workplace," she said. "Don't pretend they're men who have wives at home to do this."

One reason Mrs. Cassidy feels little guilt is that she was able to take off work 45 to watch her children in school plays, or tend them when they were sick. But other companies, particularly factories where workers' absences may slow assembly lines, are not so lenient. Several women said their employers required 24-hour notice for sick days—an impossibility with children—or docked their pay if they wanted to go to an event at their children's schools.

But even if they did not choose to work, some mothers have found that 46 working has brought unexpected benefits: a new sense of identity, a role in a broader community, pride in their independence, a temporary escape from children that may allow them to be better mothers in the time they share.

And while women may yearn for the safe world of mythic families, they 47 have seen enough of the sobering reality of divorce and widowhood to cherish the financial independence that working confers. "My mother stayed home, and when my father divorced her she had nothing to fall back on," said Donna King, a hospital laboratory supervisor who is a mother of four.

In fact, most of the women interviewed said they would prefer working to 48 staying at home—but most wanted to work part time.

These days, some more affluent and educated women say they would feel 49 embarrassed to tell their friends that they did not work. Yet many working-class mothers who have found that they are happy working treat it like a guilty secret. Mrs. Lencki dropped her voice almost to a whisper when she

---

[12]*Cub Scouts:* Young members (ages eight to ten) of the Boy Scouts.

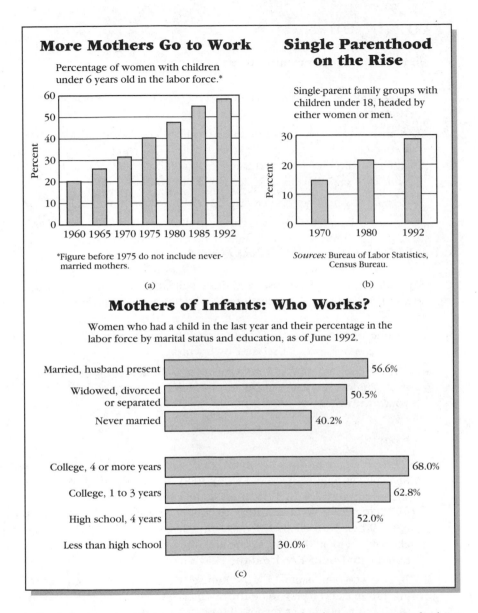

More Mothers Go to Work

Percentage of women with children under 6 years old in the labor force.*

*Figure before 1975 do not include never-married mothers.

(a)

Single Parenthood on the Rise

Single-parent family groups with children under 18, headed by either women or men.

Sources: Bureau of Labor Statistics, Census Bureau.

(b)

Mothers of Infants: Who Works?

Women who had a child in the last year and their percentage in the labor force by marital status and education, as of June 1992.

Married, husband present — 56.6%
Widowed, divorced or separated — 50.5%
Never married — 40.2%

College, 4 or more years — 68.0%
College, 1 to 3 years — 62.8%
High school, 4 years — 52.0%
Less than high school — 30.0%

(c)

talked about enjoying her job, despite her guilt that her youngest son had not had her full-time presence.

Pride, embarrassment and defiance competed as Mrs. Moorefield talked 50 about work. "For me, the ideal mother is one who is able to choose," Mrs. Moorefield said. "Even if we could financially afford that I could not work, I still think I would need at least some other contact, part time. You want to be there for your children, and on the other hand you want to be able to provide for them well. This sounds like I'm anti-family values."

READING JOURNAL

In your reading journal, discuss one of the following:

1. How your family conveyed its expectations about appropriate female/male traits and behavior

2. A time when you experienced a conflict concerning the roles society expected you to play as a female or male. (Did you find yourself pulled in different directions—by cultural expectations, on the one hand, and by your own expectations and desires, on the other?)

3. A topic of your own choice related to the article

MEANING AND TECHNIQUE

The following questions and activities will help you understand the main ideas in the article and the manner in which it was written.

1. In one or two sentences, summarize the *main idea* Chira is trying to convey in her article. Use your own words.

2. Write a one-sentence summary of each of the following paragraphs—that is, a sentence explaining the main idea of the paragraph. Be sure to use your own words.

Example:

" 'I never feel like I'm a full mom,' said Mrs. Rumsey, a 34-year-old mother of two who checks Gerber's baby food for shards of glass and signs of spoilage from 7 A.M. to 3 P.M. 'I make the cookies, the homemade costumes for Halloween. I volunteer for everything to make up to them for not being here. When I do all that, I make myself so tired that they lose a happy cheerful mom, and then I'm cheating them again. It's hard when you were raised with Donna Reed and the Beav's mom.' " (par. 11)

SUMMARY OF PARAGRAPH 11: Mrs. Rumsey describes the difficulties of working full-time and trying to be the mythical good mother and concludes that she is not fulfilling her responsibility as a parent.

a. Summary of paragraph 16: _____

_____

_____

b. Summary of paragraph 25: _____

_____

_____

c. Summary of paragraph 26: _____

_____

_____

d. Summary of paragraph 43: _____

_____

_____

3. Show that you understand the meaning of the following sentences from Chira's article by *paraphrasing,* or restating, the main ideas in your own words. You can use simpler vocabulary and leave out some details as long as you retain the general meaning of the sentences. (See the guidelines for paraphrasing on p. 258.)

Example:

"It is precisely because convictions about what kind of mother is best run so strong and deep that family values became such an explosive issue." (par. 19)

PARAPHRASE: The topic of family values is very controversial because people have fixed beliefs about what it means to be a good mother.

a. "Motherhood in America has undergone a breathtaking transformation in little more than 30 years, propelled by shrinking wages of husbands and changing social attitudes." (par. 6)

Paraphrase: _____

_____

_____

b. "Measuring themselves against such an exacting, idealized standard . . . many working women feel they fall short." (par. 26)

Paraphrase: _____

_____

_____

c. "Mrs. Cassidy, the garment worker, also believes that too many mothers become obsessed with motherhood's gestures rather than its substance." (par. 41)

Paraphrase: _____

_____

_____

d. "And while women may yearn for the safe world of mythic families, they have seen enough of the sobering reality of divorce and widowhood to cherish the financial independence that working confers." (par. 47)

Paraphrase: _____

_____

_____

4. What is the traditional image of motherhood described in the article? Why does Chira call this a "fictional ideal" (par. 5)?

DRAWING INFERENCES

The following questions and activities will help develop your ability to draw inferences—an important reading skill.

1. Two of the headings in Chira's article are "The New Reality: Harried Jugglers on a Tightrope" and "Blazing a New Path: Leaving the Land of Make-Believe." Briefly explain the meaning of each heading. (Both headings are *metaphors,* or implied comparisons, between two dissimilar things. See the discussion of metaphors on pp. 154–155.)

2. Why do you think social definitions of the "good mother" have changed over the last thirty years in the United States?

3. Look at the graphs on page 121 and answer the following questions:

   • Why do you think the percentage of working mothers has increased so dramatically since 1960?

- Why have single-parent families been on the rise?
- How do you interpret the graph titled "Mothers of Infants: Who Works?" (Consider both marital status and education.)

4. Think of a question of your own to ask your classmates about an issue raised in Chira's article.

VOCABULARY: BY THEME

Separate the following words into the columns below, one relating to character traits commonly associated with females and the other to those commonly associated with males (if you think a word relates equally to both sexes, put it in both columns). You don't necessarily have to agree with the associations; fill in the columns according to what you think most people in your native culture would say.

Then share your lists with several classmates. Discuss the extent to which the descriptions reflect stereotypes and reality.

talkative, adventurous, obstinate, illogical, dogmatic, outspoken, sensual, frivolous, reliable, even-tempered, submissive, charismatic, intuitive, decisive, nurturing, sensitive, competitive, seductive, self-reliant, creative, sentimental, jealous

Female Traits	*Male Traits*

VOCABULARY: IN CONTEXT

In this exercise, you will develop your vocabulary by using words and idioms in a realistic context.

- If you don't know the meaning of one of the following italicized vocabulary items, first find it in the reading and see if you can determine its meaning from the context. (Review the major types of context clues on pp. 263–267.)

- If the meaning is still unclear, look up the item in a dictionary or consult with a native speaker of English.

- Then, in a few sentences, describe or explain each of the following situations, ideas, and things. **Do not** just define the italicized words and expressions. Discuss personal experiences and opinions and give examples.

    1. A type of work you would find *monotonous,* and why (par. 9)

    2. An example of a *flaw* in an argument (par. 12)

    3. An example of someone *boasting* (par. 16)

    4. What you would like to do with your life *in the long run* (par. 22)

    5. Something that once *turned out* better than you had expected (par. 35)

    6. Someone you know who is *outgoing* (par. 36)

    7. What someone who is *conscientious* might do (par. 43)

    8. A *crucial* aspect of learning a foreign language (par. 43)

    9. Something that has *had an* enormous *impact* on your life (par. 43)

    10. Something you *cherish,* and why (par. 47)

DISCUSSION AND DEBATE

1. In a small group, fill in the following chart with the advantages and disadvantages—according to the women mentioned in Chira's article—of mothers working outside the home.

    Then discuss the extent to which you agree with the women. Also feel free to consider arguments not dealt with in the article and cultural patterns in your native country.

Advantages of Mothers Working Outside the Home	Disadvantages of Mothers Working Outside the Home

2. Write a list of careers traditionally associated with women and men in your native country. Then share your list with several classmates. Discuss the extent to which career options have changed over the last thirty years.

3. In a small group, analyze gender images in several magazine advertisements. Consider the following questions:

   • What types of products are geared toward females and males?

   • What traits, activities, and values are associated with each sex?

   • To what extent do the advertisements reflect gender-role stereotyping?

   After you have completed your analysis, share your findings with the rest of the class.

WRITING ACTIVITIES

1. Write a one-paragraph summary of "New Realities Fight Old Images of Mother," following the guidelines for summarizing on page 255. Remember that a summary should be *concise, accurate, objective,* and *coherent.*

2. Preparing an *outline* of your essays before you actually write them can be very helpful in clarifying, developing, and organizing your ideas.

   Imagine you and several classmates are writing an essay about a topic of your own choice related to "New Realities Fight Old Images of Mother." As a group, write an outline of the essay. (See the discussion of outlines in Appendix B.)

Then show your outline to one of the other groups and see if your classmates have any questions or suggestions.

3. Write an essay discussing the extent to which you agree with one of the following statements (or with one of the statements in activity 3 of the "Prereading Activities"). Support your arguments with examples from Chira's article and personal experiences and observations. (To help you plan, draft, and revise the essay, see Appendix A.)

   a. Families are instrumental in conveying a society's expectations about appropriate female/male traits and behavior.

   b. "I expect a significant change by 2020. A majority of men married to working wives will share equally in the responsibility of the home" (Arlie Hochschild, American sociologist).

4. Write a narrative depicting a culture in which gender roles are reversed, eliminated, or carried to an extreme. What would the culture look like? How would people act? What would they say? What opportunities and limitations would individuals have? As you write your story, try to make your descriptions as vivid as possible.

READING

PREREADING ACTIVITIES

1. In your reading journal, spend ten to fifteen minutes writing about what you like most and least about being female or male.

2. *Gender roles* are the patterns of feeling and behavior considered appropriate and inappropriate for a person's sex.

   Fill in the following chart with four or five behaviors that would be seen as *inappropriate* for females and males in your native culture.

   When you are finished, share your thoughts with several classmates.

Inappropriate Behavior for Females	*Inappropriate Behavior for Males*
1.	1.
2.	2.
3.	3.
4.	4.
5.	5.

3. Indicate the extent to which you agree with the following statements by filling in each blank with *SA* (strongly agree), *A* (agree), *U* (undecided), *D* (disagree), or *SD* (strongly disagree). Then share your responses in a small group.

a. _____ Men usually have more difficulty expressing their emotions than women.

b. _____ In my native country, there are more advantages to being female than there are to being male.

c. _____ I personally feel a certain amount of pressure to conform to traditional gender roles.

d. _____ Heterosexual males are less afraid of being considered homosexual than heterosexual females are.

e. _____ Women are more restricted by gender roles than men are.

f. _____ It is impossible for a woman and man to have a platonic (nonsexual) relationship.

g. _____ God is neither female nor male.

h. _____ Feminists are doing more to hurt women than to help them.

i. _____ The world would be a better place if there were no distinct "female" and "male" roles.

j. _____ Women generally appreciate art and beauty more than men do.

The Androgynous Male
NOEL PERRIN

Noel Perrin is a professor of English at Dartmouth College and also raises beef cattle in Vermont. He has written a number of books, including Vermont in All Weathers *(1973),* First Person Rural *(1978), and* Second Person Rural *(1980). The following essay, written in 1984, originally appeared in the "About Men" column in the magazine section of the* New York Times, *a large daily newspaper.*

The summer I was 16, I took a train from New York to Steamboat Springs, Colo., where I was going to be assistant horse wrangler[1] at a camp. The trip

---

[1] *horse wrangler:* Person who takes care of horses trained for riding.

took three days, and since I was much too shy to talk to strangers, I had quite a lot of time for reading. I read all of *Gone With the Wind.*[2] I read all the interesting articles in a couple of magazines I had, and then I went back and read all the dull stuff. I also took all the quizzes, a thing of which magazines were even fuller then than now.

The one that held my undivided attention was called "How Masculine/ 2 Feminine Are You?" It consisted of a large number of inkblots. The reader was supposed to decide which of four objects each blot most resembled. The choices might be a cloud, a steam engine, a caterpillar and a sofa.

When I finished the test, I was shocked to find that I was barely masculine 3 at all. On a scale of 1 to 10, I was about 1.2. Me, the horse wrangler? (And not just wrangler, either. That summer, I had to skin a couple of horses that died—the camp owner wanted the hides.)

The results of that test were so terrifying to me that for the first time in my 4 life I did a piece of original analysis. Having unlimited time on the train, I looked at the "masculine" answers over and over, trying to find what it was that distinguished real men from people like me—and eventually I discovered two very simple patterns. It was "masculine" to think the blots looked like man-made objects, and "feminine" to think they looked like natural objects. It was masculine to think they looked like things capable of causing harm, and feminine to think of innocent things.

Even at 16, I had the sense to see that the compilers of the test were using 5 rather limited criteria—maleness and femaleness are both more complicated that *that*—and I breathed a huge sigh of relief. I wasn't necessarily a wimp, after all.

That the test did reveal something other than the superficiality of its mak- 6 ers I realized only many years later. What it revealed was that there is a large class of men and women both, to which I belong, who are essentially androgynous. That doesn't mean we're gay, or low in the appropriate hormones, or uncomfortable performing the jobs traditionally assigned our sexes. (A few years after that summer, I was leading troops in combat and, unfashionable as it now is to admit this, having a very good time. War is exciting. What a pity the 20th century went and spoiled it with high-tech weapons.)

What it does mean to be spiritually androgynous is a kind of freedom. Men 7 who are all-male, or he-man, or 100 percent red-blooded Americans, have a little biological set that causes them to be attracted to physical power, and probably also to dominance. Maybe even to watching football. I don't say this to criticize them. Completely masculine men are quite often wonderful people: good husbands, good (though sometimes overwhelming) fathers, good members of society. Furthermore, they are often so unselfconsciously at ease

---

[2]*Gone With the Wind:* Popular novel about the American Civil War written in 1936 by the American author Margaret Mitchell.

in the world that other men seek to imitate them. They just aren't as free as us androgynes. They pretty nearly have to be what they are; we have a range of choices open.

The sad part is that many of us never discover that. Men who are not 100 8 percent red-blooded Americans—say, those who are only 75 percent red-blooded—often fail to notice their freedom. They are too busy trying to copy the he-men ever to realize that men, like women, come in a wide variety of acceptable types. Why this frantic imitation? My answer is mere speculation, but not casual. I have speculated on this for a long time.

Partly they're just envious of the he-man's unconscious ease. Mostly 9 they're terrified of finding that there may be something wrong with them deep down, some weakness at the heart. To avoid discovering that, they spend their lives acting out the role that the he-man naturally lives. Sad.

One thing that men owe to the women's movement is that this kind of 10 failure is less common than it used to be. In releasing themselves from the single ideal of the dependent woman, women have more or less incidentally released a lot of men from the single ideal of the dominant male. The one mistake the feminists have made, I think, is in supposing that *all* men need this release, or that the world would be a better place if all men achieved it. It wouldn't. It would just be duller.

So far I have been pretty vague about just what the freedom of the androgy- 11 nous man is. Obviously it varies with the case. In the case I know best, my own, I can be quite specific. It has freed me most as a parent. I am, among other things, a fairly good natural mother. I like the nurturing role. It makes me feel good to see a child eat—and it turns me to mush to see a 4-year-old holding a glass with both small hands, in order to drink. I even enjoyed sewing patches on the knees of my daughter Amy's Dr. Dentons[3] when she was at the crawling stage. All that pleasure I would have lost if I had made myself stick to the notion of the paternal role that I started with.

Or take a smaller and rather ridiculous example. I feel free to kiss cats. 12 Until recently it never occurred to me that I would want to, though my daughters have been doing it all their lives. But my elder daughter is now 22, and in London. Of course, I get to look after her cat while she is gone. He's a big, handsome farm cat named Petrushka, very unsentimental, though used from kittenhood to being kissed on the top of the head by Elizabeth. I've gotten very fond of him (he's the adventurous kind of cat who likes to climb hills with you), and one night I simply felt like kissing him on the top of the head, and did. Why did no one tell me sooner how silky cat fur is?

Then there's my relation to cars. I am completely unembarrassed by my 13 inability to diagnose even minor problems in whatever object I happen to be

---

[3]*Dr. Dentons:* Popular brand of pajamas for young children.

driving, and don't have to make some insider's remark to mechanics to try to establish that I, too, am a "Man With His Machine."

The same ease extends to household maintenance. I do it, of course. Service people are expensive. But for the last decade my house has functioned better than it used to because I've had the aid of a volume called "Home Repairs Any Woman Can Do," which is pitched just right for people at my technical level. As a youth, I'd as soon have touched such a book as I would have become a transvestite. Even though common sense says there is really nothing sexual whatsoever about fixing sinks. 14

Or take public emotion. All my life I have easily been moved by certain kinds of voices. The actress Siobhan McKenna's, to take a notable case. Give her an emotional scene in a play, and within 10 words my eyes are full of tears. In boyhood, my great dread was that someone might notice. I struggled manfully, you might say, to suppress this weakness. Now, of course, I don't see it as a weakness at all, but as a kind of fulfillment. I even suspect that the true he-men feel the same way, or one kind of them does, at least, and it's only the poor imitators who have to struggle to repress themselves. 15

Let me come back to the inkblots, with their assumption that masculine equates with machinery and science, and feminine with art and nature. I have no idea whether the right pronoun for God is He, She or It. But this I'm pretty sure of. If God could somehow be induced to take the test, God would not come out macho, and not feminismo, either, but right in the middle. Fellow androgynes, it's a nice thought. 16

READING JOURNAL

In your reading journal, discuss one of the following:

1. Whether or not the world would be a better place if more people were androgynous
2. An advantage or disadvantage of being female or male
3. A topic of your own choice related to "The Androgynous Male"

VOCABULARY: PARTS OF SPEECH

A *part of speech* refers to the grammatical function a word performs in a sentence. The four major parts of speech are *nouns, verbs, adjectives,* and *adverbs* (other parts of speech are pronouns, prepositions, and conjunctions).

The following words appear in the essay "The Androgynous Male." Fill in each of the blanks below with the appropriate part of speech. If there is no corresponding form for a word, put an asterisk (*) in the blank. Try to do this exercise first without using a dictionary.

Noun	Verb	Adjective	Adverb
Example: analysis (par. 4)	analyze	analytical	analytically
		terrifying (par. 4)	
			eventually (par. 4)
			necessarily (par. 5)
	reveal (par. 6)		
variety (par. 8)			
speculation (par. 8)			
		dominant (par. 10)	
		vague (par. 11)	
			obviously (par. 11)
	diagnose (par. 13)		
dread (par. 15)			
	repress (par. 15)		

ADDITIONAL READINGS

Cinderella

CHARLES PERRAULT

"Cinderella" is one of the best-known fairy tales in the world. In fact, researchers have discovered more than seven hundred versions of the story worldwide—in North

*and South America, Europe, the Middle East, Asia, and Africa. More than four hun-
dred years old, "Cinderella" was popularized in the West by the French writer and
critic Charles Perrault (1628–1703), who published a collection of fairy tales*
(Mother Goose Tales) *taken from European folklore.*

Once there was a nobleman who took as his second wife the proudest and 1
haughtiest woman imaginable. She had two daughters of the same character,
who took after their mother in everything. On his side, the husband had a
daughter who was sweetness itself; she inherited this from her mother, who
had been the most kindly of women.

No sooner was the wedding over than the stepmother showed her ill- 2
nature. She could not bear the good qualities of the young girl, for they made
her own daughters seem even less likable. She gave her the roughest work of
the house to do. It was she who washed the dishes and the stairs, who cleaned
out Madam's room and the rooms of the two Misses. She slept right at the top
of the house, in an attic, on a lumpy mattress, while her sisters slept in
panelled rooms where they had the most modern beds and mirrors in which
they could see themselves from top to toe. The poor girl bore everything in
patience and did not dare to complain to her father. He would only have
scolded her, for he was entirely under his wife's thumb.

When she had finished her work, she used to go into the chimney-corner 3
and sit down among the cinders, for which reason she was usually known in
the house as Cinderbottom. Her younger stepsister, who was not so rude as
the other, called her Cinderella. However, Cinderella, in spite of her ragged
clothes, was still fifty times as beautiful as her sisters, superbly dressed though
they were.

One day the King's son gave a ball, to which everyone of good family was 4
invited. Our two young ladies received invitations, for they cut quite a figure[1]
in the country. So there they were, both feeling very pleased and very busy
choosing the clothes and the hair-styles which would suit them best. More
work for Cinderella, for it was she who ironed her sisters' underwear and
goffered their linen cuffs.[2] Their only talk was of what they would wear.

"I," said the elder, "shall wear my red velvet dress and my collar of English 5
lace."

"I," said the younger, "shall wear just my ordinary skirt; but, to make up, I 6
shall put on my gold-embroidered cape and my diamond clasp, which is quite
out of the common."

The right hairdresser was sent for to supply double-frilled coifs,[3] and 7
patches were bought from the right patch-maker. They called Cinderella to

---

[1]*cut quite a figure:* Made quite an impression through their appearance.

[2]*goffered their linen cuffs:* Ironed folds into the linen cuffs of their blouse sleeves. (A cuff is the
part of the sleeve around the wrist.)

[3]*double-frilled coifs:* Tight-fitting caps with highly ornamented borders.

ask her opinion, for she had excellent taste. She made useful suggestions and even offered to do their hair for them. They accepted willingly.

While she was doing it, they said to her: 8

"Cinderella, how would you like to go to the ball?"   9

"Oh dear, you are making fun of me. It wouldn't do for me."   10

"You are quite right. It would be a joke. People would laugh if they saw a   11
Cinderbottom at the ball."

Anyone else would have done their hair in knots for them, but she had a   12
sweet nature, and she finished it perfectly. For two days they were so excited
that they ate almost nothing. They broke a good dozen laces trying to tighten
their stays[4] to make their waists slimmer, and they were never away from
their mirrors.

At last the great day arrived. They set off, and Cinderella watched them   13
until they were out of sight. When she could no longer see them, she began to
cry. Her godmother, seeing her all in tears, asked what was the matter.

"If only I could . . . If only I could . . ." She was weeping so much that she   14
could not go on.

Her godmother, who was a fairy, said to her: "If only you could go to the   15
ball, is that it?"

"Alas, yes," said Cinderella with a sigh.   16

"Well," said the godmother, "be a good girl and I'll get you there."   17

She took her into her room and said: "Go into the garden and get me a   18
pumpkin."

Cinderella hurried out and cut the best she could find and took it to her   19
godmother, but she could not understand how this pumpkin would get her to
the ball. Her godmother hollowed it out, leaving only the rind, and then
tapped it with her wand and immediately it turned into a magnificent gilded
coach.

Then she went to look in her mouse-trap and found six mice all alive in it.   20
She told Cinderella to raise the door of the trap a little, and as each mouse
came out she gave it a tap with her wand and immediately it turned into a fine
horse. That made a team of six horses, each of fine mouse-coloured grey.

While she was wondering how she would make a coachman, Cinderella   21
said to her:

"I will go and see whether there is a rat in the rat-trap, we could make a   22
coachman of him."

"You are right," said the godmother. "Run and see."   23

Cinderella brought her the rat-trap, in which there were three big rats. The   24
fairy picked out one of them because of his splendid whiskers and, when she
had touched him, he turned into a fat coachman, with the finest moustaches
in the district.

---

[4]*stays:* Corsets.

Then she said: "Go into the garden and you will find six lizards behind the watering-can. Bring them to me." 25

As soon as Cinderella had brought them, her godmother changed them into six footmen, who got up behind the coach with their striped liveries, and stood in position there as though they had been doing it all their lives. 26

Then the fairy said to Cinderella: 27

"Well, that's to go to the ball in. Aren't you pleased?" 28

"Yes. But am I to go like this, with my ugly clothes?" 29

Her godmother simply touched her with her wand and her clothes were changed in an instant into a dress of gold and silver cloth, all sparkling with precious stones. Then she gave her a pair of glass slippers, most beautifully made. 30

So equipped, Cinderella got into the coach; but her godmother warned her above all not to be out after midnight, telling her that, if she stayed at the ball a moment later, her coach would turn back into a pumpkin, her horses into mice, her footmen into lizards, and her fine clothes would become rags again. 31

She promised her godmother that she would leave the ball before midnight without fail, and she set out, beside herself with joy. 32

The King's son, on being told that a great princess whom no one knew had arrived, ran out to welcome her. He handed her down from the coach and led her into the hall where his guests were. A sudden silence fell; the dancing stopped, the violins ceased to play, the whole company stood fascinated by the beauty of the unknown princess. Only a low murmur was heard: "Ah, how lovely she is!" The King himself, old as he was, could not take his eyes off her and kept whispering to the Queen that it was a long time since he had seen such a beautiful and charming person. All the ladies were absorbed in noting her clothes and the way her hair was dressed, so as to order the same things for themselves the next morning, provided that fine enough materials could be found, and skillful enough craftsmen. 33

The King's son placed her in the seat of honour, and later led her out to dance. She danced with such grace that she won still more admiration. An excellent supper was served, but the young Prince was too much occupied in gazing at her to eat anything. She went and sat next to her sisters and treated them with great courtesy, offering them oranges and lemons which the Prince had given her. They were astonished, for they did not recognize her. 34

While they were chatting together, Cinderella heard the clock strike a quarter to twelve. She curtsied low to the company and left as quickly as she could. 35

As soon as she reached home, she went to her godmother and, having thanked her, said that she would very much like to go again to the ball on the next night—for the Prince had begged her to come back. She was in the middle of telling her godmother about all the things that had happened, when the two sisters came knocking at the door. Cinderella went to open it. 36

"How late you are!" she said, rubbing her eyes and yawning and stretching 37 as though she had just woken up (though since they had last seen each other she had felt very far from sleepy).

"If you had been at the ball," said one of the sisters, "you would not have 38 felt like yawning. There was a beautiful princess there, really ravishingly beautiful. She was most attentive to us. She gave us oranges and lemons."

Cinderella could have hugged herself. She asked them the name of the 39 princess, but they replied that no one knew her, that the King's son was much troubled about it, and that he would give anything in the world to know who she was. Cinderella smiled and said to them:

"So she was very beautiful? Well, well, how lucky you are! Couldn't I see 40 her? Please, Miss Javotte, do lend me that yellow dress which you wear about the house."

"Really," said Miss Javotte, "what an idea! Lend one's dress like that to a 41 filthy Cinderbottom! I should have to be out of my mind."

Cinderella was expecting this refusal and she was very glad when it came, 42 for she would have been in an awkward position if her sister had really lent her her frock.

On the next day the two sisters went to the ball, and Cinderella too, but 43 even more splendidly dressed than the first time. The King's son was constantly at her side and wooed her the whole evening. The young girl was enjoying herself so much that she forgot her godmother's warning. She heard the clock striking the first stroke of midnight when she thought that it was still hardly eleven. She rose and slipped away as lightly as a roe-deer. The Prince followed her, but he could not catch her up. One of her glass slippers fell off, and the Prince picked it up with great care.

Cinderella reached home quite out of breath, with no coach, no footmen, 44 and wearing her old clothes. Nothing remained of all her finery, except one of her little slippers, the fellow to the one which she had dropped. The guards at the palace gate were asked if they had not seen a princess go out. They answered that they had seen no one go out except a very poorly dressed girl, who looked more like a peasant than a young lady.

When the two sisters returned from the ball, Cinderella asked them if they 45 had enjoyed themselves again, and if the beautiful lady had been there. They said that she had, but that she had run away when it struck midnight, and so swiftly that she had lost one of her glass slippers, a lovely little thing. The Prince had picked it up and had done nothing but gaze at it for the rest of the ball, and undoubtedly he was very much in love with the beautiful person to whom it belonged.

They were right, for a few days later the King's son had it proclaimed to the 46 sound of trumpets that he would marry the girl whose foot exactly fitted the slipper. They began by trying it on the various princesses, then on the duchesses and on all the ladies of the Court, but with no success. It was brought to the two sisters, who did everything possible to force their feet into the slipper, but they could not manage it. Cinderella, who was looking on, recognized her own slipper, and said laughing:

"Let me see if it would fit me!" 47

Her sisters began to laugh and mock at her. But the gentleman who was 48 trying on the slipper looked closely at Cinderella and, seeing that she was very beautiful, said that her request was perfectly reasonable and that he had instructions to try it on every girl. He made Cinderella sit down and, raising the slipper to her foot, he found that it slid on without difficulty and fitted like a glove.

Great was the amazement of the two sisters, but it became greater still 49 when Cinderella drew from her pocket the second little slipper and put it on her other foot. Thereupon the fairy godmother came in and, touching Cinderella's clothes with her wand, made them even more magnificent than on the previous days.

Then the two sisters recognized her as the lovely princess whom they had 50 met at the ball. They flung themselves at her feet and begged her forgiveness for all the unkind things which they had done to her. Cinderella raised them up and kissed them, saying that she forgave them with all her heart and asking them to love her always. She was taken to the young Prince in the fine clothes which she was wearing. He thought her more beautiful than ever and a few days later he married her. Cinderella, who was as kind as she was beautiful, invited her two sisters to live in the palace and married them, on the same day, to two great noblemen of the Court.

Women Have What It Takes
CAROL BARKALOW

A 1980 graduate of West Point (the U.S. military academy), Carol Barkalow is currently a colonel in the U.S. Army. She has commanded an air-defense platoon in Germany and a truck unit at Fort Lee, Virginia. In 1990, she published In the Men's House, *a book about her life in the military.*

The following essay originally appeared in Newsweek *magazine in August 1991. In the essay, Barkalow refers to her service in a U.S. noncombat army unit in Saudi Arabia and Kuwait during the Persian Gulf War. This was a war between Iraq (which had invaded Kuwait in August 1990) and a military coalition consisting of the United States, Saudi Arabia, Kuwait, and many other nations. In the spring of 1991, the allied troops defeated the Iraqi military, forcing it to leave Kuwait.*

Although women in the U.S. military are currently allowed to serve in some combat units on the ground and to fly combat missions, they are prohibited from fighting in front-line ground units.

I realized I wanted a military career when I was 16, the summer between 1 my junior and senior years of high school. I had been very active in athletics. I enjoyed the discipline, the comradeship, the physicalness of sports, helping other teammates. I also wanted to serve my country. For me, the answer was the Army. My guidance counselor told me that West Point[1] was starting to accept women. I was in the first class.

As plebes,[2] we were required to greet the upperclassmen "Good morning, 2 sir." Too often we'd hear back, "Mornin', bitch." I was naive, I guess. I thought my classmates wanted the same thing I wanted. I thought they would just accept me for that. By the time we graduated, the men's attitudes had begun to mellow somewhat. The women's attitudes had changed, too. If we weren't feminists when we went in, we were when we came out. I went back for my 10-year reunion in October 1990. There was a big difference. My male classmates had changed tremendously. They recognized us as peers. I realized they had been going through their own growth a decade ago, the hell of being a cadet. The reunion was the best time I ever had at West Point.

But some of those old attitudes still linger when the question of women in 3 combat arises. It's a generational issue for the most part. Most of the senior leadership had little opportunity to work with women as peers. Many see us as a mother, a wife, a daughter—especially a daughter. They always say they wouldn't want to see their daughters in combat. What I ask them in return is, would you really want to see your *son* in combat? And isn't it the daughter's choice? One lesson our society learned in the Persian Gulf is that it is no more tragic to lose a mother, a sister, a daughter than it is to lose a father, a brother or a son—and no less so.

I volunteered to go to the Gulf. I was attached to the 24th Infantry Divi- 4 sion, the unit that spearheaded the end-around attack.[3] Our support outfit was in just as much danger as the combat element. The Iraqi weapons had just as much capability of hitting us as the men in front. The difference was that we didn't have the capability to defend ourselves like the combat troops.

One question that is always raised is whether women have what it takes to 5 kill an enemy face to face—whether we can handle that particular brand of stress. After my book came out last year, a Vietnam vet[4] named Bill Hanake came to see me. He had a leg and a foot blown off in Vietnam. I think Bill's experience is an eloquent answer to the naysayers who think women don't have what it takes for combat. Both times his unit was overrun in 'Nam, he said, it was the Viet Cong *women* who were the more disciplined, the tougher, who were the most willing to make sure their enemy wasn't going to come back at 'em.

Then there's the argument that men will be overprotective of women. 6

---

[1]*West Point:* The U.S. military academy, located north of New York City.

[2]*plebes:* First-year students at a military or naval academy.

[3]*spearheaded the end-around attack:* Led a surprise attack from the side and rear.

[4]*Vietnam vet:* Veteran of the Vietnam War (1954–1975). This was a war between South Vietnam, aided by the United States, and Communist guerrillas (Viet Cong), aided by North Vietnam. The war ended in a Communist victory.

When men are overprotective of *men,* we give them awards for valor. In May, our country awarded an Air Force pilot its second highest medal for leading a nine-hour rescue mission for a fallen flier. That wasn't looked upon as overprotective. Would it have been so if the downed flier had been a woman?

Some believe females would interfere with male bonding. In Saudi,[5] I saw a   7 new type of relationship forming between men and women, one that has traditionally been described among men. It was a nurturing relationship based upon respect, based on sharing the same hardships. The big worry before Vietnam was that blacks couldn't bond with whites. When the bullets started flying, that went away pretty fast. The same type of relationships developed in the Gulf between men and women soldiers.

Do I believe women should be allowed to serve in the infantry? Yes, if   8 qualified. The training and physical-strength standards should be uniform. We have standards that we must keep. Our military readiness should never suffer. But I saw a number of physically strong men very scared in Saudi Arabia. It's not just a matter of physical strength. It's mental and emotional strength as well. I think God knew what he was doing when he allowed women to bear the children and gave us the ability to handle that mental and emotional stress.

Pregnancy? The military doesn't have a good handle on the question. When   9 the military looks at pregnancy, it sees it as nonavailability. We had more injuries and nonavailability among men than women in Saudi. Too often, the women are the only ones held responsible for pregnancy, not the men who helped get them that way.

No normal person wants to go into combat. Soldiers are the last people   10 who want to. But we've volunteered. We understand our commitment. Everybody raises a hand, male and female, and swears to support and defend the same Constitution. Women are competent, capable and committed. We are an integral part of the best-trained military force in the world. The services should have the flexibility to assign the best-qualified person to the job, regardless of gender. That's the bottom line.

Men Have the Power—Why Would They Want to Change?

WARREN FARRELL

The following reading is part of a chapter from the book Why Men Are the Way They Are: The Male-Female Dynamic *(1986) by Warren Farrell, a psychologist and social scientist. This book focuses on the experiences of men being male, on their relation-*

---

[5]*Saudi:* Saudi Arabia, where, during the Persian Gulf War (1990–1991), a number of U.S. troops were stationed.

ships with women, and on their feelings about the women's movement. Farrell has formed more than six hundred women's and men's groups and has taught psychology, political science, and sociology at several American universities. He is best known for his work in the men's movement and for his book The Liberated Man *(1974), which explores changing male roles in the United States.*

Ralph was a forty-one-year-old man in our men's group. He was married, 1 the father of two children. He had been in the group for three months, and had hardly said a word. One evening he looked up and said, "I think I'd like to speak tonight. I'm afraid I joined this group only because my wife forced me to. She got involved in one of these women's movement operations and started changing. She called it 'growing.' About three months ago she said, 'Ralph, I'm tired of having to choose between a relationship with you and a relationship with myself.' Pretty fancy rhetoric, I thought. Then she added, 'There's a men's group forming that's meeting next Tuesday. Why don't you get involved?'

"Well, I kind of laughed her off. But a week later she started again. 'The 2 group's meeting next Tuesday. As far as I'm concerned, if you're not doing some changing in *three* months, that's the end.'

" 'The end! For the sake of a *men's group?*' I asked. 3

" 'It's symbolic, Ralph,' she said. 4

"So I figured I'd join this symbol and see what you fags[1] were talking about! 5 But the problem was, you didn't fit my image, and I began identifying with some of the things you were saying. Well, anyway, last night Ginny reminded me the three months were up tomorrow. So I think I'd like to speak up tonight."

We laughed at Ralph's motivation, but encouraged him to continue. 6

"Well, what struck me was how each of you chose different careers, but 7 you all worried about succeeding. Even you, Jim—even though you're employed and have a laid-back facade. That started me thinking about my career.

"All my life I wanted to play baseball. As a pro. When I was a sophomore in 8 high school I was pretty hot stuff, and my uncle came and scouted[2] me. Later he said, 'Ralph, you're good. Damn good. And you might make it to the pros if you really work at it. But only the best make good money for a long time. If you really want to be good to yourself, make use of your intelligence, get yourself a good job—one you can depend on for life.'

"I was surprised when my folks agreed with him. Especially Dad. Dad 9 always called me 'Ralph, who pitched the no-hitter.'[3] Dad stopped calling me that after that conversation. Maybe that turned the tide for me." Ralph hesitated, as if he were piecing something together, but he quickly withdrew from his introspection.

---

[1]*fags*: Derogatory term for homosexuals.

[2]*scouted*: Observed. (A sports scout is someone who observes and evaluates players.)

[3]*no-hitter*: Baseball term for a game in which a pitcher allows no hits (a major accomplishment).

"Anyway, I was proud of myself for making the transition like a man. I'd 10 always liked reading and learning, but just hadn't focused much on it. But I figured just for a couple of years I'd 'play the system': borrow friends' old term papers, take a look at old exams, focus my reading on the questions different teachers tended to ask, and so on. I never cheated. I just figured I'd 'play the system' for a couple of years, raise my grades, then when I got into college, I could really learn—I could do what I wanted after that.

"Well, 'playing the system' worked. I got into a top-notch university. But it 11 soon became apparent that a lot of people graduated from good universities— if I wanted to really stand out it would help to 'play the system' for just a few more years, get into a good grad school or law school, and then, once I did that, I could do with my life what I wanted after that.

"I decided on law school—but to become a social-work lawyer, so I could 12 make a real contribution to people who most needed it. But about my second or third year of law school—when my colleagues saw I was taking what they called this 'missionary law' seriously, they explained that if I really wanted to be effective as a social-work lawyer, I'd better get some experience first in the hard-knocks,[4] reality-based field of corporate law rather than ease into the namby-pamby[5] area of social-work law right away—if I didn't I wouldn't get the respect to be effective. Frankly, that made sense. So I joined a top corporate law firm in New York. I knew I could work there for a couple of years, and then really do what I wanted with my life after that.

"After a couple of years in the firm, I was doing well. But the whole 13 atmosphere of the corporate legal community made it clear that if I dropped out after two years it would be seen as a sign that I just couldn't hack the pressure. If I continued for just a couple more years, and became a junior partner—junior partners were the ones marked with potential—then I could really do what I wanted with my life after that.

"Well, it took me seven years to get the junior partnership offered to me— 14 with politics and everything. But I got it. By that time I had lost some of the desire to be a social-work lawyer—it was considered a clear step backward. In other ways I maintained that ideal—it seemed more meaningful than kowtowing to rich money. But I also knew the switch would mean forfeiting a lot of income. My wife Ginny and I had just bought a new home—which we pretty much had to do with two kids—and I knew they'd be going to college. . . . Ginny's income was only part-time now, and she was aching to travel a bit.

"By that time, I also realized that while junior partners had potential, the 15 people with the real ins in the legal community were not the junior partners, but the senior partners. I figured I had a pretty big investment in the corporate law area now—if I just stuck it out for a couple more years, I could get a

---

[4]*hard-knocks*: Competitive and rigorous (strong).

[5]*namby-pamby*: Lacking in substance (weak).

senior partnership, get a little money saved for the kids' education and travel, and *then* I could really do with my life what I wanted. . . .

"It took me eight more years to get the senior partnership. I can remember 16 my boss calling me into the office and saying, 'Ralph, we're offering you a senior partnership.' I acted real calm, but my heart was jumping toward the phone in anticipation of telling Ginny. Which I did. I told Ginny I had a surprise. I'd tell her when I got home. I asked her to get dressed real special. I refused to leak what it was about. I made reservations in her favorite restaurant, bought some roses and her favorite champagne.

"I came home real early so we'd have time to sip it together; I opened the 17 door and said, 'Guess what?' Ginny was looking beautiful. She said, 'What is it, Ralph?' I said 'I got the senior partnership!' She said, 'Oh, fine, that's great,' but there was a look of distance in her eyes. A real superficial enthusiasm, you know what I mean?"

We nodded. 18

"So I said, 'What do you mean "Oh, fine"—I've been working since the day 19 we met to get this promotion for us, and you say, "Oh, fine"?'

" 'Every time you get a promotion, Ralph,' Ginny announced, 'you spend 20 less time with me. I guess I just wish you'd have more time for me. More time to love me.'

" 'Why do you think I've been working my ass off all these years if it isn't to 21 show you how much I love you?' I said.

" 'Ralph, that's not what I mean by love. Just look at the kids, Ralph.' 22

"Well, I did look at the kids. Randy is seventeen. And Ralph, Jr., is fifteen. 23 Randy just got admitted to college—a thousand miles from here. Each year I keep promising myself that 'next year' I'll really get to know who they are. 'Next year . . .' 'Next year.' But next year he'll be in college. And I don't even know who he is. And I don't know whether I'm his dad or his piggy bank.

"I don't know where to begin with Randy, but a few weeks ago I tried to 24 change things a bit with Ralph, Jr. He was watching TV. I asked him if he wouldn't mind turning it off so we could talk. He was a little reluctant, but he eventually started telling me some of what was happening at school. We talked baseball, and I told him about some of my days pitching. He said I'd already told him. He told me about some of his activities, and I spotted a couple of areas where I thought his values were going to hurt him. So I told him. We got into a big argument. He said I wasn't talking with him, I was lecturing him . . . 'spying' on him.

"We've hardly talked since. I can see what I did wrong—boasting and 25 lecturing—but I'm afraid if I try again, he'll be afraid to say much now, and we'll just sit there awkwardly. And if he mentions those values, what do I say? I want to be honest, but I don't want to lecture. I don't even know where to begin."

Ralph withdrew from the group. He had struck so many chords it took us 26 more than ten minutes to notice that he was fighting back tears. Finally one of the men picked up on it and asked, "Ralph, is there anything else you're holding back?" Ralph said there wasn't, but his assurance rang false. We prodded.

"I guess maybe I am holding something back," he said hesitantly. "I feel like 27 I spent forty years of my life working as hard as I can to become somebody I don't even like."

When I heard that sentence fifteen years ago, I was twenty-seven. It's been 28 perhaps the most important sentence I've heard in my life: *"I feel like I've spent forty years of my life working as hard as I can to become somebody I don't even like."* Even as I heard it, the ways it was threatening to be true in my own life flashed through my mind.

Ralph continued: "I was mentioning some of my doubts to a few of my 29 associates at work. They listened attentively for a couple of minutes, then one made a joke, and another excused himself. Finally I mentioned this men's group—which I never should have done—and they just laughed me out of the office. I've been the butt of jokes ever since: 'How are the U.S. Navel Gazers[6] doing, Ralph boy?'

"Suddenly I realized. Ginny has a whole network of lady friends she can 30 talk with about all this. Yet the men I've worked with for seventeen years, sixty hours a week, hardly know me. Nor do they want to."

Ralph withdrew again. But this time he seemed to be taking in what he had 31 just said as if he were putting together his life as he was speaking. Then his face grew sad. A few of us who might otherwise have said something held back.

"I guess I could handle all this," Ralph volunteered, fighting back the tears 32 again, "but I think, for all practical purposes, I've lost Ginny in the process. And maybe I could handle that, too. But the only other people I love in this world are Randy and Ralph, Jr. And when I'm really honest with myself—I mean *really* honest—I think for all practical purposes I've lost them too—."

We started to interrupt, but Ralph stopped us, tears silently escaping his 33 eyes. "What really gets me . . . what really gets me *angry* is that I did everything I was supposed to do for forty years, did it better than almost any other man I know, and I lost everyone I love in the process, including myself. I don't mean to be philosophical, but the more I did to stand out, the more I became the same. Just one more carbon copy. Oh, I got to a high level, okay. A high-level mediocre.

"In some ways, I feel I could handle all that, too. But look at me—paid 34 more than any two of you guys put together, supposedly one of the top decision-makers in the country, and when it comes to my own home, my own life, I don't even know how to begin."

Ralph cried. For the first time in twenty-two years.   35

---

[6]*U.S. Navel Gazers*: Play on the word "naval" (relating to the navy). Ralph's colleagues think that the members of men's groups do nothing but sit around and "gaze at each other's navels."

Cartoon

CATHY GUISEWITE

1. What do you consider the main point of the cartoon?

2. To what extent do you think it is possible to raise children free from gender stereotyping?

MAKING CONNECTIONS

The following questions and activities can be used for both writing assignments and class discussions. These exercises will help develop your ability to *synthesize* what you read—to combine and integrate information and ideas from different sources.

1. Did any of the readings in this chapter make you think about gender roles in a new way? Discuss what you learned from the readings and how they affected you.

2. Write a one-paragraph *plot summary* of "Cinderella." Your goal is to give your reader a sense of the major events of the story. Start your overview in the following manner: "Cinderella is a fairy tale about . . .".

3. What types of gender stereotypes are reflected in the additional readings in this chapter? What images, values, expectations, and messages relating to gender do you find in the selections?

4. In a small group, design a questionnaire based on issues raised in this chapter. What, for example, do people see as the advantages and disadvantages of their sex? Have your subjects noticed any differences in gender roles during their lifetime?

    Distribute the questionnaire to at least ten people. Then analyze the information you receive and draw whatever conclusions you can.

5. Write an essay or give an oral presentation on a topic of your own choice relating to one or more of the readings in this chapter. Consider researching your subject in a university or public library. (*Sample topics:* The biological origins of gender differences; language differences between females and males; the "beauty trade"—diets, exercising, cosmetics, and fashion; anorexia and other eating disorders; cross-dressing; pornography; and "nontraditional" family structures.)

6. Read one of the following selections from another chapter in this book: "A Coward" (Chapter 1); "Sex, Sighs, and Conversation" (Chapter 1); "Striking a Nerve" (Chapter 2); "The New American Dreamers" (Chapter 4); "Worker Poll Shows Family, Fringes Gain Favor" (Chapter 4); or "They Get by with a Lot of Help from Their Kyoiku Mamas" (Chapter 5). Discuss the ways in which the reading reflects issues raised in this chapter. To what extent are the ideas and perspectives similar?

CHAPTER FOUR

WORK

Reading Skill:
Appreciating Figurative Language

The Russian author Maxim Gorky once wrote, "When work is a pleasure, life is a joy! When work is a duty, life is slavery." The readings and activities in this chapter explore the attitudes of many people toward their work (or future work). Focusing on the reasons some people find their jobs enjoyable and rewarding and others unenjoyable and unrewarding, this chapter examines such issues as the skills and traits necessary for success in various occupations, work vs. play, the American dream, employment benefits, the Protestant work ethic, and cross-cultural similarities and differences in work values.

Following are some of the questions you will be considering in this chapter:

- What jobs are valued most in your native culture, and why?
- Do most people see a strong connection between what they do at work and what they do in their private life?
- How do different people define success?
- What do people find stressful about their jobs?
- What have you personally liked and disliked about jobs you've had?
- What are your career goals, and how do you hope to achieve them?

In the first reading of the chapter, "The New American Dreamers," Ruth Sidel examines the ways young women in the United States define success. Next, in "Confessions of a Working Stiff," Patrick Fenton discusses a typical day at his job loading cargo for a large international airline. After that, in his article "Worker Poll Shows Family, Fringes Gain Favor," Tom Mashberg focuses on recent trends in the American workplace. Then the short story "Señor Payroll," by William E. Barrett, describes a humorous conflict between the management and employees of a Spanish gas company. Following this, the poem "To Be of Use," by Marge Piercy, explores the value of different types of work. Finally, a cartoon by P. Steiner focuses on the lives of workaholics.

BRIEF QUOTES

The following quotations will help introduce you to the topic of work. Think about these statements as you read the selections in this chapter.

"Every calling is great when greatly pursued."

—STUDS TERKEL

"One does not work to live; one lives to work."

—MAX WEBER

"Happiness is only achieved by working at what you love."

—ANZIA YEZIERSKA

"In fact, there is perhaps only one human being in a thousand who is passionately interested in his job for the job's sake."

—DOROTHY SAYERS

"Men, for the sake of getting a living, forget to live."

—MARGARET FULLER

"Ever-increasing production, the drive to make bigger and better things, have become aims in themselves, new ideals. Work has become alienated from the working person."

—ERICH FROMM

"I had a 'real' job for seven months. My soul fell asleep."

—BARBRO HEDSTROM

"The only jobs for which no man is qualified are human incubator and wet nurse. Likewise, the only job for which no woman is or can be qualified is sperm donor."

—WILMA SCOTT HEIDE

READING

PREREADING ACTIVITIES

1. In your reading journal, freewrite for ten minutes on the topic of *success.* Don't worry about spelling, grammar, punctuation, or organization. Just write for ten minutes, without stop, about whatever comes to mind when

you think about success. (For a discussion of freewriting and other prewriting strategies, see pp. 234–240.) When you have finished, share your thoughts with several classmates.

2. In a small group, discuss several of the quotations on the previous page. To what extent do you agree with the views expressed?

3. Indicate the extent to which you agree with the following statements by filling in each blank with *SA* (strongly agree), *A* (agree), *U* (undecided), *D* (disagree), or *SD* (strongly disagree). Then compare your responses in a small group.

a. _____ In my native country, women and men have equal job opportunities.

b. _____ People have the ability to control their own destinies.

c. _____ No one job has any more value than any other job.

d. _____ To get a good job in my native country, one needs a college education.

e. _____ One cannot be successful without having a well-paying job.

f. _____ With hard work and determination, most people can achieve the "American dream."

g. _____ In my native country, one's job opportunities are determined by the social class one is born into.

h. _____ It is easier for women than men to balance their careers and family life.

i. _____ Being a lawyer is more challenging than being a waitress.

j. _____ In my native country, there are many opportunities for technical and vocational training.

The New American Dreamers
RUTH SIDEL

Ruth Sidel is a professor of sociology at Hunter College of the City University of New York. She has written a number of books focusing on women's roles in society, including Women and Child Care in China: A Firsthand Report *(1972),* Women and Children Last: The Plight of Poor Women in Affluent America *(1987), and* On Her Own: Growing Up in the Shadow of the American Dream *(1990), from which the following selection is taken.*

She is the prototype of today's young woman—confident, outgoing, knowl- 1 edgeable, involved. She is active in her school, church, or community. She may have a wide circle of friends or simply a few close ones, but she is committed to them and to their friendship. She is sophisticated about the central issues facing young people today—planning for the future, intimacy, sex, drugs, and alcohol—and discusses them seriously, thoughtfully, and forth-rightly. She wants to take control of her life and is trying to figure out how to get from where she is to where she wants to go. Above all, she is convinced that if she plans carefully, works hard, and makes the right decisions, she will be a success in her chosen field; have the material goods she desires; in time, marry if she wishes; and, in all probability, have children. She plans, as the expression goes, to "have it all."

She lives in and around the major cities of the United States, in the towns of 2 New England, in the smaller cities of the South and Midwest, and along the West Coast. She comes from an upper-middle-class family, from the middle class, from the working class, and even sometimes from the poor. What is clear is that she has heard the message that women today should be the heroines of their own lives. She looks toward the future, seeing herself as the central character, planning her career, her apartment, her own success story. These young women do not see themselves as playing supporting roles in someone else's life script; it is their own journeys they are planning. They see their lives in terms of *their* aspirations, *their* hopes, *their* dreams.

Beth Conant is a sixteen-year-old high-school junior who lives with her 3 mother and stepfather in an affluent New England college town. She has five brothers, four older and one several years younger. Her mother is a librarian, and her stepfather is a stockbroker. A junior at a top-notch public high school, she hopes to study drama in college, possibly at Yale, "like Meryl Streep." She would like to live and act in England for a time, possibly doing Shakespeare. She hopes to be living in New York by the age of twenty-five, in her own apartment or condo, starting on her acting career while working at another job by which she supports herself. She wants to have "a great life," be "really independent," and have "everything that's mine—crazy furniture, everything my own style."

By the time she's thirty ("that's so boring"), she feels, she will need to be 4 sensible, because soon she will be "tied down." She hopes that by then her career will be "starting to go forth" and that she will be getting good roles. By thirty-five she'll have a child ("probably be married beforehand"), be working in New York and have a house in the country. How will she manage all this? Her husband will share responsibilities. She's not going to be a "supermom."

They'll both do child care. He won't do it as a favor; it will be their joint responsibility. Moreover, if she doesn't have the time to give to a child, she won't have one. If necessary, she'll work for a while, then have children, and after that "make one movie a year."

Amy Morrison is a petite, black, fifteen-year-old high-school sophomore 5 who lives in Ohio. Her mother works part-time, and her father works for a local art museum. She plans to go to medical school and hopes to become a surgeon. She doesn't want to marry until she has a good, secure job but indicates that she might be living with someone. She's not sure about having children but says emphatically that she wants to be successful, to make money, to have cars. In fact, originally she wanted to become a doctor "primarily for the money," but now she claims other factors are drawing her to medicine.

Jacqueline Gonzalez is a quiet, self-possessed, nineteen-year-old Mexican- 6 American woman who is a sophomore at a community college in southern California. She describes her father as a "self-employed contractor" and her mother as a "housewife." Jacqueline, the second-youngest of six children, is the first in her family to go to college. Among her four brothers and one sister, only her sister has finished high school. Jacqueline's goal is to go to law school and then to go into private practice. While she sees herself as eventually married with "one or two children," work, professional achievement, and an upper-middle-class life-style are central to her plans for her future.

If in the past, and to a considerable extent still today, women have hoped to 7 find their identity through marriage, have sought to find "validation of . . . [their] uniqueness and importance by being singled out among all other women by a man," the New American Dreamers are setting out on a very different quest for self-realization. They are, in their plans for the future, separating identity from intimacy, saying that they must first figure out who they are and that then and only then will they form a partnership with a man. Among the young women I interviewed, the New American Dreamers stand apart in their intention to make their own way in the world and determine their own destiny prior to forming a significant and lasting intimate relationship.

Young women today do not need to come from upper-middle-class homes 8 such as Beth's or middle-class homes such as Amy's or working-class homes such as Jacqueline's to dream of "the good life." Even young women with several strikes against them see material success as a key prize at the end of the rainbow. Some seem to feel that success is out there for the taking. Generally, the most prestigious, best-paying careers are mentioned; few women of any class mention traditional women's professions such as teaching or nursing. A sixteen-year-old unmarried Arizona mother of a four-and-a-half-month-old baby looks forward to a "professional career either in a bank or with a computer company," a "house that belongs to me," a "nice car," and the ability to buy her son "good clothes." She sees herself in the future as dating but not married. "There is not so much stress on marriage these days," she says.

Yet another young woman, a seventeen-year-old black unmarried mother 9
of an infant, hopes to be a "professional model," have "lots of cash," be "rich,"
maybe have another child. When asked if a man will be part of the picture, she
responds, "I don't know."

An eighteen-year-old Hispanic unmarried mother hopes to "be my own 10
boss" in a large company, have a "beautiful home," send her daughter to "the
best schools." She wants, in her words, to "do it, make it, have money."

These young women are bright, thoughtful, personable. And they are quint- 11
essentially American: they believe that with enough hard work they will "make
it" in American society. No matter what class they come from, their fantasies are
of upward mobility, a comfortable life filled with personal choice and material
possessions. The upper-middle-class women fantasize a life even more upper-
middle-class; middle-class and working-class women look toward a life of high
status in which they have virtually everything they want; and some young
women who come from families with significant financial deprivation and
numerous other problems dream of a life straight out of "Dallas," "Dynasty," or
"L.A. Law."[1] According to one young woman, some of her friends are so determined to be successful that they are "fearful that there will be a nuclear war and
that they will die before they have a chance to live their lives. If there is a
nuclear war," she explained, "they won't live long enough to be successful."

Young women are our latest true believers.[2] They have bought into the 12
image of a bright future. Many of them see themselves as professional women,
dressed in handsome clothes, carrying a briefcase to work, and coming home
to a comfortable house or condo, possibly to a loving, caring husband and a
couple of well-behaved children. How widespread is the dream? How realistic is it? What is the function of this latest American dream? What about those
young women who cling to a more traditional dream? What about those who
feel their dreams must be deferred? What about those with no dream at all?
And what about those who "share the fantasy," as the Chanel No. 5 perfume
advertisement used to say, but have little or no chance of achieving it?

Perhaps the most poignant example of the impossible dream is Simone 13
Baker, a dynamic, bright, eighteen-year-old black woman from Louisiana. Simone's mother is a seamstress who has been off and on welfare over the
years, and her father is a drug addict. Simone herself has been addicted to
drugs of one kind or another since she was five. She has been in and out of
drug-abuse facilities, and although she attended school for many years and
was passed from grade to grade, she can barely read and write. When I met
her in a drug rehabilitation center, she was struggling to become drug free so
that she could join the Job Corps,[3] finish high school, and obtain some voca-

---

[1]*"Dallas," "Dynasty," "L.A. Law"*: Popular TV shows in the 1980s and 1990s portraying "the good
life" (wealth and success).

[2]*true believers*: People who believe totally in something; zealous promoters of a particular cause.

[3]*Job Corps*: Federally supported program of job training for disadvantaged youths.

tional training. Her dream of the future is so extraordinary, given her background, that she seems to epitomize the Horatio Alger[4] myth of another era. When asked what she would like her life to be like in the future, Simone replies instantly, her eyes shining: "I want to be a model. I want to have a Jacuzzi. I want to have a *big*, BIG house and a BIG family—three girls and two boys."

"And what about the man?" I ask her. 14

"He'll be a lawyer. He'll be responsible, hardworking, and sensitive to my 15 feelings. Everything will be fifty-fifty. And he'll take the little boys out to play football and I'll have the girls inside cooking. That would be a dream come true!"

Simone's dream is an incredible mixture of the old and the new—a Dick- 16 and-Jane reader[5] updated. And she's even mouthing the supreme hope of so many women in this age of the therapeutic solution to personal problems—that she'll find a man who is "sensitive" to her "feelings." She has lived a life far from the traditional middle class and yet has the quintessential image of the good life as it has been formulated in the last quarter of the twentieth century. But for Simone, it is virtually an impossible dream. One wishes that that were not so; listening to her, watching her excitement and hope at the mere thought of such a life, one gets caught up and wants desperately for it all to happen. The image is clear: the white house in the suburbs with the brass knocker on the front door, the leaves on the lawn in the fall, the boys playing football with this incredibly wonderful husband/father, and Simone sometimes the successful model, other times at home, cooking with her daughters. But we know how very unlikely it is that this particular dream will come true. And yet, maybe . . .

A key message the New American Dreamers are both receiving and send- 17 ing is one of optimism—the sense that they can do whatever they want with their lives. Many Americans, of course—not just young people or young women—have a fundamentally optimistic attitude toward the future. Historically, Americans have believed that progress is likely, even inevitable, and that they have the ability to control their own destinies. . . . In looking toward the future, young men clearly dream of "the good life," of upward mobility and their share of material possessions. While young women historically have had far less control over their lives than men, for the past twenty-five years they have been urged to take greater control, both in the workplace and in their private lives, and they have clearly taken the message very much to heart.

---

[4]*Horatio Alger* (1834–1899): American writer of more than one hundred novels for boys portraying characters who rise from poverty to success through hard work and self-reliance (the "rags-to-riches" myth).

[5]*Dick-and-Jane reader*: Popular elementary school reader in the 1950s and 1960s portraying a white middle-class family with traditional values (the mother stays at home and the father works).

Angela Dawson, a sixteen-year-old high-school junior from southern Cali- 18
fornia, sums up the views of the New American Dreamers: "It's your life. You
have to live it yourself. You must decide what you want in high school, plan
your college education, and from there you can basically get what you want.
If you work hard enough, you will get there. You must be in control of your
life, and then somehow it will all work out."

READING JOURNAL

In your reading journal, discuss one of the following:

1. Your major career goals
2. A job that is held in high esteem and one that is held in low esteem in your
   native country, and why
3. A topic of your own choice related to Sidel's essay

MEANING AND TECHNIQUE

The following questions and activities will help you understand the main
ideas in the essay and the manner in which it was written.

1. In one or two sentences, explain the *main idea* you think Sidel is trying to
   convey in "The New American Dreamers." Use your own words.

FIGURES OF SPEECH

Authors often use *figures of speech,* or *figurative language,* to make their
writing lively and memorable. Figures of speech are imaginative comparisons between two essentially dissimilar things. Such comparisons help
readers create mental images, or pictures, and think about ideas in new
ways.

The two most common types of figurative, or nonliteral, language are
similes and *metaphors.* A *simile* is an explicit, or direct, comparison between two dissimilar things using *like* or *as.* A *metaphor* is an implied, or
indirect, comparison between two dissimilar things not using *like* or *as.*

Here are several examples:

1. **Similes**

   • Their marriage is *like* a storm.

   • Their marriage is *as* rough *as* a storm.

FIGURES OF SPEECH *Continued*

---

2. **Metaphors**

- Their marriage *is* a storm.
- Their stormy marriage led to a divorce.
- Their marriage is full of thunder and lightning.

When writers use similes and metaphors, they usually compare one thing to another that is familiar to the reader. This helps writers to convey their ideas—especially abstract and complex ones—and to do so in a vivid manner (assuming, of course, that the figures of speech are original and not trite, or clichéd). Since figures of speech are based on *images,* or mental pictures, and appeal to people's imaginations, they allow writers to create complex associations that transcend the power of literal language.

To fully understand and evaluate what writers are saying, it is important to be aware of how they use figurative language.

---

2. What does Sidel mean by the phrase "the New American Dreamers"? How do the aspirations of these women differ from those of women forty years ago?

3. Summarize the views of the New American Dreamers about marriage.

4. In "The New American Dreamers," Sidel develops several metaphors to convey her ideas. With a partner, locate the metaphor in each of the sentences below. What two things are being compared? What idea is Sidel trying to convey?

Example:

"She looks toward the future, seeing herself as the central character, planning her career, her apartment, her own success story." (par. 2)

COMPARISON: The life of young women and a story (their life is a story in which they are the main character).

MAIN IDEA: The young women want to control their future and achieve success on their own terms.

a. "These young women do not see themselves as playing supporting roles in someone else's life script." (par. 2)

Comparison: _____

Main idea: _____

_____

b. "The New American Dreamers are setting out on a very different quest for self-realization." (par. 7)

Comparison: _____

Main idea: _____

_____

c. "Young women . . . see material success as a key prize at the end of the rainbow." (par. 8)

Comparison: _____

Main idea: _____

_____

d. "Simone's dream is an incredible mixture of the old and the new—a Dick-and-Jane reader updated." (par. 16)

Comparison: _____

Main idea: _____

_____

DRAWING INFERENCES

Often writers will not state every idea explicitly, or directly. That is, they will say some things implicitly, or indirectly, allowing the reader to draw his or her own conclusions. For example, in paragraph 4 of "The New American Dreamers," Sidel says that Beth Conant doesn't want to be a "supermom." Sidel never directly states that being a supermom involves having a career and also taking primary care of the children, but this can be *inferred* from the context.

In order to draw inferences, you need to pay special attention to the hints a writer provides. Combining these hints, or suggestions, with your own knowledge and experience will help you understand what you are reading more fully.

The following questions and activities will assist in developing your ability to understand unstated meanings implied by clues—that is, to draw inferences.

1. The title of Sidel's essay is "The New American Dreamers." Do you consider this an effective title? Why or why not? After you have answered this

question, write down two titles of your own that you think would be appropriate for the essay.

2. Briefly compare your attitude toward the future with that of the New American Dreamers. Do you share their sense of optimism? Why or why not?

3. In paragraph 7, Sidel says that the New American Dreamers, in their plans for the future, are "separating identity from intimacy." What does she mean by this? How important is the separation of identity and intimacy in your own life?

4. Think of a question of your own to ask your classmates about an issue raised in Sidel's essay.

VOCABULARY: CONNOTATIONS

Earlier in this chapter, you examined several *figures of speech* (similes and metaphors) in "The New American Dreamers." In order to fully understand figures of speech, or figurative language, you need to be aware of the *connotations* of words.

Connotations are the implied, or suggested, meanings of a word as opposed to its literal dictionary definition, or *denotation* (of course, many words have more than one denotation). For example, the denotation of *skeleton* is the rigid, supportive framework of an organism; however, the connotations of *skeleton* are disease, war, death, and poison. (Naturally, these associations can differ within and between cultures.)

Often words with a similar meaning have very different connotations, or emotional associations—for instance, *sweat* and *perspire, kill* and *murder,* and *woman* and *lady.*

- *Sweat* and *perspire* both refer to the production of moisture by the skin. *Perspire,* however, is more neutral than *sweat,* which is a graphic, colloquial term, often implying hard work.

- *Kill* and *murder* both mean to deprive of life. *Kill,* however, is more neutral than *murder,* which implies secrecy, planning, motive, and moral responsibility.

- *Woman* and *lady* both refer to an adult female. *Woman,* however, is more neutral than *lady,* which implies refinement, gentle manners, and cultivated taste. (To some people, *lady* is a negative term, connoting, or suggesting, a quiet, dainty, often docile woman.)

Look at the following pairs of words; one word from each pair is taken from Sidel's essay. Decide which word connotes a more positive feeling. Write this word in the blank. If you feel the two words are equally positive, write both in the blank. (Try to do this exercise first without using a dictionary.)

1. prototype (par. 1)   ideal   _____

2. interested in   committed to (par. 1) _____

3. sophisticated (par. 1)   knowledgeable   _____

4. desire   aspiration (par. 2)   _____

5. petite (par. 5)   delicate   _____

6. self-centered   self-possessed (par. 6) _____

7. quest (par. 7)   search   _____

8. valued   prestigious (par. 8)   _____

9. poignant (par. 13)   interesting   _____

10. aggressive   dynamic (par. 13)   _____

VOCABULARY: IN CONTEXT

In this exercise, you will develop your vocabulary by using words and idioms in a realistic context.

- If you don't know the meaning of one of the following italicized vocabulary items, first find it in the reading and see if you can determine its meaning from the context. (Review the major types of context clues on pp. 263–267.)
- If the meaning is still unclear, look up the item in a dictionary or consult with a native speaker of English.
- Then, in a few sentences, describe or explain each of the following situations, ideas, and things. **Do not** just define the italicized words and expressions. Discuss personal experiences and opinions and give examples.

    1. Someone you know who is *outgoing* (par. 1)
    2. Something you are very *committed to* (par. 1)
    3. One of your major *aspirations* in life (par. 2)

4. Several *prestigious* careers in your native culture (par. 8)

5. One or two possible results of severe financial *deprivation* (par. 11)

6. Someone you know who has a *dynamic* personality (par. 13)

7. Something you are very *sensitive to* (par. 15)

8. Something that is *inevitable,* and why (par. 17)

9. Something you *take* very much *to heart* (par. 17)

10. Something that once *worked out* very well for you (par. 18)

DISCUSSION AND DEBATE

1. With several classmates, discuss the attitude of the New American Dreamers toward the future. To what extent do you agree with Angela Dawson's comments in the last paragraph of the essay? How realistic is her view?

2. In a small group, discuss your career goals. Focus on the type of work you'd like to do in the future, and why. Consider several of the following questions:

   • Have you already decided on a particular career? If so, how?

   • Do you feel any pressure to pursue a certain career?

   • How do you plan to achieve your career goals?

   • What challenges and difficulties do you anticipate in realizing your dreams?

   • What is your personal definition of success?

3. What types of jobs are valued most and least in your native culture? Fill in the following blanks with eight occupations ranked in order of prestige from top to bottom. Then share your list with several classmates.

Job Prestige

1. _____

2. _____

3. _____

4. _____

5. _____

6. _____

7. _____

8. _____

4. In a small group, go to a university or public library and research the "American dream" from the point of view of various individuals (those native to a particular country and/or immigrants). Try to find one or two collections of oral histories in which people discuss the extent to which they have achieved their dreams.

    When you have completed your research, share your findings with the rest of the class.

WRITING ACTIVITIES

1. Authors often use *figures of speech,* or *figurative language,* to make their descriptions vivid and to communicate their ideas. The most common figures of speech are *similes* (explicit comparisons) and *metaphors* (implied comparisons).

    Review the discussion of figures of speech on pp. 154–155. Then write three similes and three metaphors that convey the essence of six of the following items: an exciting job, a boring job, stress, competition, success, a goal or dream, marriage, social class, material possessions. Use your imagination; try to come up with graphic, colorful images.

    Example:

    money

    "Money is a type of drug—the more you use, the more you need." (This is a metaphor.)

2. With several classmates, write a (one or two paragraph) definition of "success." Feel free to include examples of what success is and is not.

    When you have finished, share your definition with the rest of the class.

    > To help you plan, draft, and revise one of the following essays, see Appendix A.

3. Write an essay based on one of the quotations on page 148 or on one of the statements in activity 3 of the "Prereading Activities." Back up your points with examples from "The New American Dreamers" and personal experiences and observations. Try to develop one or two *figures of speech* (similes and metaphors) to help convey your ideas and add color to your writing.

4. Write a personal essay based on one of the following: (1) your career goals (feel free to discuss ways to achieve these goals and any challenges and difficulties you anticipate) or (2) any jobs you've personally had that you liked and/or disliked.

READING

PREREADING ACTIVITIES

1. In your reading journal, write for ten to fifteen minutes about one of the following:

   a. The type of job you would find unpleasant and unfulfilling

   b. A time when you felt like a prisoner—that is, trapped by something (a job, relationship, decision, and so on)

2. The contemporary American sociologist and educator John Feig has observed, "The idea that work per se is morally good and that there is a direct relation between hard work and success—the cornerstone of what came to be known as the Puritan, the Protestant, or simply, the work ethic—has left an indelible imprint on the American psyche."

   Discuss this quotation with several classmates. Focus on the relationship between work and morality and effort and success. Do you have a similar work ethic in your native country?

3. Indicate the extent to which you agree with the following statements by filling in each blank with *SA* (strongly agree), *A* (agree), *U* (undecided), *D* (disagree), or *SD* (strongly disagree). Then share your responses in a small group.

   a. _____ If people don't like their job, they should look for a new one.

   b. _____ Very few people are passionately interested in their job.

   c. _____ Most people do not mind performing the same task over and over again.

   d. _____ Blue-collar workers should be paid as much as white-collar workers (blue-collar work involves manual labor; white-collar work does not).

   e. _____ Two of the most important factors in determining job satisfaction are independent decision making and creativity.

f. _____ The management of most companies is very concerned about the psychological and physical well-being of its employees.

g. _____ The majority of people find their jobs disagreeable and meaningless; they work just to make money.

h. _____ Whether or not a job is interesting depends mainly on one's attitude.

i. _____ If most people didn't have to work to make a living, they wouldn't.

j. _____ The two most important things in life are love and work.

Confessions of a Working Stiff

PATRICK FENTON

Born in 1941, Patrick Fenton dropped out of high school when he was sixteen. After a series of factory jobs, he became a cargo loader at New York's John F. Kennedy Airport—a job he held for eight years. "Confessions of a Working Stiff," Fenton's first published piece, originally appeared in New York *magazine in April 1973. (A "working stiff" is a common laborer, or one who does unskilled physical work.) The essay describes one day in the life of a cargo loader. Since 1973, Fenton has been a freelance writer and frequent speaker at schools and colleges.*

The Big Ben[1] is hammering out its 5:45 alarm in the half-dark of another   1
Tuesday morning. If I'm lucky, my car down in the street will kick over for me.
I don't want to think about that now; all I want to do is roll over into the
warm covers that hug my wife. I can hear the wind as it whistles up and down
the sides of the building. Tuesday is always the worst day—it's the day the
drudgery, boredom, and fatigue start all over again. I'm off from work on
Sunday and Monday, so Tuesday is my blue Monday.

I make my living humping cargo for Seaboard World Airlines, one of the big   2
international airlines at Kennedy Airport. They handle strictly all cargo. I was
once told that one of the Rockefellers[2] is the major stockholder for the airline,
but I don't really think about that too much. I don't get paid to think. The big
thing is to beat that race with the time clock every morning of your life so the
airline will be happy. The worst thing a man could ever do is to make sugges-

---

[1]*Big Ben:* The clock in the tower of the Houses of Parliament in London.
[2]*Rockefellers:* Wealthy American family of bankers, industrialists, and philanthropists.

tions about building a better airline. They pay people $40,000 a year to come up with better ideas. It doesn't matter that these ideas never work; it's just that they get nervous when a guy from South Brooklyn or Ozone Park[3] acts like he actually has a brain.

I throw a Myadec high-potency vitamin into my mouth to ward off one of 3 the ten colds I get every year from humping mailbags out in the cold rain at Kennedy. A huge DC-8 stretch jet awaits impatiently for the 8,000 pounds of mail that I will soon feed its empty belly. I wash the Myadec down with some orange juice and grab a brown bag filled with bologna and cheese. Inside the lunch bag there is sometimes a silly note from my wife that says, "I Love You—Guess Who?" It is all that keeps me going to a job that I hate.

I've been going there for seven years now and my job is still the same. It's 4 weary work that makes a man feel used up and worn out. You push and you pull all day long with your back. You tie down pallets[4] loaded with thousands of pounds of freight. You fill igloo-shaped containers with hundreds of boxes that all look the same. If you're assigned to work the warehouse, it's really your hard luck. This is the job all the men hate most. You stack box upon box until the pallet resembles the exact shape of the inside of the plane. You get the same monotonous feeling an adult gets when he plays with a child's blocks. When you finish one pallet, you find another and start the whole dull process over again.

The airline pays me $192 a week for this. After they take out taxes and 5 $5.81 for the pension, I go home with $142. Once a month they take out $10 for term life insurance, and $5.50 for union dues. The week they take out the life insurance is always the worst: I go home with $132. My job will never change. I will fill up the same igloos with the same boxes for the next 34 years of my life, I will hump the same mailbags into the belly of the plane, and push the same 8,000-pound pallets with my back. I will have to do this until I'm 65 years old. Then I'll be free, if I don't die of a heart attack before that, and the airline will let me retire.

In the winter the warehouse is cold and damp. There is no heat. The large 6 steel doors that line the warehouse walls stay open most of the day. In the cold months, wind, rain and snow blow across the floor. In the summer the warehouse becomes an oven. Dust and sand from the runways mix with the toxic fumes of fork lifts, leaving a dry, stale taste in your mouth. The high windows above the doors are covered with a thick, black dirt that kills the sun. The men work in shadows with the constant roar of jet engines blowing dangerously in their ears.

Working the warehouse is a tedious job that leaves a man's mind empty. If 7 he's smart he will spend his days wool-gathering. He will think about pretty girls that he once knew, or some other daydream of warm, dry places where

---

[3]*South Brooklyn or Ozone Park*: Predominantly working-class areas in New York City.
[4]*pallets:* Portable platforms for moving cargo.

you never had a chill. The worst thing he can do is think about his problems. If he starts to think about how he is going to pay the mortgage on the $30,000 home that he can't afford, it will bring him down. He will wonder why he comes to the cargo airline every morning of his life, and even on Christmas Day. He will start to wonder why he has to listen to the deafening sound of the jets as they rev up their engines. He will wonder why he crawls on his hands and knees, breaking his back a little bit more every day.

To keep his kids in that great place in the country in the summer, that 8 great place far away from Brooklyn and the South Bronx, he must work every hour of overtime that the airline offers him. If he never turns down an hour, if he works some 600 hours over, he can make about $15,000. To do this he must turn against himself, he must pray that the phone rings in the middle of the night, even though it's snowing out and he doesn't feel like working. He must hump cargo late into the night, eat meatball heroes[5] for supper, drink coffee that starts to taste like oil, and then hope that his car starts when it's time to go home. If he gets sick—well, he better not think about that.

All over Long Island, Ozone Park, Brooklyn, and as far away as the Bronx, 9 men stir in the early morning hours as a new day begins. Every morning is the same as the last. Some of the men drink beer for breakfast instead of coffee. Way out in Bay Shore a cargoman snaps open a can of Budweiser. It's 6 A.M., and he covers the top of the can with his thumb in order to keep down the loud hiss as the beer escapes. He doesn't want to awaken his children as they dream away the morning in the next room. Soon he will swing his Pinto wagon up onto the crowded Long Island Expressway and start the long ride to the job. As he slips the car out of the driveway he tucks another can of beer between his legs.

All the men have something in common: they hate the work they are doing 10 and they drink a little too much. They come to work only to punch a timecard that has their last name on it. At the end of the week they will pick up a paycheck with their last name on it. They will never receive a bonus for a job well done, or even a party. At Christmastime a card from the president of the airline will arrive at each one of their houses. It will say Merry Christmas and have the president's name printed at the bottom of it. They know that the airline will be there long after they are dead. Nothing stops it. It runs nonstop, without sleep, through Christmas Day, New Year's Eve, Martin Luther King's birthday, even the deaths of Presidents.

It's seven in the morning and the day shift is starting to drift in. Huge 11 tractors are backing up to the big-mouth doors of the warehouse. Cattle trucks bring tons of beef to feed its insatiable appetite for cargo. Smoke-covered trailers with refrigerated units packed deep with green peppers sit with their diesel engines idling. Names like White, Mack, and Kenworth are

---

[5]*heroes:* Sandwiches on long rolls split lengthwise (also called grinders or submarines).

welded to the front of their radiators, which hiss and moan from the overload. The men walk through the factory-type gates of the parking lot with their heads bowed, oblivious of the shuddering diesels that await them.

Once inside the warehouse they gather in groups of threes and fours like 12 prisoners in an exercise yard. They stand in front of the two time clocks that hang below a window in the manager's office. They smoke and cough in the early morning hour as they await their work assignments. The manager, a nervous-looking man with a stomach that is starting to push out of his belt, walks out with the pink work sheets in his hand.

Eddie, a young Irishman with a mustache, has just bolted in through the 13 door. The manager has his timecard in his hand, holding it so no one else can hit Eddie in.[6] Eddie is four minutes late by the time clock. His name will now go down in the timekeeper's ledger. The manager hands the card to him with a "you'll be up in the office if you don't straighten out" look. Eddie takes the card, hits it in, and slowly takes his place with the rest of the men. He has been out till four in the morning drinking beer in the bars of Ozone Park; the time clock and the manager could blow up, for all he cares. "Jesus," he says to no one in particular, "I hope to Christ they don't put me in the warehouse this morning."

Over in another group, Kelly, a tall man wearing a navy knit hat, talks to the 14 men. "You know, I almost didn't make it in this morning. I passed this green VW on the Belt Parkway. The girl driving it was singing. Jesus, I thought to myself, it must be great going somewhere at 6:30 in the morning that makes you want to sing." Kelly is smiling as he talks. "I often think, why the hell don't you keep on going, Kelly? Don't get off at the cargo exit, stay on. Go anywhere, even if it's only Brooklyn. Christ, if I was a single man I think I would do just that. Some morning I'd pass this damn place by and drive as far away as Riverhead. I don't know what I'd do when I got there—maybe I'd pick up a pound of beefsteak tomatoes from one of those roadside stands or something."

The men laugh at Kelly but they know he is serious. "I feel the same way 15 sometimes," the man next to him says. "I find myself daydreaming a lot lately; this place drives you to that. I get up in the morning and I just don't want to come to work. I get sick when I hit that parking lot. If it wasn't for the kids and the house I'd quit." The men then talk about how hard it is to get work on "the outside." They mention "outside" as if they were in a prison.

Each morning there is an Army-type roll call[7] from the leads. The leads are 16 foremen who must keep the men moving; if they don't, it could mean their jobs. At one time they had power over the men but as time went by the company took away their little bit of authority. They also lost the deep interest, even enjoyment, for the hard work they once did. As the cargo airline grew, it beat this out of them, leaving only apathy. The ramp area is located in

---

[6]hit in: Punch in (to record the time when someone begins work).

[7]*roll call:* A reading aloud of a list of names to see who is present.

the backyard of the warehouse. This is where the huge jets park to unload their 70,000-pound payloads. A crew of men fall in behind the ramp lead as he mopes out of the warehouse. His long face shows the hopelessness of another day.

A brutal rain has started to beat down on the oil-covered concrete of the 17 ramp as the 306 screeches in off the runway. Its engines scream as they spit off sheets of rain and oil. Two of the men cover their ears as they run to put up a ladder to the front of the plane. The airline will give them ear covers only if they pay for half of them. A lot of men never buy them. If they want, the airline will give them two little plugs free. The plugs don't work and hurt the inside of the ears.

The men will spend the rest of the day in the rain. Some of them will set up 18 conveyor belts and trucks to unload the thousands of pounds of cargo that sit in the deep belly of the plane. Then they will feed the awkward bird until it is full and ready to fly again. They will crawl on their hands and knees in its belly, counting and humping hundreds of mailbags. The rest of the men will work up topside on the plane, pushing 8,000-pound pallets with their backs. Like Egyptians building a pyramid, they will pull and push until the pallet finally gives in and moves like a massive stone sliding through sand. They don't complain too much; they know that when the airline comes up with a better system some of them will go.

The old-timers at the airline can't understand why the younger men stay 19 on. They know what the cargo airline can do to a man. It can work him hard but make him lazy at the same time. The work comes in spurts. Sometimes a man will be pushed for three hours of sweat, other times he will just stand around bored. It's not the hard work that breaks a man at the airline, it's the boredom of doing the same job over and over again.

At the end of the day the men start to move in off the ramp. The rain is still 20 beating down at their backs but they move slowly. Their faces are red and raw from the rain-soaked wind that has been snapping at them for eight hours. The harsh wind moves in from the direction of the city. From the ramp you can see the Manhattan skyline, gray- and blue-looking, as it peeks up from the west wall of the warehouse. There is nothing to block the winter weather as it rolls in like a storm across a prairie. They head down to the locker room, heads bowed, like a football team that never wins.

With the workday almost over, the men move between the narrow, gray 21 rows of lockers. Up on the dirty walls that surround the lockers someone has written a couple of four-letter words.[8] There is no wit to the words; they just say the usual. As they strip off their wet gear the men seem to come alive.

"Hey, Arnie! You want to stay four hours? They're asking for overtime down 22 in Export," one of the men yells over the lockers.

---

[8]*Four-letter words:* Obscene words.

Arnie is sitting about four rows over, taking off his heavy winter clothing. 23
He thinks about this for a second and yells back, "What will we be doing?"

"Working the meat trailer." This means that Arnie will be humping huge 24
sides of beef off rows of hooks for four hours. Blood will drip down onto his
clothes as he struggles to the front of the trailer. Like most of the men, he
needs the extra money, and knows that he should stay. He has Master Charge,
Korvettes, Times Square Stores, and Abraham & Straus[9] to pay.

"Nah, I'm not staying tonight. Not if it's working the meat trailer. Don 25
wanted to stop for a few beers at The Owl; maybe I'll stay tomorrow night."

It's four o'clock in the afternoon now—the men have twelve minutes to go 26
before they punch out. The airline has stopped for a few seconds as the men
change shifts. Supervisors move frantically across the floor pushing the fresh
lot of new men who have just started to come in. They hand out work sheets
and yell orders: "Jack, get your men into their rain gear. Put three men in the
bellies to finish off the 300 flight. Get someone on the pepper trailers, they've
been here all morning."

The morning shift stands around the time clock with three minutes to go. 27
Someone says that Kevin Delahunty has just been appointed to the Fire
Department. Kevin, a young Irishman from Ozone Park, has been working the
cargo airline for six years. Like most of the men, he has hated every minute of
it. The men are openly proud of him as they reach out to shake his hand.
Kevin has found a job on "the outside." "Ah, you'll be leaving soon," he tells
Pat. "I never thought I'd get out of here either, but you'll see, you're going to
make it."

The manager moves through the crowd handing out timecards and stops 28
when he comes to Kevin. Someone told him Kevin is leaving. "Is that right,
Delahunty? Well I guess we won't expect you in tomorrow, will we? Going to
become a fireman, eh? That means you'll be jumping out of windows like a
crazy man. Don't act like you did around here," he adds as he walks back to
his office.

The time clock hits 4:12 and the men pour out of the warehouse. Kevin 29
will never be back, but the rest of them will return in the morning to grind
out another eight hours. Some of them will head straight home to the bills,
screaming children, and a wife who tries to understand them. They'll have a
Schaefer or two, then they'll settle down to a night of *The Courtship of
Eddie's Father, The Rookies, Here's Lucy,*[10] and the late news.

Some of them will start to fill up the cargo bars that surround Kennedy 30
Airport. They will head to places like Gaylor's on Rockaway Boulevard or The
Dew Drop Inn down near Farmers Boulevard. They will drink deep glasses of

---

[9]*Korvettes, . . .* : Popular chain stores. (The men need to pay the bills for merchandise they've
charged at these stores.)

[10]*The Courtship of Eddie's Father, . . .* : Popular television shows.

whiskey and cold mugs of Budweiser. The Dew Drop has a honky-tonk[11] mood of the Old West to it. The barmaid moves around like a modern-day Katie Elder.[12] Like Brandy, she's a fine girl, but she can out-curse any cargoman. She wears a low-cut blouse that reveals most of her breasts. The jukebox will beat out some Country & Western as she says, "Ah, hell, you played my song." The cargomen will hoot and holler as she substitutes some of her own obscene lyrics.

They will drink late into the night, forgetting time clocks, Master Charge, First National City,[13] Korvettes, mortgages, cars that don't start, and jet engines that hurt their ears. They will forget about damp, cold warehouses, winters that get longer and longer every year, minutes that drift by like hours, supervisors that harass, and the thought of growing old on a job they hate. At midnight they will fall dangerously into their cars and make their way up onto the Southern State Parkway. As they ride into the dark night of Long Island they will forget it all until 5:45 the next morning—when the Big Ben will start up the whole grind all over again. 31

READING JOURNAL

In your reading journal, discuss one of the following:

1. Why some jobs are more enjoyable and rewarding than others

2. A job that you very much liked or disliked

3. A topic of your own choice related to "Confessions of a Working Stiff"

MEANING AND TECHNIQUE

The following questions and activities will help you understand the main ideas in the essay and the manner in which it was written.

1. In one or two sentences, write down the *main point* you think Fenton is trying to make in "Confessions of a Working Stiff." Use your own words.

2. What are the chief things Fenton dislikes about his job?

3. According to Fenton, what more than anything else breaks the spirit of workers at the cargo airline? Why do you think this is so?

---

[11]*honky-tonk:* Cheap, noisy nightclub or dance hall.

[12]*Katie Elder:* Barroom prostitute of the old American West (late nineteenth century).

[13]*First National City:* A large bank that issues credit cards.

FIGURES OF SPEECH

One way to convey one's ideas and add vividness to one's writing is through *figures of speech*—imaginative comparisons between two essentially dissimilar things. The two most common figures of speech are *similes* and *metaphors.* A *simile* is an explicit comparison between two dissimilar things using *like* or *as* ("My life is like a roller coaster"). A *metaphor* is an implied comparison between two dissimilar things not using *like* or *as* ("My life is a roller coaster").

4. With one or two classmates, review the discussion of figures of speech, or figurative language, on pages 154–155. Then read through paragraphs 3, 11, 12, 18, and 20, each of which contains at least one instance of figurative language. Find one of the similes or metaphors in each paragraph and write it in the blank below. Then answer the following questions: What two things are being compared? What idea is Fenton trying to convey? Is the same image (mental picture) repeated in any of the paragraphs?

Example:

"As they strip off their wet gear, the men seem to come alive." (par. 21)

COMPARISON: Men and dead bodies coming to life.

MAIN IDEA: Knowing that their long, hard day is over (a time of emotional "death"), the men become more active.

a. Simile/metaphor in paragraph 3: _____

_____

Comparison: _____

Main Idea: _____

_____

b. Simile/metaphor in paragraph 11: _____

_____

Comparison: _____

Main Idea: _____

_____

c. Simile/metaphor in paragraph 12: _____

_____

Comparison: _____

Main Idea: _____

_____

d. Simile/metaphor in paragraph 18: _____

_____

Comparison: _____

Main Idea: _____

_____

e. Simile/metaphor in paragraph 20: _____

_____

Comparison: _____

Main Idea: _____

_____

DRAWING INFERENCES

The following questions and activities will help develop your ability to draw inferences—an important reading skill.

1. How does the title "Confessions of a Working Stiff" relate to the main idea of the essay? Write down two other titles that would also be appropriate.

2. Why do you think the airline company gets nervous "when a guy from South Brooklyn or Ozone Park acts like he actually has a brain" (par. 2)?

TONE

The *tone* of a piece of writing is the author's attitude toward a subject as reflected in the choice of words and details. Tone can be defined by using such adjectives as *angry, nostalgic, distant, playful, optimistic, sarcastic,*

TONE *Continued*

---

formal, matter-of-fact, surprised, serious, enthusiastic, and *critical.* A writer's tone depends on his or her audience, subject matter, and purpose. Learning to recognize the tone of a piece of writing is essential to understanding and evaluating the ideas an author is trying to convey. (For a more complete discussion of tone, see pp. 58–59.)

---

3. What is the overall tone of "Confessions of a Working Stiff"? Try to think of two or three adjectives that describe Fenton's attitude toward his work. Support your answer with examples from the essay.

4. Think of a question of your own to ask your classmates about an issue raised in Fenton's essay.

VOCABULARY: FIGURES OF SPEECH

In "Confessions of a Working Stiff," Fenton uses many *figures of speech* (similes and metaphors) to convey his ideas and add color to his writing.

With a partner, review the discussion of figurative, or nonliteral, language on pages 154–155. Then show that you understand the meaning of the following similes and metaphors by restating the main idea of each in simple, literal language.

Example:

"They [the cargo loaders] head down to the locker room, heads bowed, like a football team that never wins." (par. 20)

RESTATEMENT: They return to the locker room feeling demoralized.

1. A huge DC-8 jet "awaits impatiently for the 8,000 pounds of mail that I will soon feed its empty belly." (par. 3)

   Restatement: _____

   _____

2. "Cattle trucks bring tons of beef to feed its [the warehouse's] insatiable appetite for cargo." (par. 11)

   Restatement: _____

   _____

3. "Once inside the warehouse they [the cargo loaders] gather in groups of threes and fours like prisoners in an exercise yard." (par. 12)

Restatement: _____

_____

4. "Like Egyptians building a pyramid, they [the cargo loaders] will pull and push until the pallet finally gives in and moves like a massive stone sliding through sand." (par. 18)

Restatement: _____

_____

VOCABULARY: IN CONTEXT

In this exercise, you will develop your vocabulary by using words and idioms in a realistic context.

- If you don't know the meaning of one of the following italicized vocabulary items, first find it in the reading and see if you can determine its meaning from the context. (Review the major types of context clues on pp. 263–267.)
- If the meaning is still unclear, look up the item in a dictionary or consult with a native speaker of English.
- Then, in a few sentences, describe or explain each of the following situations, ideas, and things. **Do not** just define the italicized words and expressions. Discuss personal experiences and opinions and give examples.

  1. A type of work that is *drudgery* for you, and why (par. 1)
  2. A reason someone might experience *fatigue* (par. 1)
  3. How you are currently *making* or are hoping in the future to *make a living* (par. 2)
  4. What it means if a person has a lot of *hard luck* (par. 4)
  5. Why an employee might receive a *bonus* (par. 10)
  6. Something for which you or someone you know has an *insatiable* appetite (par. 11)
  7. Why being *oblivious of* (or *to*) something might cause a problem (par. 11)
  8. Something that might cause a person to *shudder* (par. 11)

9. How a teacher might deal with *apathy* in a student (par. 16)

10. An example of a supervisor *harassing* an employee (par. 31)

DISCUSSION AND DEBATE

1. In a small group, discuss any jobs you've personally had (part-time or full-time) that you liked or disliked. If you've never had a job, describe the type of work you think you'd find rewarding and the type you think you'd find unrewarding.

2. Imagine you and several classmates are members of a management consultant firm that has been hired by Seaboard World Airlines to help improve the morale of the cargo loaders at the company.

   First analyze the problems Fenton and his co-workers have been complaining about. Take into consideration the work environment, the company's treatment of its workers, and the workers' feelings and attitudes.

   Then make any recommendations you feel would enhance worker satisfaction and productivity. Be as specific as possible.

   When you have finished, share your suggestions with the rest of the class.

Problems	*Recommendations*

3. In a small group, write a list of the major skills and traits you think would be necessary for someone to be successful at *four* of the following jobs and positions: actor, psychiatrist, fashion designer, college president, police officer, politician, minister, stockbroker, soccer player, CEO (Chief Executive Office) of a computer firm.

   Then compare your lists with those of the other groups in the class.

WRITING ACTIVITIES

1. Although *similes* usually use the word *like* ("The meat tasted like a rubber boot"), they sometimes appear in the form *as . . . as* ("The meat was as tough as a rubber boot").

   Fill in the following blanks with a phrase that completes the simile. Use your fantasy; try to come up with original comparisons that evoke vivid images.

   When you have finished, share your similes with several classmates. Also discuss the words that might appear in the blanks if you were using your native language.

   a. as happy as _____

   _____

   b. as crazy as _____

   _____

   c. as interesting as _____

   _____

   d. as stubborn as _____

   _____

   e. as funny as _____

   _____

   f. as ugly as _____

   _____

   g. as easy as _____

h. as difficult as _____

2. Imagine you and several classmates are cargo loaders at Seaboard World Airlines. You are depressed about the poor working conditions and the oppressive nature of the job. You have spoken with your manager several times, but he or she has not been very responsive.

   As a group, write a letter to the manager in which you express your concerns and argue the necessity of improving the work environment. Be sure to provide specific recommendations. (Consider including one or two figures of speech—similes and metaphors—to enhance your description of the workplace.)

3. Go through the employment ads of a local newspaper (usually found in the "Classified" or "Help Wanted" section) and find a position that looks interesting to you. Imagine you are applying for this position. You already have a résumé and now need to write a cover letter describing why you are interested in the job and what your qualifications for it are. Remember that you will probably be one of many people applying for the position.

   Write a cover letter (no more than one typed, single-spaced page), and then show your letter and the original ad to several classmates.

4. Write an essay exploring why some jobs are more satisfying than others. What factors contribute most to making a job enjoyable and fulfilling? To making a job disagreeable and unrewarding? Support your points with examples from "Confessions of a Working Stiff" and personal experiences and observations. (To help you plan, draft, and revise the essay, see Appendix A.)

READING

PREREADING ACTIVITIES

1. In your reading journal, spend ten to fifteen minutes writing about how important a high-paying job is to you.

2. Determine how important the following factors would be to you if you were deciding whether or not to accept a particular job offer: job security, control of work schedule, open communications with co-workers and supervisors, control over work content, salary, fringe benefits, effect on personal/family life. Rank the factors in the blanks below (1 = most impor-

tant, 7 = least important). Then share your response with the rest of the class.

Most Important Reasons to Accept a Job

1. _____

2. _____

3. _____

4. _____

5. _____

6. _____

7. _____

3. Indicate the extent to which you agree with the following statements by filling in each blank with *SA* (strongly agree), *A* (agree), *U* (undecided), *D* (disagree), or *SD* (strongly disagree). Then share your responses in a small group.

a. _____ Most people see a strong connection between what they do at work and what they do in their private lives.

b. _____ In my native country, wives and husbands usually share the housework.

c. _____ The majority of unemployed people could find a job if they really wanted to.

d. _____ Most people are concerned with "keeping up with the Joneses" (following the latest fashions and having as many material possessions as their neighbors).

e. _____ Every job should provide at least six weeks of paid vacation.

f. _____ In my native country, many parents place their children in day care.

g. _____ My career will always be the most important thing in my life.

h. _____ In my native country, most people work too much.

i. _____ Most people would prefer to work fewer hours for less money.

j. _____ In my native country, unemployment is a major problem.

Worker Poll Shows Family, Fringes Gain Favor
TOM MASHBERG

The following article, written by Tom Mashberg, a staff writer for the Boston Globe, *first appeared in this large daily newspaper in September 1993. The article examines the types of jobs and employment benefits ("fringes," or "fringe benefits") that are becoming more attractive to American workers.*

American workers are sacrificing fatter paychecks and the fast track[1] for more fun on the job and more time with their families, according to a major survey of life in the American workplace. 1

Three in five employees say they feel "used up" by the end of the day—a day that piles up an average of $8\frac{1}{2}$ hours at work and 6 more hours of commuting, chores and children. A similar majority say they have seen a co-worker lose a job in recent years, and are deeply nervous about the economy and their own job security. 2

The survey of 3,381 workers nationwide, by the New York–based Families and Work Institute, confirms some trends that have been chronicled informally for years. Managers with families of their own, for instance, are far more patient with employees who lose job time because of child-related problems. And when it comes to cooking, cleaning, shopping, and child care, women in two-income couples are four times more likely than men to carry the load. 3

But the most profound finding, labor specialists and workers say, is that most employees say they prefer a decent supervisor and a chance at a home life over big money and responsibility. 4

The pattern makes sense to Anne McGrath, a 39-year-old data analyst with Hale & Dorr in Boston. She said she could easily earn more than her $30,000 a year as an executive secretary in another office. But the law firm's fringe benefits—emergency on-site day care, flexible work hours and a computer terminal in the home—have kept her in place for seven years. 5

"Let's face it: data analysis is pretty dry," she said. "I used to be a career-first person—I wanted to be a flight attendant—but I've changed. I seek fulfillment from family." 6

---

[1]*fast track:* Path to rapid advancement and success.

Punctuating the changes in McGrath's life was the survey's finding that 87 7
percent of American workers live with at least one family member (4 percent
have roommates and just 9 percent live alone). According to the Bureau of
Labor Statistics, the number of workers who live with family members is 15
percent higher than it was in a 1990 survey, before recession and downsizing[2]
rippled through the American workforce, forcing many children and parents
to live together to cut costs.

A result, the survey said, is that finding time for spouses, children, parents 8
or partners is becoming a priority.

"It's a profound new path after 15 turbulent years in the workplace," said 9
Ellen Galinsky, who directed the survey. "For years, people were living and
breathing their careers. Now they're saying, 'I just won't put aside my family
life.' "

Fandi Pleskow of Needham, a 35-year-old mother of three who trained as 10
a pediatric surgeon, says she took the path of fewer hours despite her
original ambitions of becoming well-known, even famous, in the field of
gastroenterology.[3]

"I guess I fit the bill exactly," said Pleskow, who now works a flexible 11
schedule as a researcher at the New England Medical Center in Boston. "I
turned my whole career around: I could earn twice the money in a less joyful
atmosphere; I've put my ambitions aside in favor of my family life, and my
husband . . . he's wonderful, but I'm the one who sweeps the house."

MOMENTUM GROWING

The survey found that the family-first trend is gaining momentum among 12
younger men. About one-third of men under 40 said they would consider
giving up both promotions and pay increases in favor of a better home life—
twice the number of men who felt that way five years ago.

"I used to think I'd put up with endless hours forever," said John Costello, 13
an engineer with Polaroid Corp. in Waltham who has declined offers of better
pay from other companies. "I once saw myself as a manager. Now I manage
my family."

Costello, 38, says he took the job at Polaroid for reasons big and small. The 14
office is within biking distance of his Belmont home, and the company even
installed new showers. More importantly, he said, his bosses have children
and never scowl when he needs a morning off.

"I took a half-day last week," he said. "It's viewed more positively here, and 15
believe me I've seen it viewed negatively elsewhere. It's not that I've dropped
my career. I'm doing well here and the fringe benefits are great. But family is
first."

---

[2]*downsizing:* Reducing the number of employees at a company.
[3]*gastroenterology:* Study of the stomach and intestines.

According to the survey, that view is gaining among managers, but is not as 16
universal as workers would like. Forty percent of the working parents questioned said they still felt they were breaking unspoken rules of the workplace
by taking time off from the job to care for their children.

A MORALE-BOOSTER

"I wouldn't say all employers have caught on to this," said Whit Browne, a 17
Wakefield consultant who helps businesses with employee needs. "But the
ones who listen are learning that simple things like on-site child care work
wonders for morale."

In day care, at least, companies seem to be coming around. The survey 18
noted that parents with youngsters tend to miss a week more each year due
to absenteeism than workers without children.

As a result, more and more companies are investing in day care. Blue Cross 19
and Blue Shield of Massachusetts yesterday opened its first day-care center, in
Quincy, with spaces for 20 children. The company said it received nearly 70
applications and hopes to expand to 60 spaces in the next few weeks.

"Sure it's a response," said Susan Leahy, a spokeswoman for the giant health 20
insurer. "Our workers tell us what they need."

Specialists said the survey's results offer other insights into a work force 21
where the presence of women has risen from 40 percent to 48 percent in 15
years. Not since the Department of Labor's Quality of Employment Survey,
conducted in 1977, they say, has such a broad-based survey been conducted
of workers' lives.

The discoveries included changes in the work environment. Workers are 22
crediting their employers with more flexibility and with trying to make the
workplace more open and comfortable.

OPEN DIALOGUE PRAISED

Asked why they had taken their most recent jobs, 65 percent of those sur- 23
veyed cited open communications; 60 percent cited the effect of family life;
and 59 percent management quality. Only 35 percent of workers rated salary
as very important.

"A lot of this stems from the psychologists—that total-quality and team- 24
management stuff,"[4] said Browne. "If people buy into it then they have huge
motivational rewards. They feel like they've practically signed the products
they've made."

It was that kind of environment that drew Michael Berry, a Cambridge father 25
of two, to Thinking Machines Corp., a high-tech firm near his home that tries to

---

[4]*total-quality and team-management stuff:* Business approaches that stress the active participation of employees in determining company policy and success.

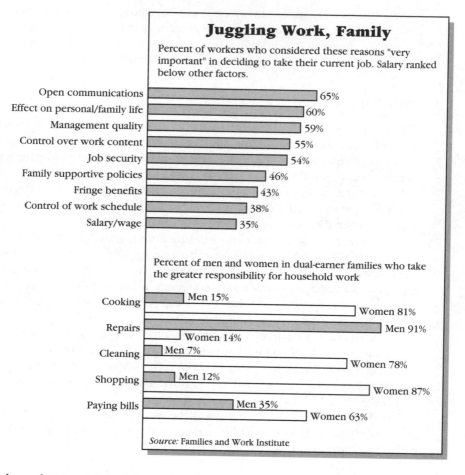

Juggling Work, Family

Percent of workers who considered these reasons "very important" in deciding to take their current job. Salary ranked below other factors.

Open communications	65%
Effect on personal/family life	60%
Management quality	59%
Control over work content	55%
Job security	54%
Family supportive policies	46%
Fringe benefits	43%
Control of work schedule	38%
Salary/wage	35%

Percent of men and women in dual-earner families who take the greater responsibility for household work

Cooking	Men 15%	Women 81%
Repairs	Men 91%	Women 14%
Cleaning	Men 7%	Women 78%
Shopping	Men 12%	Women 87%
Paying bills	Men 35%	Women 63%

Source: Families and Work Institute

keep the mood light. Like many workers in the survey, Berry said he did not give up the urge to get ahead. He just took his ambition to a new setting.

"I took a pay cut—very willingly—to work in a friendly environment," he 26 said. "I've had fun, but I don't feel like I gave up all the traditional rewards. I can get those here."

He also gets to enjoy a bit of quirkiness. Like the day a co-worker raised a 27 French flag in the lunchroom and declared one of the tables a French-only zone. Even the food was French.

"It's the kind of thing that adds extra appeal," he said. 28

MORE EMPLOYEE CONTROL

Browne said this type of workplace approach, which can give employees 29 control over their own hours, work teams and even their spots on the assembly line, has angered unions.

"The survey points up the weakened position of unions," he said, noting 30 that they now represent only 15 percent of the labor force. "They're ceding almost everything to managers."

Still, the heart of the survey was its focus on the way employees balance 31 work and family concerns. Despite the big changes in the office place, 66 percent of employed parents with young children surveyed said they still lacked time at home with their children.

Deirdre Mailing, a dental hygienist in Medway and new mother, said her 32 key was finding a likable place and a livable schedule, and not worrying too much about advancement above all else.

"I've been told that I could make more money elsewhere," she said. "But 33 we have a great group of girls here and we work well together. We make time for our kids. Who needs anything else?"

READING JOURNAL

In your reading journal, discuss one of the following:

1. The extent to which you agree with the following statement by Max Weber (an early twentieth-century German sociologist and political economist): "One does not work to live; one lives to work."

2. How important your career is in your life

3. A topic of your own choice related to Mashberg's article

VOCABULARY: IDIOMS

Earlier in this chapter, you focused on two types of figurative, or nonliteral, language: *similes* and *metaphors* (see pp. 154–155). Idiomatic expressions are another type of figurative language. For example, if someone says to you, "Break a leg!" he or she is not literally telling you to break your leg; rather, the person is wishing you good luck on something you are about to do.

With several classmates, try to guess the meaning of the following idioms from the context. (See pp. 263–267 for the major types of context clues.) If the meaning is still unclear after examining the context, try to find the idiom in a dictionary or consult with your teacher.

> carry the load (par. 3), make sense (par. 5), fit the bill (par. 11), put up with something (par. 13), take time off (par. 16), work wonders (par. 17), buy into something (par. 24), make money (par. 33)

Now write a short narrative or dialogue between two people in which you use as many of the idioms as possible (in any order).

When you have finished, share your narrative or dialogue with the rest of the class.

ADDITIONAL READINGS

Señor Payroll

WILLIAM E. BARRETT

The American author William E. Barrett (1900–1986) is best known for his novels The Left Hand of God, The Lilies of the Field, *and* The Glory Tent. *The following short story, first published in 1943, is a humorous account of a management-employee conflict at a Spanish gas company.*

Larry and I were Junior Engineers in the gas plant, which means that we were clerks. Anything that could be classified as paper work came to the flat double desk across which we faced each other. The Main Office downtown sent us a bewildering array of orders and rules that were to be put into effect. 1

Junior Engineers were beneath the notice of everyone except the Mexican laborers at the plant. To them we were the visible form of a distant, unknowable paymaster. We were Señor Payroll.[1] 2

Those Mexicans were great workmen; the aristocrats among them were the stokers,[2] big men who worked Herculean eight-hour shifts in the fierce heat of the retorts.[3] They scooped coal with huge shovels and hurled it with uncanny aim at tiny doors. The coal streamed out from the shovels like black water from a high-pressure nozzle, and never missed the narrow opening. The stokers worked stripped to the waist, and there was pride and dignity in them. Few men could do such work, and they were the few. 3

The Company paid its men only twice a month, on the fifth and on the twentieth. To a Mexican, this was absurd. What man with money will make it last fifteen days? If he hoarded money beyond the spending of three days, he was a miser—and when, Señor, did the blood of Spain flow in the veins of misers? Hence, it was the custom for our stokers to appear every third or fourth day to draw the money due to them. 4

There was a certain elasticity in the Company rules, and Larry and I sent the necessary forms to the Main Office and received an "advance" against a man's pay check. Then, one day, Downtown[4] favored us with a memorandum: 5

"There have been too many abuses of the advance-against-wages privilege. Hereafter, no advance against wages will be made to any employee except in a case of genuine emergency." 6

---

[1]*Señor Payroll:* Mr. Payroll.

[2]*stokers:* People whose job is to supply a furnace with fuel.

[3]*retorts:* Bottlelike instruments used in laboratories to heat substances (this is a *metaphor,* or implied comparison, to emphasize the difficult working conditions).

[4]*Downtown:* The company management.

We had no sooner posted the notice when in came stoker Juan Garcia. He 7 asked for an advance. I pointed to the notice. He spelled it through slowly, then said, "What does this mean, this 'genuine emergency'?"

I explained to him patiently that the Company was kind and sympathetic, 8 but that it was a great nuisance to have to pay wages every few days. If someone was ill or if money was urgently needed for some other good reason, then the Company would make an exception to the rule.

Juan Garcia turned his hat over and over slowly in his big hands. "I do not 9 get my money?"

"Next payday, Juan. On the twentieth." 10

He went out silently and I felt a little ashamed of myself. I looked across the 11 desk at Larry. He avoided my eyes.

In the next hour two other stokers came in, looked at the notice, had it 12 explained and walked solemnly out; then no more came. What we did not know was that Juan Garcia, Pete Mendoza, and Francisco Gonzalez had spread the word, and that every Mexican in the plant was explaining the order to every other Mexican. "To get money now, the wife must be sick. There must be medicine for the baby."

The next morning Juan Garcia's wife was practically dying, Pete Mendoza's 13 mother would hardly last the day, there was a veritable epidemic among children, and, just for variety, there was one sick father. We always suspected that the old man was really sick; no Mexican would otherwise have thought of him. At any rate, nobody paid Larry and me to examine private lives; we made out our forms with an added line describing the "genuine emergency." Our people got paid.

That went on for a week. Then came a new order, curt and to the point: 14 "Hereafter, employees will be paid ONLY on the fifth and the twentieth of the month. No exceptions will be made except in the cases of employees leaving the service of the Company."

The notice went up on the board, and we explained its significance gravely. 15 "No, Juan Garcia, we cannot advance your wages. It is too bad about your wife and your cousins and your aunts, but there is a new rule."

Juan Garcia went out and thought it over. He thought out loud with Men- 16 doza and Gonzalez and Ayala, then, in the morning, he was back. "I am quitting this company for different job. You pay me now?"

We argued that it was a good company and that it loved its employees like 17 children, but in the end we paid off, because Juan Garcia quit. And so did Gonzalez, Mendoza, Obregon, Ayala and Ortez, the best stokers, men who could not be replaced.

Larry and I looked at each other; we knew what was coming in about three 18 days. One of our duties was to sit on the hiring line early each morning, engaging transient workers for the handy gangs.[5] Any man was accepted who

---

[5]*handy gangs:* Employees doing various small jobs, such as maintenance and repair of machines.

could walk up and ask for a job without falling down. Never before had we been called upon to hire such skilled virtuosos as stokers for handy-gang work, but we were called upon to hire them now.

The day foreman was wringing his hands and asking the Almighty if he was 19 personally supposed to shovel this condemned coal, while there in a stolid, patient line were skilled men—Garcia, Mendoza, and others—waiting to be hired. We hired them, of course. There was nothing else to do.

Every day we had a line of resigning stokers, and another line of stokers 20 seeking work. Our paper work became very complicated. At the Main Office they were jumping up and down. The procession of forms showing Juan Garcia's resigning and being hired over and over again was too much for them. Sometimes Downtown had Garcia on the payroll twice at the same time when someone down there was slow in entering a resignation. Our phone rang early and often.

Tolerantly and patiently we explained: "There's nothing we can do if a man 21 wants to quit, and if there are stokers available when the plant needs stokers, we hire them."

Out of chaos, Downtown issued another order. I read it and whistled. Larry 22 looked at it and said, "It is going to be very quiet around here."

The order read: "Hereafter, no employee who resigns may be rehired 23 within a period of 30 days."

Juan Garcia was due for another resignation, and when he came in we 24 showed him the order and explained that standing in line the next day would do him no good if he resigned today. "Thirty days is a long time, Juan."

It was a grave matter and he took time to reflect on it. So did Gonzalez, 25 Mendoza, Ayala and Ortez. Ultimately, however, they were all back—and all resigned.

We did our best to dissuade them and we were sad about the parting. This 26 time it was for keeps and they shook hands with us solemnly. It was very nice knowing us. Larry and I looked at each other when they were gone and we both knew that neither of us had been pulling for Downtown to win this duel. It was a blue day.

In the morning, however, they were all back in line. With the utmost 27 gravity, Juan Garcia informed me that he was a stoker looking for a job.

"No dice, Juan," I said. "Come back in thirty days. I warned you." 28

His eyes looked straight into mine without a flicker. "There is some mis- 29 take, Señor," he said. "I am Manuel Hernandez. I work as the stoker in Pueblo, in Santa Fe, in many places."

I stared back at him, remembering the sick wife and the babies without 30 medicine, the mother-in-law in the hospital, the many resignations and the rehirings. I knew that there was a gas plant in Pueblo, and that there wasn't any in Santa Fe; but who was I to argue with a man about his own name? A stoker is a stoker.

So I hired him. I hired Gonzalez, too, who swore that his name was Carrera, 31 and Ayala, who had shamelessly become Smith.

Three days later the resigning started. 32

Within a week our payroll read like a history of Latin America. Everyone 33 was on it: Lopez and Obregon, Villa, Diaz, Batista, Gomez, and even San Martín and Bolívar. Finally Larry and I, growing weary of staring at familiar faces and writing unfamiliar names, went to the Superintendent and told him the whole story. He tried not to grin, and said, "Damned nonsense!"

The next day the orders were taken down. We called our most prominent 34 stokers into the office and pointed to the board. No rules any more.

"The next time we hire you hombres,"[6] Larry said grimly, "come in under the 35 names you like best, because that's the way you are going to stay on the books."[7]

They looked at us and they looked at the board; then for the first time in 36 the long duel, their teeth flashed white. "Sí, Señores," they said.

And so it was. 37

To Be of Use
MARGE PIERCY

The following poem, by the American poet and novelist Marge Piercy, appears in a collection of her poetry titled Circles on the Water *(1972). As you read the poem, focus on the* similes *and* metaphors *Piercy develops to convey her ideas.*

The people I love the best
jump into work head first
without dallying in the shadows
and swim off with sure strokes almost out of sight.
They seem to become natives of that element,
the black sleek heads of seals
bouncing like half-submerged balls.

I love people who harness themselves, an ox to a heavy cart,
who pull like water buffalo, with massive patience,
who strain in the mud and the muck to move things forward,
who do what has to be done, again and again.

I want to be with people who submerge
in the task, who go into the fields by harvest
and work in a row and pass the bags along,
who are not parlor generals[1] and field deserters
but move in a common rhythm
when the food must come in or the fire be put out.

---

[6]*hombres:* Spanish for "guys" or "fellows."

[7]*on the books:* Officially recorded or registered.

[1]*parlor generals:* Generals who stay indoors (in parlors, or conference rooms).

The work of the world is common as mud.
Botched, it smears the hands, crumbles to dust.
But the thing worth doing well done
has a shape that satisfies, clean and evident.
Greek amphoras[2] for wine or oil,
Hopi[3] vases that held corn, are put in museums
but you know they were made to be used.
The pitcher cries for water to carry
and a person for work that is real.

Cartoon
P. STEINER

1. What do you consider the main point of the cartoon?

2. What is the source of the humor?

[2]*amphoras:* Ancient Greek jars or vases.

[3]*Hopi:* Native American people living primarily in northeastern Arizona.

MAKING CONNECTIONS

The following questions and activities can be used for both writing assignments and class discussions. These exercises will help develop your ability to *synthesize* what you read—to combine and integrate information and ideas from different sources.

1. Which of the readings in this chapter did you like best, and why? What did you like least, and why?

2. Review the discussion of *figures of speech,* or *figurative language,* on pages 154–155. Then read through paragraphs 3, 4, 26, and 33 of "Señor Payroll" and locate the figure(s) of speech in each. What two things are being compared? What idea is Barrett trying to convey? (If you have time, also discuss the similes and metaphors in Marge Piercy's poem "To Be of Use"—another of the additional readings.)

3. Using as evidence examples from the readings in this chapter and personal experiences and observations, discuss one of the following:

   a. Why some jobs are more enjoyable and rewarding than others

   b. How you would define "success"

   c. What you see as the "ideal" job

4. In a small group, design a questionnaire based on issues raised in this chapter. What, for example, do people like and dislike about their jobs? What advice do they have for someone interested in the same line of work?

   Distribute the questionnaire to at least ten people. Then analyze the information you receive and draw whatever conclusions you can.

5. Write an essay or give an oral presentation on a topic of your own choice related to one or more of the readings in this chapter. Consider researching your subject in a university or public library. (*Sample topics:* The Protestant work ethic, the American dream, affirmative action, migrant farmworkers, day care, employment benefits, labor unions, and unemployment.)

6. Read one of the following selections from another chapter in this book: "American Values and Assumptions" (Chapter 1); "Striking a Nerve" (Chapter 2); "New Realities Fight Old Images of Mother" (Chapter 3); "Women Have What It Takes" (Chapter 3); "Men Have the Power—Why Would They Want to Change?" (Chapter 4); or "They Get by with a Lot of Help from Their Kyoiku Mamas" (Chapter 5). Discuss the ways in which the reading reflects issues raised in this chapter. To what extent are the ideas and perspectives similar?

CHAPTER FIVE

EDUCATION

Reading Skill:
Guessing the Meaning of Unfamiliar Words and Expressions from Their Context

Bel Kaufman, an American writer and teacher, once said, "Education is not a product (mark, diploma, job, money, in that order); it is a process, a never-ending one." To what extent does education represent a "product"? To what extent is it a "process"? The readings and activities in this chapter consider these questions by exploring the major goals of education and the problems associated with primary and secondary education in different countries. In addition, the chapter deals with such issues as cross-cultural similarities and differences in educational theory and practice; the ways in which schools teach values, beliefs, and skills; and the roles of students and teachers.

Following are some of the questions you will be considering in this chapter:

- What does it mean to be an "educated" person?
- What are the strengths and weaknesses of the educational system in your native country?
- To what extent are students in your native culture encouraged to express their opinions and disagree with their classmates and teachers?
- Should schools have a fixed, required curriculum?
- Does most real learning take place inside or outside the classroom?

- What are your personal career goals, and how will your education help you achieve them?

In the first reading of the chapter, "School Is Bad for Children," John Holt discusses the negative effects of the American school system and his recommendations for improvement. Next, in "They Get by with a Lot of Help from Their Kyoiku Mamas," Carol Simons analyzes the effects of competition and pressure on students in Japanese schools and the roles Japanese mothers play in educating their children. After that, in "The Teacher Who Changed My Life," Nicholas Gage pays tribute to the seventh-grade English teacher who inspired him to become a journalist. Then, in "Reading, Writing, and Arithmetic and, Now, Right and Wrong," Kate Stone Lombardi focuses on the pros and cons of "values education" according to teachers and parents. Following this, the Hopi folktale "Coyote and the Crying Song" raises questions about how people learn and fail to learn. Finally, a cartoon by Charles H. Schulz pokes fun at a student's notion of a good essay.

BRIEF QUOTES

The following quotations will help introduce you to the topic of education. Think about these statements as you read the selections in this chapter.

"Imagination is more important than knowledge."

—ALBERT EINSTEIN

"A teacher is one who is present when learning takes place."

—*ESKIMO PROVERB*

"Tell me and I forget. Teach me and I remember. Involve me and I learn."

—BENJAMIN FRANKLIN

"That is what learning is. You suddenly understand something that you've understood all your life, but in a new way."

—DORIS LESSING

"Education is an admirable thing, but it is well to remember from time to time that nothing that is worth knowing can be taught."

—OSCAR WILDE

"The greatest danger of traditional education is that learning may remain purely verbal."

—MIRRA KOMAROVSKY

"Education makes a people easy to lead, but difficult to drive; easy to govern, but impossible to enslave."

—HENRY PETER BROUGHAM

"The true test of intelligence is not how much we know how to do, but how we behave when we don't know what to do."

—JOHN HOLT

READING

PREREADING ACTIVITIES

1. In your reading journal, write for ten to fifteen minutes about something you didn't like at a school you once attended.

2. In a small group, discuss several of the quotations on pages 189–190. Do you agree with the views expressed?

3. Indicate the extent to which you agree with the following statements by filling in each blank with *SA* (strongly agree), *A* (agree), *U* (undecided), *D* (disagree), or *SD* (strongly disagree). Then compare your responses with those of several classmates.

   a. _____ Most schools are more harmful than helpful to students.

   b. _____ Schools should abolish compulsory attendance.

   c. _____ Students should feel free to disagree with their teachers in class.

   d. _____ As part of their formal education, students should be required to do some type of socially useful work in the community.

   e. _____ Schools should not have a fixed, required curriculum.

   f. _____ Most formal education involves passive learning.

   g. _____ High school students should be required to take courses in religion, politics, art, music, and sex education.

   h. _____ Cooperation, obedience, and respect for authority should be encouraged in all school systems.

   i. _____ Most real learning does not take place at school.

   j. _____ Students can learn as much from each other as they can from their teachers.

GUESSING MEANING FROM CONTEXT

In this chapter, you will be learning how to guess the meaning of an unknown word or expression from its *context*—the sentence and paragraph in which the unfamiliar item appears. This is a very important skill for improving your vocabulary and reading comprehension.

Practice this skill now by reading the following essay *without* using a dictionary. Don't worry if there are a number of words you are unfamiliar with. You will usually be able to understand the general sense of a passage without knowing the exact meaning of each word. If you come across a word or expression you are not familiar with, try to figure out its general meaning from the other words in the paragraph. You will be able to do this most of the time.

Use a dictionary to check the meanings of words only *after* you have finished reading the whole essay. (At this point, you might want to read through the discussion of *context clues* in Appendix F.)

School Is Bad for Children
JOHN HOLT

John Holt (1923–1985), an American teacher for many years at the elementary and secondary school levels, was a vocal critic of the educational system in the United States. In addition to lecturing nationally and internationally about educational reform, he wrote a number of books, including How Children Fail *(1964),* How Children Learn *(1967),* Instead of Education *(1976), and* Learning All the Time *(1989). The following essay first appeared in the magazine the* Saturday Evening Post *in February 1969.*

Almost every child, on the first day he sets foot in a school building, is   1 smarter, more curious, less afraid of what he doesn't know, better at finding and figuring things out, more confident, resourceful, persistent and independent than he will ever be again in his schooling—or, unless he is very unusual and very lucky, for the rest of his life. Already, by paying close attention to and interacting with the world and people around him, and without any school-type formal instruction, he has done a task far more difficult, complicated and abstract than anything he will be asked to do in school, or than any of his teachers has done for years. He has solved the mystery of language. He has discovered it—babies don't even know that language exists—and he has found out how it works and learned to use it. He has done it by exploring, by experimenting, by developing his own model of the grammar of language, by trying it out and seeing whether it works, by gradually changing it and refining it until it does work. And while he has been doing this, he has been learning other things as well, including many of the "concepts" that the schools think only they can teach him, and many that are more complicated than the ones they do try to teach him.

In he comes, this curious, patient, determined, energetic, skillful learner. 2 We sit him down at a desk, and what do we teach him? Many things. First, that learning is separate from living. "You come to school to learn," we tell him, as if the child hadn't been learning before, as if living were out there and learning were in here, and there were no connection between the two. Secondly, that he cannot be trusted to learn and is no good at it. Everything we teach about reading, a task far simpler than many that the child has already mastered, says to him, "If we don't make you read, you won't, and if you don't do it exactly the way we tell you, you can't." In short, he comes to feel that learning is a passive process, something that someone else does *to* you, instead of something you do for yourself.

In a great many other ways he learns that he is worthless, untrustworthy, fit 3 only to take other people's orders, a blank sheet for other people to write on. Oh, we make a lot of nice noises in school about respect for the child and individual differences, and the like. But our acts, as opposed to our talk, say to the child, "Your experience, your concerns, your curiosities, your needs, what you know, what you want, what you wonder about, what you hope for, what you fear, what you like and dislike, what you are good at or not so good at—all this is of not the slightest importance, it counts for nothing. What counts here, and the only thing that counts, is what we know, what we think is important, what we want you to do, think and be." The child soon learns not to ask questions—the teacher isn't there to satisfy his curiosity. Having learned to hide his curiosity, he later learns to be ashamed of it. Given no chance to find out who he is—and to develop that person, whoever it is—he soon comes to accept the adults' evaluation of him.

He learns many other things. He learns that to be wrong, uncertain, con- 4 fused, is a crime. Right Answers are what the school wants, and he learns countless strategies for prying these answers out of the teacher, for conning her into thinking he knows what he doesn't know. He learns to dodge, bluff, fake, cheat. He learns to be lazy. Before he came to school, he would work for hours on end, on his own, with no thought of reward, at the business of making sense of the world and gaining competence in it. In school he learns, like every buck private,[1] how to goldbrick, how not to work when the sergeant isn't looking, how to know when he is looking, how to make him think you are working even when he is looking. He learns that in real life you don't do anything unless you are bribed, bullied or conned into doing it, that nothing is worth doing for its own sake, or that if it is, you can't do it in school. He learns to be bored, to work with a small part of his mind, to escape

---

[1]*buck private:* Person of lowest rank in the army and marine corps.

from the reality around him into daydreams and fantasies—but not like the fantasies of his preschool years, in which he played a very active part.

The child comes to school curious about other people, particularly other 5 children, and the school teaches him to be indifferent. The most interesting thing in the classroom—often the only interesting thing in it—is the other children, but he has to act as if these other children, all about him, only a few feet away, are not really there. He cannot interact with them, talk with them, smile at them. In many schools he can't talk to other children in the halls between classes; in more than a few, and some of these in stylish suburbs, he can't even talk to them at lunch. Splendid training for a world in which, when you're not studying the other person to figure out how to do him in,[2] you pay no attention to him.

In fact, he learns how to live without paying attention to anything going on 6 around him. You might say that school is a long lesson in how to turn yourself off, which may be one reason why so many young people, seeking the awareness of the world and responsiveness to it they had when they were little, think they can only find it in drugs. Aside from being boring, the school is almost always ugly, cold, inhuman—even the most stylish, glass-windowed, $20-a-square-foot schools.

And so, in this dull and ugly place, where nobody ever says anything very 7 truthful, where everybody is playing a kind of role, as in a charade, where the teachers are no more free to respond honestly to the students than the students are free to respond to the teachers or each other, where the air practically vibrates with suspicion and anxiety, the child learns to live in a daze, saving his energies for those small parts of his life that are too trivial for the adults to bother with, and thus remain his. It is a rare child who can come through his schooling with much left of his curiosity, his independence or his sense of his own dignity, competence and worth.

So much for criticism. What do we need to do? Many things. Some are 8 easy—we can do them right away. Some are hard, and may take some time. Take a hard one first. We should abolish compulsory school attendance. At the very least we should modify it, perhaps by giving children every year a large number of authorized absences. Our compulsory school-attendance laws once served a humane and useful purpose. They protected children's right to some schooling, against those adults who would otherwise have denied it to them in order to exploit their labor, in farm, store, mine or factory. Today the laws help nobody, not the schools, not the teachers, not the children. To keep kids in school who would rather not be there costs the schools an enormous amount of time and trouble—to say nothing of what it costs to repair the damage that these angry and resentful prisoners do every time they get a chance. Every teacher knows that any kid in class who, for whatever reason, would rather not be there not only doesn't learn anything himself but makes it

[2]*do him in:* Cheat or swindle him. (To "do someone in" can also mean to kill a person.)

a great deal tougher for anyone else. As for protecting the children from exploitation, the chief and indeed only exploiters of children these days *are* the schools. Kids caught in the college rush more often than not work 70 hours or more a week, most of it on paper busywork. For kids who aren't going to college, school is just a useless time waster, preventing them from earning some money or doing some useful work, or even doing some true learning.

Objections. "If kids didn't have to go to school, they'd all be out in the 9 streets." No, they wouldn't. In the first place, even if schools stayed just the way they are, children would spend at least some time there because that's where they'd be likely to find friends; it's a natural meeting place for children. In the second place, schools wouldn't stay the way they are, they'd get better, because we would have to start making them what they ought to be right now—places where children would *want* to be. In the third place, those children who did not want to go to school could find, particularly if we stirred up our brains and gave them a little help, other things to do—the things many children now do during their summers and holidays.

There's something easier we could do. We need to get kids out of the 10 school buildings, give them a chance to learn about the world at first hand. It is a very recent idea, and a crazy one, that the way to teach our young people about the world they live in is to take them out of it and shut them up in brick boxes. Fortunately, educators are beginning to realize this. In Philadelphia and Portland, Oregon, to pick only two places I happen to have heard about, plans are being drawn up for public schools that won't have any school buildings at all, that will take the students out into the city and help them to use it and its people as a learning resource. In other words, students, perhaps in groups, perhaps independently, will go to libraries, museums, exhibits, courtrooms, legislatures, radio and TV stations, meetings, businesses and laboratories to learn about their world and society at first hand. A small private school in Washington is already doing this. It makes sense. We need more of it.

As we help children get out into the world, to do their learning there, we 11 can get more of the world into the schools. Aside from their parents, most children never have any close contact with any adults except people whose sole business is children. No wonder they have no idea what adult life or work is like. We need to bring a lot more people who are *not* full-time teachers into the schools, and into contact with the children. In New York City, under the Teachers and Writers Collaborative, real writers, working writers—novelists, poets, playwrights—come into the schools, read their work, and talk to the children about the problems of their craft. The children eat it up. In another school I know of, a practicing attorney from a nearby city comes in every month or so and talks to several classes about the law. Not the law as it is in books but as he sees it and encounters it in his cases, his problems, his work. And the children love it. It is real, grown-up, true, not *My Weekly Reader,*[3] not "social studies," not lies and baloney.

---

[3]*My Weekly Reader:* Popular weekly magazine for elementary school students.

Something easier yet. Let children work together, help each other, learn 12
from each other and each other's mistakes. We now know, from the experience of many schools, both rich-suburban and poor-city, that children are
often the best teachers of other children. What is more important, we know
that when a fifth- or sixth-grader who has been having trouble with reading
starts helping a first-grader, his own reading sharply improves. A number of
schools are beginning to use what some call Paired Learning. This means that
you let children form partnerships with other children, do their work, even
including their tests, together, and share whatever marks or results this work
gets—just like grownups in the real world. It seems to work.

Let the children learn to judge their own work. A child learning to talk 13
does not learn by being corrected all the time—if corrected too much, he
will stop talking. *He* compares, a thousand times a day, the difference between
language as he uses it and as those around him use it. Bit by bit, he makes the
necessary changes to make his language like other people's. In the same way,
kids learning to do all the other things they learn without adult teachers—to
walk, run, climb, whistle, ride a bike, skate, play games, jump rope—compare
their own performance with what more skilled people do, and slowly make
the needed changes. But in school we never give a child a chance to detect
his mistakes, let alone correct them. We do it all for him. We act as if we
thought he would never notice a mistake unless it was pointed out to him, or
correct it unless he was made to. Soon he becomes dependent on the expert.
We should let him do it himself. Let him figure out, with the help of other
children if he wants it, what this word says, what is the answer to that
problem, whether this is a good way of saying or doing this or that. If right
answers are involved, as in some math or science, give him the answer book,
let him correct his own papers. Why should we teachers waste time on such
donkey work? Our job should be to help the kid when he tells us that he can't
find a way to get the right answer. Let's get rid of all this nonsense of grades,
exams, marks. We don't know now, and we never will know, how to measure
what another person knows or understands. We certainly can't find out by
asking him questions. All we find out is what he doesn't know—which is what
most tests are for, anyway. Throw it all out, and let the child learn what every
educated person must someday learn, how to measure his own understanding, how to know what he knows or does not know.

We could also abolish the fixed, required curriculum. People remember 14
only what is interesting and useful to them, what helps them make sense of
the world, or helps them get along in it. All else they quickly forget, if they
ever learn it at all. The idea of a "body of knowledge," to be picked up in
school and used for the rest of one's life, is nonsense in a world as complicated and rapidly changing as ours. Anyway, the most important questions
and problems of our time are not *in* the curriculum, not even in the hotshot
universities, let alone the schools.

Children want, more than they want anything else, and even after years of 15
miseducation, to make sense of the world, themselves, and other human

beings. Let them get at this job, with our help if they ask for it, in the way that makes most sense to them.

READING JOURNAL

In your reading journal, discuss one of the following:

1. Your reaction to Holt's comments about the negative effects of schools
2. A time when you learned something important at school
3. A topic of your own choice related to Holt's essay

MEANING AND TECHNIQUE

The following questions and activities will help you understand the main ideas in the essay and the manner in which it was written.

1. In one or two sentences, write down the *main point* you think Holt is making in the essay. Use your own words.
2. Describe the structure of the essay. What are its major divisions?
3. What does Holt mean when he says that "school is a long lesson in how to turn yourself off" (par. 6)?
4. Why does Holt think students should have more contact with the world outside the classroom?

DRAWING INFERENCES

In order to fully understand and evaluate a piece of writing, it is important to be aware of ideas that are not stated directly. Often writers will formulate their ideas indirectly, providing hints or suggestions to lead their reader to a certain conclusion. For example, in paragraph 14 of "School Is Bad for Children," Holt states that "the most important questions and problems of our time are not *in* the curriculum, not even in the hotshot universities, let alone the schools." He never directly states that the most important things people learn are in the real world, not in educational institutions, but this can be *inferred* from the context. (The reader can also infer that Holt does not think much of prestigious universities.)

Recognizing the implied ideas in a reading passage involves the ability to "read between the lines"—that is, to combine the hints a writer provides with one's own knowledge and experience to draw inferences. The following questions and activities will help you develop this reading skill.

1. Summarize Holt's argument in favor of abolishing compulsory school attendance. To what extent do you agree with him?

2. In paragraph 10, Holt supports the notion of schools without school buildings. Do you see any drawbacks to these "schools without walls," as some people call them?

3. Why does Holt believe schools should get rid of exams and grades? Do you think this is a good idea? Why or why not?

4. Think of a question of your own to ask your classmates about an issue raised in Holt's essay.

VOCABULARY: SYNONYMS

Synonyms are words or phrases that have the same (or nearly the same) meaning. Sometimes the vocabulary items are so close in meaning that they can be used interchangeably—for example, *"On the whole/by and large,* I feel younger than I did ten years ago." However, because most synonyms do not have exactly the same meaning in all senses, they cannot always be used in the same context. For instance, one can speak of a *tender* or *caring* relationship between two people, but one cannot refer to meat as *caring* (of course, meat can be *tender*).

Look at the following sentences from Holt's essay. Try to figure out the meaning of each italicized word from the *context*—that is, from the other words in the paragraph. (See the major types of context clues on pp. 263–267.)

Then write down two or three synonyms for each italicized word. Make sure the synonyms you choose not only have the same meaning as the italicized word but also can be used in the same sentence. (If you use a dictionary to help you, remember that most dictionaries focus on the meanings of words and not on the contexts in which the words are used.)

1. Children learn language by "trying it out and seeing whether it works, by gradually changing it and *refining* it until it does work." (par. 1)

   Synonyms: _____

2. The student "soon comes to accept the adults' *evaluation* of him." (par. 3)

   Synonyms: _____

3. "The child comes to school curious about other people, . . . and the school teaches him to be *indifferent*." (par. 5)

   Synonyms: _____

4. The silence children face at school is "*splendid* training" for the real world. (par. 5)

   Synonyms: _____

5. "Aside from being boring, the school is almost always ugly, cold, *inhuman*." (par. 6)

   Synonyms: _____

6. "The child learns to live in a daze, saving his energies for those small parts of his life that are too *trivial* for the adults to bother with." (par. 7)

   Synonyms: _____

7. "We should *abolish* compulsory school attendance." (par. 8)

   Synonyms: _____

8. "Our *compulsory* school-attendance laws once served a humane and useful purpose." (par. 8)

   Synonyms: _____

VOCABULARY: IN CONTEXT

In this exercise, you will develop your vocabulary by using words and idioms in a realistic context.

- If you don't know the meaning of one of the following italicized vocabulary items, first find it in the reading and see if you can determine its meaning from the context. (Review the major types of context clues on pp. 263–267.)
- If the meaning is still unclear, look up the item in a dictionary or consult with a native speaker of English.
- Then, in a few sentences, describe or explain each of the following situations, ideas, and things. **Do not** just define the italicized words and expressions. Discuss personal experiences and opinions and give examples.

1. An example of someone being *resourceful* (par. 1)

2. The extent to which high school students and teachers *interact* in the classroom in your native country (par. 1)

3. A time when you worked for hours *on end* (par. 4)

4. Something that might cause someone to feel *in a daze* (par. 7)

5. Something you think should be *abolished,* and why (par. 8)

6. An example of a law that serves a *humane* purpose (par. 8)

7. A time when you felt *resentful* of something (par. 8)

8. An example of *exploitation* (par. 8)

9. A time when you *encountered* a problem due to cross-cultural differences (par. 11)

10. Something that would help people from different cultures *get along* (par. 14)

DISCUSSION AND DEBATE

1. In a small group, fill in the following chart with Holt's major criticisms of schools and your reactions to these criticisms. Consider at least six aspects of schooling that Holt attacks. Be sure to discuss your own experiences. (If you have time, also consider Holt's recommendations for improvement.)

Holt's Criticisms of Schools	*Your Reactions*
1. _____	1. _____
2. _____	2. _____
3. _____	3. _____
4. _____	4. _____
5. _____	5. _____
6. _____	6. _____
7. _____	7. _____
8. _____	8. _____

2. With several classmates, discuss educational practices and norms in your native culture. Consider such questions as the following:

   • How much stress is placed on note taking, memorization, and recitation?

   • Do students actively participate in classroom discussions and express viewpoints that differ from those of the teacher?

   • How formal is the relationship between students and teachers?

   • What types of activities (individual and group) are common in the classroom?

3. Imagine you are a teacher at any type of educational institution—an elementary or secondary school, college, language institute, and so forth. You plan to take about fifteen minutes of class time to deal with a specific topic related to the course you are teaching: a skill, concept, historical figure or period, grammatical point, and so on.

   Think about different ways to approach the subject and to engage the students' attention. Then come to class and "teach" your students. (This can be done with your own class as a whole or in small groups.)

   After all of the sessions have taken place, discuss the various approaches to teaching and learning.

4. Observe a class at any educational institution. Concentrate on what is being taught, how it is being taught, and on the nature of the student-student and student-teacher interaction.

   Then share your observations and reactions with several classmates.

WRITING ACTIVITIES

1. Imagine you and several classmates are members of a committee that is writing a statement for a university catalog about the marks, or qualities, of an "educated" person. As a group, write such a statement (two or three paragraphs long), and then share it with the rest of the class.

To help you plan, draft, and revise the following writing assignment(s), see Appendix A.

---

2. Imagine you are one of several high school students who has been invited to speak at a national conference of secondary school teachers in your native country. You have been asked to discuss what you consider the strengths and weaknesses of your high school education up until this point.

Write a short speech titled "A Talk to Teachers" in which you address this issue. Then read your speech to the high school teachers (the rest of the class) and respond to any questions they might have.

3. Write an essay focusing on any differences you noticed in educational practices, rules, and norms while studying in a foreign country (or in part of your native country that is culturally different from where you grew up). What was your reaction to these cultural differences? Were they a source of confusion or frustration?

READING

PREREADING ACTIVITIES

1. In your reading journal, write for ten to fifteen minutes about one type of pressure you experienced during a particular stage of your education. What was the source of the pressure, and how did you deal with it?

2. What do you consider one or two of the biggest problems with the educational system in your native culture? Share your thoughts with several classmates.

3. Indicate the extent to which you agree with the following statements by filling in each blank with *SA* (strongly agree), *A* (agree), *U* (undecided), *D* (disagree), or *SD* (strongly disagree). Then compare your responses in a small group.

a. _____ Most high school students don't study enough.

b. _____ In most schools, there is too much pressure.

c. _____ A good score on a national examination should be the main factor in accepting students to universities.

d. _____ The schools in my native country provide equal educational opportunities for all people.

e. _____ Elementary school students should have at least three hours of homework a day.

f. _____ One of the best ways to learn a second language is to memorize grammar rules and vocabulary.

g. _____ A competitive school system is necessary to prepare students for the competition they will face in the real world.

h. _____ Most fathers are more actively involved than mothers in their children's education.

i. _____ In my native country, a college education is more important for men than for women.

j. _____ Examinations should be an important part of all school systems in admitting, grading, and graduating students.

GUESSING MEANING FROM CONTEXT

As with the previous selection in this chapter, "School Is Bad for Children," try to read the following essay *without* using a dictionary. If you come across a word or expression you are unfamiliar with, see if you can guess its general meaning from the *context*—the other words in the paragraph. Trying to figure out the meanings of unknown words without using a dictionary is one of the best ways to improve your vocabulary and reading comprehension. Feel free to use a dictionary to check the meanings of words *after* you have finished reading the whole essay. (See the discussion of context clues in Appendix F.)

They Get by with a Lot of Help from Their Kyoiku Mamas
CAROL SIMONS

Carol Simons is an American freelance writer who has published numerous articles on such issues as education, horticulture, and popular technology. She has lived with her children and husband in many parts of Asia, including Hong Kong, Thailand, Malaysia, Vietnam, India, and, for six years, Japan. The following essay, published in 1987 in the Smithsonian *magazine, grew out of her family's experiences with the educational system in Japan.*

Two-year-old Hiromasa Itoh doesn't know it yet, but he's preparing for one of the most important milestones of his life, the examination for entry into first grade. Already he has learned to march correctly around the classroom in time with the piano and follow the green tape stuck to the floor—ignoring the red, blue, and yellow tapes that lead in different directions. With the other 14 children in his class at a central Tokyo nursery school, he obeys the "cleaning-up music" and sings the good-bye song. His mother, observing through a one-way glass window, says that it's all in preparation for an entrance examination in two or three years, when Hiromasa will try for admission to one of Tokyo's prestigious private schools.

Forty-five minutes south of the capital city by train, in the small suburb of 2 Myorenji, near Yokohama, 13-year-old Naoko Masuo returns from school, slips quietly into her family's two-story house, and settles into her homework. She is wearing a plaid skirt and blue blazer, the uniform of the Sho-ei Girls School, where she is a seventh grader. "I made it," her smile seems to say. For three years, when she was in fourth through sixth grades in public school, Naoko's schedule was high-pressure: she would rush home from school, study for a short time, and then leave again to attend *juku,* or cram school, three hours a day three times a week. Her goal was to enter a good private school, and the exam would be tough.

Her brother, Toshihiro, passed a similar exam with flying colors several 3 years ago and entered one of the elite national schools in Tokyo. The summer before the exam, he went to *juku* eight hours a day. Now, as a high school graduate, he is attending prep school, preparing for university entrance exams that he will take in March.

Little Hiromasa, Naoko, and Toshihiro are all on the Japanese road to 4 success. And alongside them, in what must surely be one of the world's greatest traffic jams, are thousands of the nation's children, each one trying to pass exams, enter good schools, and attain the good jobs that mark the end of a race well run.

But such children are by no means running as independents.[1] They are 5 guided and coached, trained and fed every step of the way by their mothers, who have had sharp eyes on the finish line right from the start.

No one doubts that behind every high-scoring Japanese student—and they 6 are among the highest scoring in the world—there stands a mother, supportive, aggressive and completely involved in her child's education. She studies, she packs lunches, she waits for hours in lines to register her child for exams, and waits again in the hallways for hours while he takes them. She denies herself TV so her child can study in quiet, and she stirs noodles at 11:00 P.M. for the scholar's snack. She shuttles youngsters from exercise class to rhythm class to calligraphy and piano, to swimming and martial arts. She helps every day with homework, hires tutors and works part-time to pay for *juku.* Sometimes she enrolls in "mother's class" so she can help with the drills at home.

---

[1]*running as independents:* Working by themselves (independents are political candidates in the United States who do not declare membership in either of the two main political parties— Democratic and Republican).

So accepted is this role that it has spawned its own label, *kyoiku mama* 7 (education mother). This title is not worn openly. Many Japanese mothers are embarrassed or modest and simply say, "I do my best." But that best is a lot, because to Japanese women, motherhood is a profession, demanding and prestigious, with education of the child the number one responsibility. Cut-throat competition in postwar Japan has made her job harder than ever. And while many critics tend to play down the idea of the perpetually pushy mother, there are those who say that a good proportion of the credit for Japan's economic miracle can be laid at her feet.

"Much of a mother's sense of personal accomplishment is tied to the 8 educational achievements of her children, and she expends a great effort helping them," states *Japanese Education Today,* a major report, issued in January 1987, by the U.S. Department of Education. "In addition, there is considerable peer pressure on the mother. The community's perception of a woman's success as a mother depends in large part on how well her children do in school."

Naoko's and Toshihiro's mother, Mieko Masuo, fully feels the responsibility 9 of the role of the education mother, although she would be the last to take credit for her children's accomplishments. This 46-year-old homemaker with a B.A. in psychology is a whiz[2] at making her family tick. She's the last one to go to bed at night ("I wait until my son has finished his homework. Then I check the gas and also for fire. My mother stayed up and my husband's mother, and it's the custom for me too") and the first one up in the morning, at 6. She prepares a traditional breakfast for the family, including *miso*[3] soup, rice, egg, vegetable, and fish. At the same time, she cooks lunch for her husband and Naoko, which she packs in a lunch box, or *o-bento.* She displays the *o-bento* that Naoko will carry to school. In the pink plastic box, looking like a culinary jigsaw puzzle, are fried chicken, boiled eggs, rice, lotus roots, mint leaves, tomatoes, carrots, fruit salad, and chopsticks. No pb&j[4] sandwiches in brown bags for this family.

"Every morning, every week, every year, I cook rice and make *o-bento*," 10 Mrs. Masuo says with a laugh, winking at Naoko. "I wouldn't want to give her a *tenuki o-bento.*" Naturally. Everyone knows that a "sloppy lunch box" indicates an uncaring mother.

But Mrs. Masuo doesn't live in the kitchen. She never misses a school 11 mother's meeting. She knows all the teachers well, has researched their backgrounds and how successful their previous students have been in passing exams. She has carefully chosen her children's schools and *juku* and has spent

---

[2]*whiz:* Abbreviation for *wizard.* "To be a whiz at something" means to be talented or skilled in something.

[3]*miso:* Thick, fermented paste made of soybeans and rice.

[4]*pb&j:* Peanut butter and jelly sandwiches—one of the most popular lunches for schoolchildren in the United States.

hours accompanying them to classes. "It's a pity our children have to study so much," she apologizes, "but it's necessary." She says that someday she'd like to get a part-time job—perhaps when exams are over. "But at the moment I must help my children. So I provide psychological help and *o-bento* help." Then she laughs.

Toshihiro says that it was his mother who drilled him in elementary school   12 and instilled in him his good work habits. And he says it was she who "forced" him to go to *juku* from fifth grade on, even though he hated it and "missed being able to play after school." And it was she who made sure the money was set aside to pay for his many lessons—up to $12,000 for two years before he took the junior high exam. Mrs. Masuo explains that her husband, who works for an oil company, didn't feel *juku* was necessary "because he didn't go when he was young." But, like most Japanese husbands, he works late and doesn't get involved in the children's activities. "So what happened was that Toshihiro just started to go, and afterward the subject was raised. Naoko, being the second, was no problem."

Some evenings she went with Naoko to *juku.* Mother and daughter walked   13 the 15 minutes down the hill to the train station and took the Tokyo line four stops to Yokohama, then walked past the brightly lit shops and kiosks and along the glittering lanes that make so many of Japan's shopping streets look like Coney Island.[5] They passed sake[6] shops and bakeries, Kentucky Fried Chicken and a clanging *pachinko*[7] parlor, and turned in at the modern high-rise, where the *juku* occupies two floors.

Naoko studied Japanese, math, and science. Today, in her former math   14 class, the *juku* teacher rapidly explains algebra problems to 50 fifth-graders. He lectures; they listen. In a science class down the hall, a young teacher is explaining photosynthesis and pretends to be a drooping plant. Seated at long tables, the children listen attentively, occasionally giggling at his antics. It is almost 8:30 P.M. and many of them haven't been home since breakfast.

"Yes, it's difficult," says Masato Nichido, assistant director of the *juku.* "But   15 most of these children like *juku* better than public school. These children want to study more. And whether they want to or not is beside the point. They must, in order to pass exams."

It is this prospect of exams, known in Japan as "examination hell," that has   16 prompted Yukiko Itoh to expose little Hiromasa to early training in the hope that he will get into a prestigious private school. Just over 10 percent of Tokyo's children attend private schools, some of which run from first grade through high school and even through university. Assuming there are no major mishaps, a child who enters one of these schools can pass the rest of his

---

[5]*Coney Island:* Amusement center in New York City.

[6]*sake:* Japanese liquor made from fermented rice, usually served warm.

[7]*pachinko:* Popular pinball game in Japan.

academic career without the fierce examinations children such as the Masuos must face.

Like most Japanese mothers, Mrs. Itoh spends most of her time with Hiromasa and her six-month-old daughter, Emi. Baby-sitters and play groups are not part of her life. She has dinner with the children well before her husband comes home from work. She takes them to the park, to swimming lessons and music, much of the time carrying her baby in a pack on her back. Indeed, a young mother with an infant in a sling and a toddler by the hand, walking along a subway platform or a city street, is a sight that evokes the very essence of motherhood to most Japanese. 17

This physical tie between mother and child is only a small part of the strong social relationship that binds members of the family together in mutual dependency and obligation. It's the mother's job to foster this relationship. From the beginning, the child is rarely left alone, sleeps with the parents, is governed with affectionate permissiveness, and learns through low-key signals what is expected and what to expect in return. 18

Many American children are also raised with affection and physical contact, but the idea is to create independent youngsters. Discipline begins early. Children have bedrooms separate from their parents. They spend time playing alone or staying with strangers and learn early that the individual is responsible for his own actions. An American mother, in disciplining, is more likely to scold or demand; a Japanese mother is apt to show displeasure with a mild rebuke, an approach that prompted one American six-year-old to tell his own mother: "If I had to be gotten mad at by someone, I wish it would be by a Japanese." 19

Even a casual observer is struck by the strong yet tender mother-child connection. A Japanese senior high school teacher said that many wives, including his own, sleep in a room with their children and not with their husbands. "Is it the same in America?" he asked. At a dinner party, a businessman made his wife's excuses: "I'm sorry she couldn't come tonight. My son has an exam tomorrow." Even if the excuse were not true, the use of it says a lot. 20

YOU MUST DO WELL OR PEOPLE WILL LAUGH

The relationship of dependency and obligation fostered in the child by the mother extends to family, school, company, and country and is the essence of Japanese society. The child is taught early that he must do well or people will laugh at him—and laugh at his mother as well. "Most Japanese mothers feel ashamed if their children do not do well at school," said one mother. "It is our responsibility to see that the child fulfills his responsibility." Bad behavior may bring shame, but good behavior has its own rewards. One woman described a friend by saying, "Her son studied very hard in order to get into a good high school and he got in. She is very clever." 21

This attitude is precisely what gives education mothers such as Mrs. Masuo 22
and her *o-bento* philosophy such esteem and why they take such pride in
their role, even if they don't admit it. Their goal is clear: success in entrance
exams, a good school, a good college, and a good job. (For daughters the goal
has a twist: good schools lead to good husbands.)

For the majority of students who go the public school route, test scores 23
become key, and it is this fact that motivates many of the 11- and 12-year-olds
traveling home from *juku* on evening trains. Many try out for the elite national junior high schools which, because of the demand, grant entrance on a
combination of scores and a lottery. Three years later they test again, for
placement in high schools, which, unlike the egalitarian lower grades, are
organized according to ability. And three years after that, they test for college.

Passing the final obstacle isn't easy: only about half get into college on their 24
first try. Many try again, for a year or two attending prep schools and *juku*,
memorizing facts for exams to come. Such students are called *ronin*, literally
"masterless samurai,"[8] and even are referred to in government statistics by
this term.

A $5 BILLION-A-YEAR INDUSTRY

But "exam hell" doesn't stop with college. Companies and government minis- 25
tries administer highly competitive tests to prospective employees, sometimes only to graduates of the prestigious universities—a system that increases the pressure even more.

This competition at all levels has generated the "*juku* boom," a $5 billion- 26
a-year industry of prep schools for *ronin*, cram schools, tutors, and special
courses. Over the past ten years, the number of children attending *juku* has
increased by half—now more than 16 percent of the primary school children
and 45 percent of junior high students. Attending *juku* can cost well over
$200 a month.

Even the *juku* compete with each other—there are now 36,000 of them in 27
Japan. One Tokyo *juku* administers practice exams to 20,000 youngsters on
Sundays. Some of the more famous cram schools give their own admissions
tests, prompting jokes about going to *juku* for *juku.* Can a student get into a
prestigious high school or college with just the information learned in public
school? "Highly unlikely," said one local public high school teacher. "The
exams are very severe."

So, in the evenings and on Saturdays and Sundays, subway platforms are 28
crowded with students of all ages. Dressed in casual clothes or sober midnight blue school uniforms and lugging heavy black leather book bags, they
are traveling to the thousands of cram schools tucked into office buildings,
down side lanes, and in every corner of every neighborhood.

---

[8]*samurai:* Japanese warrior class that arose in the twelfth century and was abolished in 1868.

Sometimes children are launched into the system when they are barely old 29 enough to walk, some of them starting "school" when they are still in diapers. They learn to obey such commands as how to clench and open their fists. "The future of a child here begins with conception," said one Tokyo mother. "Schools, after-school schools, calligraphy, piano, exercises—Japanese mothers don't waste any time." A documentary film on nursery schools by the Japan Broadcasting Company depicted a typical week for a five-year-old named Yasukata and his mother. Every morning he went to kindergarten. Three afternoons a week he attended "special strengthening class" ($500 a month), which included rhythm exercises, simple academics, and etiquette. His mother waited two and a half hours while he took the class. On another afternoon, she took him to athletics, and on another to drawing. Such preparations, the mother said, would help her son "jump the puddles"[9] ahead of him. By the program's end, Yasukata was one of 1,066 to "challenge" the prestigious Keio private school—which continues through university—and one of the 132 first-graders to gain entrance. On the same program, a mother of twin girls, both of whom had also been accepted to a famous private school, said, "It's as though I have received a long distance ticket to life."

Hoping for the same ticket are many of the mothers sitting on the benches 30 in the large gymnasium at a branch of the ponderously named Japan Athletic Club Institute for Education of Infants (JAC for short), the school that Hiromasa attends. They are watching an afternoon class of about 50 four-year-olds in their regulation red-and-blue shorts and T-shirts. The children have finished exercising and are beginning a "voice obedience" session. Abreast in a straight line, the group is told to "hop forward to the beat of the tambourine, jump in place to the tweet of the whistle." It sounds easy, but not everyone arrives at the finish line at the same time, indicating a slipup in obeying the tweets and beats. Some private primary schools might use such exercises in their entrance exams, so practice is considered essential.

Watching the mothers watch their children, JAC director, Naomi Ooka, 31 says he is dismayed by the pressure of the exams on the mothers and their children. In his view, modern Japanese mothers and children spend too much time together. "It's not good," he says.

Today, more and more educators and parents are questioning the high- 32 pressure system that gives rise to such popular sayings as "Sleep four hours, pass; sleep five hours, fail." Educationists speak of lost childhoods, kids never getting a chance to play, "eating facts" to pass exams, and the production of students who memorize answers but can't create ideas. They cite the cruelty of students who take pleasure when their classmates fail, increasing delinquency, and high incidence of bullying in the schools.

---

[9]*"jump the puddles":* A play on the English expression "to jump [or leap] over a hurdle," meaning to overcome an obstacle.

Not surprisingly, Japanese mothers have been among the major critics, 33 perhaps because they bear much of the brunt and witness the effects of the pressure on their children. "My son kept getting headaches and then he didn't want to go to school," said one mother. "So I stopped the *juku*." Recently, such mothers have gained an ally in Prime Minister Yasuhiro Nakasone,[10] whose government has been seeking ways to depressurize the education system. Nevertheless, many doubt that his efforts will have any effect in a society dedicated to hard work and competition.

For on a measuring stick, the competition has surely paid off. In math and 34 science, Japanese children rank highest in the world. They do long division before American children, take more years of a foreign language (English), learn chemistry earlier, and are overflowing with factual knowledge about history, geography, scientific formulas, and other bits of information that to many Americans would seem encyclopedic.

And the accomplishments don't stop there. A stunning 94 percent of 35 Japanese youth go to high school. Some 90 percent graduate (compared with 76 percent in the United States) and are well qualified to take their place in the work force. At the college level, the comparison shifts: only 29 percent of Japanese high school graduates go on to college (compared with 58 percent of American graduates). It is here, at the highest level, that Japanese education is considered inferior to that in the United States. The Japanese college years are often referred to as a "four-year vacation," although a well-earned vacation since the years through high school produce students who shine.

Among the Japanese who are beginning to fight the system are the increas- 36 ing numbers who have lived abroad. Quite simply, they want their children to have more time to play; they want them to learn more and memorize less; they want them to be more creative and independent. Critics say that small families, small houses, and modern conveniences lead to children being babied by mothers who don't have enough to do; and that mothers themselves are stifled at an age when women should have more freedom.

Chikako Ishii claims to know a better life. She spent several years in New 37 York City with her family and is an outspoken opponent of the education mother and the highly competitive education system. "I don't think women like this role," she says, "but the competition is pushing them into it."

Mrs. Ishii teaches Parent Effectiveness Training, an approach to learning 38 that emphasizes the individuality of the child. It's an idea long accepted in the West but anathema in group-oriented Japan, where one of the most repeated proverbs is the "nail that protrudes will be hammered down." Her two sons go to neighborhood schools. Masahiro, 12, is in the sixth grade and Hideaki, 14, is in the eighth, where he is ranked number one in his class. They do not

---

[10]*Yasuhiro Nakasone:* Prime minister of Japan, 1982–1987.

attend *juku* and do not have tutors. "So far they're both doing well," remarks their mother. "I am watching to see how they develop."

Like those around them, the Ishiis have high expectations for their chil- 39
dren, but their wait-and-see approach is baffling to many. "She's brave," said one young mother. "It's fine, I suppose," allowed another. "But what if she fails?"

READING JOURNAL

In your reading journal, discuss one of the following:

1. Your reactions to the *juku* system as described in the essay

2. What you currently find stressful about your educational studies

3. A topic of your own choice related to the reading

MEANING AND TECHNIQUE

The following questions and activities will help you understand the main ideas in the essay and the manner in which it was written.

1. In one or two sentences, write down the *main idea* (or *ideas*) you think Simons is trying to convey in the essay. Use your own words.

2. Good writers provide sufficient details (examples, facts, reasons, anecdotes, and so on) to back up, or support, their points. What types of *supporting detail* does Simons use to back up her main ideas? Do you feel she provides enough evidence?

3. In paragraphs 4 and 5, Simons uses several *metaphors* to describe the Japanese educational system. A metaphor is an implied comparison between two essentially dissimilar things—for example, "Love is a flower in bloom" or "I've lived my life in a prison." (See the discussion of *figures of speech*, including similes and metaphors, on pp. 154–155.)

    With a partner, write a list of all the metaphors you can find in paragraphs 4 and 5. Why do you think Simons makes these comparisons? What images do they evoke?

    Next, in the spaces below, write down two metaphors that you feel capture the essence of the educational system in your native country.

Metaphor: _____

Metaphor: _____

DRAWING INFERENCES

The following questions and activities will help develop your ability to draw inferences—an important reading skill.

1. The title of this essay is a play on the line "I get by with a little help from my friends," from a song by the British music group the Beatles (*to get by* means "to manage"). What point is Simons trying to make with this title? Write down two other titles that would also be appropriate for the essay.

2. What do you consider a strength and a weakness of the *juku* system as described in the essay?

3. In paragraph 8, Simons writes that in Japan, "the community's perception of a woman's success as a mother depends in large part on how well her children do in school." How do you think this perception affects the lives of Japanese women?

TONE

The tone of a piece of writing is the author's attitude toward his or her subject and audience as reflected in the choice of words and details. When people speak, their tone of voice can reveal a lot about how they are feeling. Similarly, when people write, their "voice" can express a wide range of tones, or feelings, such as *excitement, disappointment, anger, confidence, surprise, irritation*, and *nostalgia*. Some statements a writer makes are *subjective*—reflecting personal feelings and interpretations. Others are more *objective*—stressing facts rather than personal feelings and judgments. (For a more complete discussion, see pp. 58–59.)

---

4. Do you have any sense of how Simons feels about the issues she discusses? If so, through what words and details? How would you describe the overall tone of the essay? How objective is it?

5. Think of a question of your own to ask your classmates about an issue raised in the essay.

VOCABULARY: DEFINITIONS OF TERMS

Often writers will define terms that they think might be unfamiliar to their audience. Sometimes they will provide the definitions *directly* and other times *indirectly*.

In "Kyoiku Mamas," Simons introduces a number of Japanese words: *juku*, *kyoiku mama, miso, o-bento, tenuki o-bento, sake, pachinko, ronin,* and *samurai.* Some of these words are defined and some are not.

With a partner, review the strategies on pages 265–267 for defining words. Then fill in the chart below by locating all of the Japanese terms in the essay and discussing (1) how certain words are defined (directly or indirectly and the particular method) and (2) why you think certain words are not defined.

Word	Meaning	Method of Definition (or Reason for No Definition)
Example: *juku* (2)	cram school	direct definition introduced with "or"
kyoiku mama (par. 7)		
miso (par. 9)		
o-bento (par. 9)		
tenuki o-bento (par. 10)		
sake (par. 13)		
pachinko (par. 13)		
ronin (par. 24)		
samurai (par. 24)		

VOCABULARY: IN CONTEXT

In this exercise, you will develop your vocabulary by using words and idioms in a realistic context.

- If you don't know the meaning of one of the following italicized vocabulary items, first find it in the essay and see if you can determine its meaning from the context. (Review the major types of context clues on pp. 263–267.)

- If the meaning is still unclear, look up the item in a dictionary or consult with a native speaker of English.

- Then, in a few sentences, describe or explain each of the following situations, ideas, and things. **Do not** just define the italicized words and expressions. Discuss personal experiences and opinions and give examples.

  1. Something on which you *expend* great *effort* (par. 8)

  2. An example of something that is *beside the point* (par. 15)

  3. A sight that *evokes* the essence of motherhood or fatherhood in your native country (par. 17)

  4. Something you *take pride in,* and why (par. 22)

  5. A behavior that you consider a breach of *etiquette* (par. 29)

  6. An example of juvenile *delinquency* (par. 32)

  7. Something a *bully* might do (par. 32)

  8. The extent to which your studying hard now will *pay off* later (par. 34)

  9. Something that *stifles* learning (par. 36)

  10. An idea that is *anathema* in your native country (par. 38)

DISCUSSION AND DEBATE

1. With several classmates, fill in the chart below with the advantages and disadvantages of the *juku* system according to different people mentioned in "Kyoiku Mamas." You may also include arguments not discussed in the essay.

   As you fill in the chart, consider the following questions:

   - What are the effects of the *juku* system on children, parents, and education in general?

   - Do you have a similar system in your native country?

   - If you are Japanese, do you feel Simons accurately portrays your educational system? Do you disagree with any statements made by her or other people in the essay? Has anything changed since the essay was written?

Advantages of Juku	Disadvantages of Juku

2. Do you have a national examination for entrance to universities in your native country? Do students compete against each other for a limited number of acceptances? What is the nature of the examination, its significance, and your opinion of standardized national testing in general? Consider these questions in a small group.

3. Imagine you and several classmates are members of a college admissions committee meeting to discuss guidelines for accepting students. What do you consider the most important factors in admitting a student to your college? What do you consider less important? After you have formulated your admissions policy, share it with the rest of the class.

WRITING ACTIVITIES

1. In what ways can competition between students affect their education? What, for example, is the effect of competition on students' attitudes and learning styles?

    Divide a sheet of paper into two columns. On one side, list potential positive results of competition, and on the other side, list possible negative results.

    Then write one or two paragraphs discussing whether you feel there are more positive or more negative effects of competition on education.

2. Imagine that, for a college student handbook, you and several classmates are writing an entry on stress management. Briefly identify the major types of stress students typically experience. Then consider ways to reduce this stress so that students can more fully enjoy their university experience.

   When you are done, share your entry with the other groups in the class.

| To help you plan, draft, and revise the following essays, see Appendix A. |

3. Write a personal essay based on one of the following:

   a. The types of pressure you've experienced during various stages of your education

   b. Your parents' involvement in your formal education

4. Write an essay discussing the extent to which you agree with one of the following quotations (or with one of the statements in activity 3 of the "Prereading Activities"). Support your arguments with examples from "Kyòiku Mamas" and personal experiences and observations.

   a. "Education is not a product (mark, diploma, job, money, in that order); it is a process, a never-ending one" (Bel Kaufman, contemporary American author and educator).

   b. "The purpose of education, finally, is to create in a person the ability to look at the world for himself, to make his own decisions, to say to himself this is black or this is white, to decide for himself whether there is a God in heaven or not" (James Baldwin, twentieth-century American writer).

READING

PREREADING ACTIVITIES

1. In your reading journal, spend ten to fifteen minutes writing about a former teacher you liked or disliked.

2. Write a list of what you consider the main aims, or goals, of education. Discuss your list with several classmates. Then have one person from each group summarize the discussion for the rest of the class.

3. Indicate the extent to which you agree with the following statements by filling in each blank with *SA* (strongly agree), *A* (agree), *U* (undecided), *D*

(disagree), or *SD* (strongly disagree). Then compare your responses in a small group.

a. _____ Bilingual education facilitates immigrant children's adjustment to a new culture.

b. _____ In today's society, there are not enough positive role models for children.

c. _____ Most teachers are very concerned about their students' progress.

d. _____ In my native country, teachers are respected and well paid.

e. _____ Every high school student should have a part-time job at some point.

f. _____ Teachers should be friends with their students.

g. _____ High schools should have different programs for students interested in going on to college and those pursuing a vocational or technical career.

h. _____ In my native country, it is hard to get a good job without a college education.

i. _____ All high school students should be required to participate in an extracurricular activity, such as music lessons, a sport, or a club.

j. _____ In my native country, females and males receive an equal education.

GUESSING MEANING FROM CONTEXT

As with the previous two selections in this chapter, try to read the following essay *without* using a dictionary. If you come across a word or expression you are not familiar with, see if you can figure out its general meaning from the *context*—the other words in the paragraph. You will be able to do this most of the time. Use a dictionary to check the meanings of words only *after* you have finished reading the whole essay. (See the discussion of context clues in Appendix F.)

The Teacher Who Changed My Life
NICHOLAS GAGE

Nicholas Gage was born in Greece in 1939 and immigrated to the United States in 1949. He was an investigative reporter for the New York Times *newspaper for ten years and has written a number of books, the best known being* Eleni, *about the torture and execution of his mother in 1948 by Greek Communist guerrillas, and* A Place for Us, *about his adjustment to life in the United States. The following essay, adapted from this latter book, first appeared in* Parade *magazine in December 1989.*

The person who set the course of my life in the new land I entered as a 1 young war refugee—who, in fact, nearly dragged me onto the path that would bring all the blessings I've received in America—was a salty-tongued,[1] no-nonsense schoolteacher named Marjorie Hurd. When I entered her classroom in 1953, I had been to six schools in five years, starting in the Greek village where I was born in 1939.

When I stepped off a ship in New York Harbor on a gray March day in 1949, 2 I was an undersized 9-year-old in short pants who had lost his mother and was coming to live with the father he didn't know. My mother, Eleni Gatzoyiannis, had been imprisoned, tortured and shot by Communist guerrillas for sending me and three of my four sisters to freedom. She died so that her children could go to their father in the United States.

The portly, bald, well-dressed man who met me and my sisters seemed a 3 foreign, authoritarian figure. I secretly resented him for not getting the whole family out of Greece early enough to save my mother. Ultimately, I would grow to love him and appreciate how he dealt with becoming a single parent at the age of 56, but at first our relationship was prickly, full of hostility.

As Father drove us to our new home—a tenement in Worcester, Mass.— 4 and pointed out the huge brick building that would be our first school in America, I clutched my Greek notebooks from the refugee camp, hoping that my few years of schooling would impress my teachers in this cold, crowded country. They didn't. When my father led me and my 11-year-old sister to Greendale Elementary School, the grim-faced Yankee[2] principal put the two of us in a class for the mentally retarded. There was no facility in those days for non-English-speaking children.

By the time I met Marjorie Hurd four years later, I had learned English, 5 been placed in a normal, graded class and had even been chosen for the college preparatory track in the Worcester public school system. I was 13 years old when our father moved us yet again, and I entered Chandler Junior

---

[1]*salty-tongued:* Witty and provocative; having a mischievous charm.

[2]*Yankee:* Someone born or living in New England.

High shortly after the beginning of seventh grade. I found myself surrounded by richer, smarter and better-dressed classmates who looked askance at my strange clothes and heavy accent. Shortly after I arrived, we were told to select a hobby to pursue during "club hour" on Fridays. The idea of hobbies and clubs made no sense to my immigrant ears, but I decided to follow the prettiest girl in my class—the blue-eyed daughter of the local Lutheran[3] minister. She led me through the door marked "Newspaper Club" and into the presence of Miss Hurd, the newspaper adviser and English teacher who would become my mentor and my muse.

A formidable, solidly built woman with salt-and-pepper hair, a steely eye   6
and a flat Boston accent, Miss Hurd had no patience with layabouts. "What are all you goof-offs[4] doing here?" she bellowed at the would-be journalists. "This is the Newspaper Club! We're going to put out a *newspaper.* So if there's anybody in this room who doesn't like work, I suggest you go across to the Glee Club[5] now, because you're going to work your tails off here!"

I was soon under Miss Hurd's spell. She did indeed teach us to put out a   7
newspaper, skills I honed during my next 25 years as a journalist. Soon I asked the principal to transfer me to her English class as well. There, she drilled us on grammar until I finally began to understand the logic and structure of the English language. She assigned stories for us to read and discuss; not tales of heroes, like the Greek myths I knew, but stories of underdogs—poor people, even immigrants, who seemed ordinary until a crisis drove them to do something extraordinary. She also introduced us to the literary wealth of Greece— giving me a new perspective on my war-ravaged, impoverished homeland. I began to be proud of my origins.

One day, after discussing how writers should write about what they know,   8
she assigned us to compose an essay from our own experience. Fixing me with a stern look, she added, "Nick, I want you to write about what happened to your family in Greece." I had been trying to put those painful memories behind me and left the assignment until the last moment. Then, on a warm spring afternoon, I sat in my room with a yellow pad and pencil and stared out the window at the buds on the trees. I wrote that the coming of spring always reminded me of the last time I said goodbye to my mother on a green and gold day in 1948.

I kept writing, one line after another, telling how the Communist guerrillas   9
occupied our village, took our home and food, how my mother started planning our escape when she learned that the children were to be sent to re-education camps behind the Iron Curtain and how, at the last moment, she couldn't escape with us because the guerrillas sent her with a group of

---

[3]*Lutheran:* Relating to the Protestant churches that follow the teachings of Martin Luther (1483–1546).

[4]*goof-offs:* Those who avoid work or responsibility.

[5]Glee Club: Chorus that usually sings short pieces.

women to thresh wheat in a distant village. She promised she would try to get away on her own, she told me to be brave and hung a silver cross around my neck, and then she kissed me. I watched the line of women being led down into the ravine and up the other side, until they disappeared around the bend—my mother a tiny brown figure at the end who stopped for an instant to raise her hand in one last farewell.

I wrote about our nighttime escape down the mountain, across the 10 minefields and into the lines of the Nationalist soldiers, who sent us to a refugee camp. It was there that we learned of our mother's execution. I felt very lucky to have come to America, I concluded, but every year, the coming of spring made me feel sad because it reminded me of the last time I saw my mother.

I handed in the essay, hoping never to see it again, but Miss Hurd had it 11 published in the school paper. This mortified me at first, until I saw that my classmates reacted with sympathy and tact to my family's story. Without telling me, Miss Hurd also submitted the essay to a contest sponsored by the Freedoms Foundation at Valley Forge, Pa., and it won a medal. The Worcester paper wrote about the award and quoted my essay at length. My father, by then a "five-and-dime-store chef,"[6] as the paper described him, was ecstatic with pride, and the Worcester Greek community celebrated the honor to one of its own.

For the first time I began to understand the power of the written word. A 12 secret ambition took root in me. One day, I vowed, I would go back to Greece, find out the details of my mother's death and write about her life, so her grandchildren would know of her courage. Perhaps I would even track down the men who killed her and write of the crimes. Fulfilling that ambition would take me 30 years.

Meanwhile, I followed the literary path that Miss Hurd had so forcefully set 13 me on. After junior high, I became the editor of my school paper at Classical High School and got a part-time job at the Worcester *Telegram and Gazette.* Although my father could only give me $50 and encouragement toward a college education, I managed to finance four years at Boston University with scholarships and part-time jobs in journalism. During my last year of college, an article I wrote about a friend who had died in the Philippines—the first person to lose his life working for the Peace Corps[7]—led to my winning the Hearst Award for College Journalism. And the plaque was given to me in the White House by President John F. Kennedy.

For a refugee who had never seen a motorized vehicle or indoor plumbing 14 until he was 9, this was an unimaginable honor. When the Worcester paper ran a picture of me standing next to President Kennedy, my father rushed out

---

[6]*"five-and-dime-store chef"*: Owner of a variety store selling inexpensive items.

[7]*Peace Corps*: Organization created by President John F. Kennedy in 1961 to train American volunteers to work with people of developing nations.

to buy a new suit in order to be properly dressed to receive the congratulations of the Worcester Greeks. He clipped out the photograph, had it laminated in plastic and carried it in his breast pocket for the rest of his life to show everyone he met. I found the much-worn photo in his pocket on the day he died 20 years later.

In our isolated Greek village, my mother had bribed a cousin to teach her 15
to read, for girls were not supposed to attend school beyond a certain age. She had always dreamed of her children receiving an education. She couldn't be there when I graduated from Boston University, but the person who came with my father and shared our joy was my former teacher, Marjorie Hurd. We celebrated not only my bachelor's degree but also the scholarships that paid my way to Columbia's Graduate School of Journalism. There, I met the woman who would eventually become my wife. At our wedding and at the baptisms of our three children, Marjorie Hurd was always there, dancing alongside the Greeks.

By then, she was Mrs. Rabidou, for she had married a widower when she 16
was in her early 40s. That didn't distract her from her vocation of introducing young minds to English literature, however. She taught for a total of 41 years and continually would make a "project" of some balky student in whom she spied a spark of potential. Often these were students from the most troubled homes, yet she would alternately bully and charm each one with her own special brand of tough love until the spark caught fire. She retired in 1981 at the age of 62 but still avidly follows the lives and careers of former students while overseeing her adult stepchildren and driving her husband on camping trips to New Hampshire.

Miss Hurd was one of the first to call me on Dec. 10, 1987, when President 17
Reagan,[8] in his television address after the summit meeting with Gorbachev,[9] told the nation that Eleni Gatzoyiannis' dying cry, "My children!" had helped inspire him to seek an arms agreement "for all the children of the world."

"I can't imagine a better monument for your mother," Miss Hurd said with 18
an uncharacteristic catch in her voice.

Although a bad hip makes it impossible for her to join in the Greek danc- 19
ing, Marjorie Hurd Rabidou is still an honored and enthusiastic guest at all family celebrations, including my 50th birthday picnic last summer, where the shish kebab[10] was cooked on spits, clarinets and *bouzoukis*[11] wailed, and

---

[8]*President Reagan:* Ronald Reagan, actor and fortieth president of the United States (1981–1989).

[9]*Gorbachev:* Mikhail Gorbachev, general secretary of the Communist party of the Soviet Union (1985–1991) and president of the Soviet Union (1990–1991).

[10]*shish kebab:* Cubes of meat (and often vegetables) roasted on a long metal pin; popular in Turkey and Greece.

[11]*bouzoukis:* Greek string instruments resembling a mandolin, or small round-bodied guitar.

costumed dancers led the guests in a serpentine line around our Colonial farmhouse, only 20 minutes from my first home in Worcester.

My sisters and I felt an aching void because my father was not there to lead 20 the line, balancing a glass of wine on his head while he danced, the way he did at every celebration during his 92 years. But Miss Hurd was there, surveying the scene with quiet satisfaction. Although my parents are gone, her presence was a consolation, because I owe her so much.

This is truly the land of opportunity, and I would have enjoyed its bounty 21 even if I hadn't walked into Miss Hurd's classroom in 1953. But she was the one who directed my grief and pain into writing, and if it weren't for her I wouldn't have become an investigative reporter and foreign correspondent, recorded the story of my mother's life and death in *Eleni* and now my father's story in *A Place for Us,* which is also a testament to the country that took us in. She was the catalyst that sent me into journalism and indirectly caused all the good things that came after. But Miss Hurd would probably deny this emphatically.

A few years ago, I answered the telephone and heard my former teacher's 22 voice telling me, in that won't-take-no-for-an-answer tone of hers, that she had decided I was to write and deliver the eulogy at her funeral. I agreed (she didn't leave me any choice), but that's one assignment I never want to do. I hope, Miss Hurd, that you'll accept this remembrance instead.

READING JOURNAL

In your reading journal, discuss one of the following:

1. A person who has been influential in shaping the course of your life
2. The qualities of a "good" teacher or student
3. A topic of your own choice related to Gage's essay

VOCABULARY: GUESSING MEANING FROM CONTEXT

By using *context clues,* you will be able to figure out the general meaning of an unknown word or expression most of the time. When you use context clues, you use the words you are familiar with in a sentence or paragraph to make an educated guess about the meaning of an unfamiliar vocabulary item. Remember that what is usually most important in understanding a reading passage is not an *exact* definition of the unknown word or expression but a *general* sense of its meaning.

With a partner, review the four major types of context clues on pages 263–267. Then try to determine the meaning of the following italicized words and expressions from Gage's essay by analyzing the *context* (sentence and paragraph) in which they appear.

First write a definition, synonym, or description of each word or expression. Then list the context clues that helped you figure out the meaning of the vocabulary item.

When you have finished, check your answers in a dictionary.

Example:

"But Miss Hurd was there [at Nicholas's birthday party], surveying the scene with quiet satisfaction. Although my parents are gone, her presence was a *consolation,* because I owe her so much." (par. 20)

Consolation means comfort.

CONTEXT CLUES: The word *although* signals a contrast. Nicholas is feeling sad because his parents are no longer living and cannot celebrate his fiftieth birthday with him. The fact, however, that his favorite teacher, Miss Hurd, is at the party is a *consolation,* or comfort.

1. "Ultimately, I would grow to love him and appreciate how he dealt with becoming a single parent at the age of 56, but at first our relationship was *prickly,* full of hostility." (par. 3)

    Prickly means _____

    Context clues: _____

    _____

2. "I found myself surrounded by richer, smarter and better-dressed classmates who *looked askance* at my strange clothes and heavy accent." (par. 5)

    Look askance means _____

    Context clues: _____

    _____

3. "So if there's anybody in this room who doesn't like work, I suggest you go across to the Glee Club now, because you're going to *work your tails off* here!" (par. 6)

    Work one's tail off means _____

Context clues: _____

_____

4. "She did indeed teach us to put out a newspaper, skills I *honed* during my next 25 years as a journalist." (par. 7)

   Hone means _____

   Context clues: _____

   _____

5. "I handed in the essay, hoping never to see it again, but Miss Hurd had it published in the school paper. This *mortified* me at first, until I saw that my classmates reacted with sympathy and tact to my family's story." (par. 11)

   Mortify means _____

   Context clues: _____

   _____

6. "Often these were students from the most troubled homes, yet she would alternately *bully* and charm each one with her own special brand of tough love until the spark caught fire." (par. 16)

   Bully means _____

   Context clues: _____

   _____

7. "She retired in 1981 at the age of 62 but still *avidly* follows the lives and careers of former students." (par. 16)

   Avidly means _____

   Context clues: _____

   _____

8. "She was the *catalyst* that sent me into journalism and indirectly caused all the good things that came after." (par. 21)

   Catalyst means _____

   Context clues: _____

   _____

ADDITIONAL READINGS

Reading, Writing, and Arithmetic and, Now, Right and Wrong

KATE STONE LOMBARDI

The following article, by Kate Stone Lombardi, an American freelance writer, origi-
nally appeared in the large daily newspaper the New York Times *in November 1992.*
The article explores a current educational debate in the United States: whether
schools should focus on traditional academic subjects (especially the three R's of
reading, writing, and arithmetic) or on the development of moral values.

Forget for the moment why Johnny can't read.[1] Consider instead why 1
Johnny can't tell right from wrong. Can he be taught to make morally informed decisions? And should he be taught tolerance for those different from
himself?

Mirroring a nationwide trend, many schools in Westchester County[2] are 2
grappling with these questions. Educators are studying and, in some cases,
implementing a re-introduction of moral and democratic values into both the
curriculum and the school setting.

For many parents and teachers, the focus represents a long-overdue recog- 3
nition of the schools' critical role in combatting what they see as a deteriorat-
ing moral climate surrounding children. But others are balking at what they
see as the schools' intrusion into what has historically been the role of the
family. And some argue that an emphasis on values detracts from the schools'
principal job of teaching academic subjects.

Critical to the debate, of course, is just what—or whose—values will be 4
taught. Evelyn Stock, a former member of the Scarsdale School Board, described the quandary by recalling a retreat that board members took some
years ago to study the issue.

"CORE VALUES"

"It was easy to get the first few, like respect yourself, or respect others, but 5
when we started to get into things like patriotism, we were still coming off

---

[1]*Johnny can't read:* The author is referring to the well-known book *Why Johnny Can't Read*
(1955), by the American writer Rudolph Flesch (1911–1986). This book attacked the way
reading was taught in American schools.

[2]*Westchester County:* Part of New York State north of Manhattan.

the Vietnam War,[3] and it was controversial. Charity was another one. It meant different things to different people," she said.

Despite the difficulty some communities have in coming to a consensus, 6 many people argue that there are some basic principles almost everybody can agree on.

"People have become more comfortable talking about this," said Maureen 7 Grolnick, principal of Bronxville High School. "One needn't be embarrassed by it; it's not a cliché value of 'law and order' or 'motherhood and apple pie.'[4] There are some values around decency and responsibility toward oneself and others that we share pretty much across the board and that don't need to get us into a terribly painful conflict about what is the role of the school or the role of the family," she said.

The State Department of Education has held several conferences on values 8 education. The most recent was last week in Albany, and several Westchester school districts were represented. The State Board of Regents[5] has also taken a strong interest in the issue. It has identified what it calls "core values" on which it says there is universal agreement. These include responsibility, honesty, self-discipline, self-respect, respect for others, commitment to equality, justice, rule of law and the work ethic.

REACTION TO NEW FOCUS IS MIXED

"After four decades of neglect, values education is being emphasized again in 9 many public schools of New York State," said Emlyn I. Griffith, a member of the State Board of Regents. "The Regents strongly support this initiative. The Regents have defined basic core values as principles of intrinsic enduring worth—the standards of conduct required of everyone in a self-governing society," he said.

Values education can occur on two levels. First, children can be given 10 moral or ethical guidance and taught critical thinking. Second, the atmosphere for learning can be one that underscores the importance of values. That is, not only should Johnny theoretically learn how to respect other people but he should also do so while not wearing a cap in class, putting his feet up on his desk or using abusive language toward the teacher.

The reaction to the new focus on values is mixed. For some it is a welcome 11 relief.

"I'm finding that there is a visceral response to being given permission and 12

---

[3]*Vietnam War:* War between South Vietnam, aided by the United States, and Communist guerrillas, aided by North Vietnam (1954–1975). The war ended in a Communist victory.

[4]*"motherhood and apple pie":* Symbols of traditional American values.

[5]*State Board of Regents:* Group of people governing the schools of a state.

validation for teaching values in the school," said Tom Laconna, a professor at the State University of New York at Cortland and a leading expert in the field. "There has been a mounting frustration in the face of a tidal wave of cultural and moral sleaze that has been washing over us, Madonna's sex book[6] being the latest example. There is a deep anger on the part of parents and teachers that significant social institutions have not been able to address this."

SOME PARENTAL OPPOSITION

While some administrators might welcome the license to re-emphasize values, parents are not always quite so sanguine. Mark Soss, principal at the Roaring Brook Elementary School in Chappaqua, described an incident where a fourth grader had come to school wearing a T-shirt that bore a statement that was blatantly sexual in nature. The principal asked the child to turn the shirt inside out and asked that he not wear it to school again. To his surprise, the child's parents objected to Mr. Soss's position, saying it was an infringement on their child's freedom of speech. 13

George Cohen, a human relations specialist for the White Plains Public Schools, has faced similar dilemmas. Mr. Cohen says he has seen a breakdown of discipline among students, with foul language used in the classrooms and a lack of respect for authority so basic that some children are willing to ignore direct requests from administrators and teachers. Children also show a lack of fear of any disciplinary action. Compounding the difficulty, he says, is the attitude of some parents. 14

"In the old days, if the school disciplined you, you were also going to get punished at home," Mr. Cohen said. "Now if the school punishes you, the parents run to the rescue. They keep the school from doing anything that sends the message that you have to be responsible for your own behavior," he said. 15

That is not to say that all parents oppose values in the schools. Many embrace the schools' interest in this area. 16

VALUES START IN THE FAMILY

"Our P.T.A.[7] believes values should be a marriage of both the schools' responsibility and the family's. That way kids get the message louder and clearer," said Caren Fried, chairwoman of the parent education committee for the Chappaqua P.T.A. Mrs. Fried's committee is organizing a Parenting Symposium titled "Values Start in the Family . . . Then What?" for parents in the district next month. 17

---

[6]*Madonna's sex book:* Book published by the pop-rock star Madonna in 1992 that contains many sexually explicit photographs.

[7]*P.T.A.:* Parent-teacher association—local organization working for the improvement of schools.

The implementation of values education varies widely in the district. In 18 White Plains, second graders are taught Socratic[8] reasoning: they are given a text and are taught how to question its assumptions. At higher grade levels, in an attempt to reduce racial tension and promote tolerance, students with different backgrounds participate in ethnic sharing panels.

In Croton, students are trained in hands-on democracy. The traditional 19 student council at Croton-Harmon High School has been replaced by a school governance congress, where various "stakeholders," that is, students, teachers, administrators, parent representatives and custodial and secretarial representatives, meet weekly to make decisions affecting the school community. The congress has decided a host of issues, including academic eligibility for participation in extracurricular activities and whether suspensions should take place in or out of the school building. "The congress gives students the skills they need to participate in a democratic society," said Sherry King, Superintendent of the Croton Schools.

In Chappaqua, the district has developed what it calls standards of excel- 20 lence, by which the graduates of Horace Greeley High School will be evaluated. Students will be assessed in areas of "personal growth" and "responsible citizenship" as well as for academic excellence.

But some parents are uncomfortable with the concept of giving equal 21 weight to the more nebulous areas of personal growth and citizenship and believe that children will actually be evaluated for their "political correctness."[9]

"The irony of this development is that you have a group of educational 22 professionals whose left-of-center political orientation dominates the educational establishment, introducing a concept of 'growth of ethical reasoning' to an educational system which their liberal forefathers assured us needed to be free of any religious orientation to be truly liberal and democratic minded," said Paul Atkinson, a Chappaqua parent with two children in the school system. "They're reintroducing school prayer[10] on their terms."

Mr. Atkinson also said that he believed the central mission of the schools 23 was becoming distorted by the emphasis on values. "It detracts both in time and in orientation from the teacher's basic role. It's a lot easier for a teacher to worry about a child's self-development than to sit down and work with a child who is having trouble learning some fundamental reading or writing skills," he said.

But proponents of values education are not discouraged by a certain 24 amount of parental disapproval.

---

[8]*Socratic:* Relating to Socrates (470?–399 B.C.), a prominent Greek philosopher.

[9]*"political correctness":* Attempt to avoid language and behavior that might offend a particular social or cultural group (for example, the politically correct term for *handicapped* is *physically challenged*).

[10]*school prayer:* Group recitation of prayer in public schools, which was ruled unconstitutional in 1963.

"Conflict is inherent in everything," said Georgine Hyde, vice president of 25 the New York State School Board Association and area director for the region that includes Westchester. "I consider character development and values education a part of the educational sequence. Do we ask parents if we have to teach reading or writing? A child is not born with math skills or reading skills, and a child is not born with values. If you are not developing a whole child, you are only bringing him part of an education."

The debate over the importance of values education is not a new one. Even 26 Aristotle[11] bemoaned the moral state of his day's youth. Like other educational trends, this one has come in and out of favor with administrators. It has also appeared in different guises.

In the 1970's, for instance, a program known as "values clarification" be- 27 came popular. In this model, values were viewed to be relative. Students were given moral quandaries, and asked for their responses. There were no right or wrong responses, the point was simply that the students should "clarify" their positions, or know where they stood.

The current resurgence in values education follows a relatively dormant 28 period in the 1980's, but in this incarnation, values are not a matter of opinion but clearly a matter of right and wrong.

"There is a tremendous amount of interest in this right now," said Tom 29 Laconna. "What's different about the current scene is that values are seen as having objective worth. They are good for the individual, good for the whole human community and therefore they have a claim on our collective conscience."

Coyote and the Crying Song

The following is a folktale of the Hopi Indians, a Native American people living in northeastern Arizona. The folktale appears in a book titled People of the Short Blue Corn: Tales and Legends of the Hopi Indians, *edited by Harold Courlander, a noted folklorist who has written many books dealing with the oral literature of people around the world.*

A common figure in Native American folklore is the coyote—usually portrayed as a trickster and troublemaker. As you read the tale below, think about how it reflects the process of learning. What does the story have to teach about the ways people learn and fail to learn? What other lessons are taught in "Coyote and the Crying Song"?

Coyote once lived on Second Mesa[1] near the village of Shipaulovi. The 1 dove also lived near Shipaulovi. It was harvest time, and the dove was in the

---

[11]*Aristotle* (384–322 B.C.): Prominent Greek philosopher.

[1]*Mesa:* Hill with a flat top and one or more steep sides, common in the southwestern United States.

field collecting the seeds of the kwakwi grass.[2] To separate the seeds from the stalks, she had to rub the tassels vigorously. But the kwakwi grass was sharp, and the dove cut her hands. She began to moan: "Hu-hu-huuu! Hu-hu-huuu! Ho-uuu, ho-uuu, ho-uuu!"

It happened that Coyote was out hunting, and he heard the voice of the 2 dove. To Coyote, the moaning sounded like music. "What a fine voice," he said to himself, approaching the place where the dove was working. He stopped nearby, listening with admiration as the dove moaned again: "Hu-hu-huuu! Hu-hu-huuu! Ho-uuu, ho-uuu, ho-uuu!"

Coyote spoke, saying, "The song is beautiful. Sing it again." 3

The dove said, "I am not singing; I am crying." 4

Coyote said, "I know a song when I hear one. Sing it once more." 5

"I am not singing," the dove said. "I was gathering seeds from the kwakwi 6 grass and I cut myself. Therefore, I am crying."

Coyote became angry. "I was hunting," he said, "and I heard your song. I 7 came here thinking, 'The music is beautiful.' I stood and listened. And now you tell me you are not singing. You do not respect my intelligence. Sing! It is only your voice that keeps me from eating you. Sing again!"

And now, because she feared for her life, the dove began once more to 8 moan: "Hu-hu-huuu! Hu-hu-huuu! Ho-uuu, ho-uuu, ho-uuu!"

Coyote listened carefully. He memorized the song. And when he thought 9 he had it in mind, he said, "First I will take the song home and leave it there safely. Then I will continue hunting."

He turned and ran, saying the words over and over so that he would not 10 forget them. He came to a place where he had to leap from one rock to another, but he missed his footing and fell. He got to his feet. He was annoyed. He said, "Now I have lost the song." He tried to remember it, but all he could think of was "Hu-hu."

So he went back and said angrily to the dove, "I was taking the song home, 11 but I fell and lost it. So you must give it to me again."

The dove said, "I did not sing; I only cried." 12

Coyote bared his teeth. He said, "Do you prefer to be eaten?" 13

The dove quickly began to moan: "Hu-hu-huuu! Hu-hu-huuu! Ho-uuu, ho- 14 uuu, ho-uuu!"

"Ah, now I have it," Coyote said, and once more he started for home. In his 15 haste he slipped and tumbled into a gully. When he regained his footing, the song was gone. Again he had lost it. So he returned to the place where the dove was working.

"Your song is very slippery," he said. "It keeps getting away. Sing it again. 16 This time I shall grasp it firmly. If I can't hold onto it this time I shall come and take you instead."

---

[2]*kwakwi grass:* Hopi name for a common type of grass in the southwestern United States.

"I was not singing; I was crying," the dove said, but seeing Coyote's anger 17
she repeated her moaning sounds.

And this time Coyote grasped the song firmly as he ran toward his home 18
near Shipaulovi. When he was out of sight, the dove thought that it would be
best for her to leave the kwakwi field. But before she left she found a stone
that looked like a bird. She painted eyes on it and placed it where she had
been working. Then she gathered up her kwakwi seeds and went away.

Coyote was tired from so much running back and forth. When he was 19
almost home, he had to jump over a small ravine, but he misjudged the
distance and fell. Now Coyote was truly angry, for the song had been lost
again. He went back to the kwakwi field. He saw the stone that the dove had
placed there. He saw the painted eyes looking at him.

"Now you have done it," he said. "There is no purpose in looking at me that 20
way. I am a hunter. Therefore, I hunt." He leaped forward and his jaws
snapped. But the stone bird was very hard. Coyote's teeth broke and his
mouth began to bleed. "Hu-hu-huuu!" he moaned. "Hu-hu-huuu! Ho-uuu, ho-
uuu, ho-uuu!"

Just at that moment a crow alighted in the kwakwi field. He said, "Coyote, 21
that is a beautiful song you are singing."

Coyote replied, "How stupid the crow people are that they can't tell the 22
difference between singing and crying!"

Cartoon
CHARLES M. SCHULZ

1. What is the source of the humor in this "Peanuts" cartoon?

2. In your native culture, what are considered the characteristics of a well-
   written essay?

3. Should a teacher take into consideration such factors as effort and potential
   in grading an essay?

MAKING CONNECTIONS

The following questions and activities can be used for both writing assignments and class discussions. These exercises will help develop your ability to *synthesize* what you read—to combine and integrate information and ideas from different sources.

1. Which of the first three selections in this chapter did you like best, and why? Which did you like least, and why?

2. The American writer and educator William Zinsser has written, "What I wish for all students is some release from the clammy grip of the future. I wish them a chance to savor each segment of their education as an experience in itself and not as a grim preparation for the next step. I wish them the right to experiment, to trip and fall, to learn that defeat is as instructive as victory and is not the end of the world."

   How do you think the authors of the first three selections in this chapter would respond to Zinsser's ideas about education? Do you see any connection between his views and those expressed in the fable "Coyote and the Crying Song"?

3. Using as evidence examples from the readings in this chapter and personal experiences and observations, discuss one of the following:

   a. The major goals of education

   b. The positive and/or negative effects of education

   c. The most serious problems in elementary and/or secondary schools in your native country

4. In a small group, formulate a list of questions to ask students at your educational institution about major issues raised in this chapter.

   Then interview several students and, as a group, report your findings to the rest of the class.

5. Write an essay or give an oral presentation on a topic of your own choice relating to one or more of the readings in this chapter. Consider researching your subject in a university or public library. (*Sample topics:* Bilingual education; multicultural education; sex education; political correctness; the political abuses of education; and an educational theorist, such as John Dewey, Horace Mann, E. D. Hirsh, Paulo Freire, A. S. Neill, or Maria Montessori.)

6. Read (or reread) the essay "American Values and Assumptions" in Chapter 1. How do the cultural patterns discussed in this piece relate to educational values and practices in your native country?

APPENDIX A

THE WRITING PROCESS

Most experienced writers do not write in a simple, linear manner; for them, writing is a whole process of discovering ideas, developing and organizing them, and revising material to achieve the best effect. Writers do not wave a magic wand and create a polished essay out of thin air. Good writing takes a lot of time and practice.

No two people write in the same way. Some outline their ideas before writing about them, some don't. Some write their introduction first, some at the end. Some revise their essay as they go along, some at a later point. Not all authors follow the same method, and individual authors often write in different ways for different purposes. Every writer must discover the approach that works best on any particular occasion. Still, most experienced writers find that they pass through certain stages while writing an essay:

1. **Exploring and planning:** discovering, focusing, finding support for, and organizing ideas
2. **Drafting:** getting ideas and supporting details down on paper in rough form
3. **Revising:** rethinking and rewriting drafts to improve the content, focus, and structure
4. **Editing and proofreading:** checking for effective word choice and sentence structure, as well as correct grammar, spelling, punctuation, and mechanics

As you can see in the accompanying diagram, the four stages of the writing process overlap; that is, writers go back and forth, planning, drafting, revising, and editing material. Planning is not over when drafting begins; drafting is not

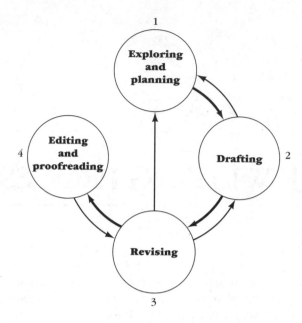

over when revising begins; and revising is not necessarily over when editing begins.

Following is a brief discussion of the four main stages of the writing process.

1. EXPLORING AND PLANNING

Most writers find it helpful to explore their ideas and plan their essay to some extent before starting the first draft. Following are six *prewriting strategies* that can assist you in exploring ideas and planning essays. A type of "thinking on paper," these techniques can help you:

- Discover ideas and relationships among them
- View a topic from different perspectives
- Think creatively and associate ideas freely
- Find a focus for your writing
- Find details to support your ideas
- Organize your ideas and supporting details

The six prewriting strategies discussed below are *freewriting, brainstorming, clustering, cubing, using the journalist's questions,* and *informal outlining.*

GUIDELINES FOR USING PREWRITING STRATEGIES

- Let your ideas flow freely. Don't worry about grammar, spelling, or organization (you can work on these later).
- Don't discard an idea because you think it is "stupid" or "trivial." When you think about a topic, write down everything that comes to mind, even if it doesn't seem important at the time. You will often end up using many of these ideas, details, and associations.
- Try a variety of prewriting strategies to see which best suit your writing style. To help explore a topic, many writers start with one technique and then, when they run out of ideas, switch to another.

Freewriting

One of the best ways to generate ideas for essays is by *freewriting.* When you freewrite, you write nonstop for a certain amount of time (usually around ten minutes) about anything that comes to mind when you think about a subject.

GUIDELINES FOR FREEWRITING

- Write down your ideas in whatever manner and order they come. Don't worry about complete sentences, grammar, spelling, or punctuation.
- Continue writing for the entire amount of time; *don't stop at all.* If you can't think of anything to say, just keep repeating a word or writing something like "I'm sure I have more ideas." Usually while you're doing this, another idea will come and you'll be able to continue.
- When your time is up, read what you've written and underline an idea you'd like to pursue. Then freewrite on this idea or use one of the other prewriting strategies to explore the idea further.

Following is an example of someone's freewriting on the topic of culture shock.

When I think of culture shock, <u>I imagine a roller coaster ride—up and down, faster and slower, going around and around.</u> Sometimes I feel this way—one moment happy and excited and the next lonely and depressed. Some of my friends have told me they feel the same way too. I thought I was the only one. It makes me feel better to know other people are having the same problems. Culture shock. Culture shock. I think of a flower in a small pot that's placed in a bigger one. I come from a small town of thirty thousand people, and now I'm living in a big city of two million. I'm a little flower in a big pot.

Brainstorming

To help discover ideas and relationships among them, many writers find it useful to *brainstorm* a topic—to make a list of everything that comes to mind when they think about a subject.

GUIDELINES FOR BRAINSTORMING

1. Write a list of everything you can think of—ideas, experiences, examples, and associations—related to a particular topic. Don't be concerned about the order of ideas or how important they seem.

2. Read through your list and look for patterns. Try to make connections among items by grouping them into categories. Then put an asterisk (*) next to the ideas that seem the most interesting or important.

3. After brainstorming your topic, you might want to explore a particular aspect of it further by using one of the other prewriting strategies.

Following is an example of someone's brainstorming the topic of culture shock.

Culture Shock (random list)
    homesick, lonely
    symptoms: physical (insomnia, upset stomach) and emotional (boredom, tension, depression)
    language difficulty
    different values, customs, and expectations (religion, education, food, family)
    criticizing the new culture
    daily problems (finances, finding an apartment, work, school, making friends)

Culture Shock (grouped list)

CAUSES OF CULTURE SHOCK

  homesick, lonely

  language difficulty

*different values, customs, and expectations (religion, education, food, family)

*daily problems (finances, finding an apartment, work, school, making friends)

EFFECTS OF CULTURE SHOCK

  symptoms: physical (insomnia, upset stomach) and emotional (boredom, tension, depression)

  criticizing the new culture

Clustering

Like freewriting and brainstorming, *clustering* (also called *mapping)* is a means of rapidly generating ideas and discovering relationships among them. Unlike the first two invention techniques, however, clustering provides a sketch or map of the connections among ideas and details. Many writers find that this process of visually exploring a subject helps them think more creatively and associate ideas more freely.

GUIDELINES FOR CLUSTERING

1. Write your topic in the middle of an unlined sheet of paper and draw a circle around it.

2. Draw a line from your topic to an idea suggested by it and circle this idea.

3. Continue associating to further ideas, details, and experiences. Circle each item and draw a line back to the idea that suggested it and to other related ideas.

4. When you finish with one major division, or branch, of your topic, return to the center and start again with another idea. Repeat the process until you run out of ideas.

5. When you are done, look over your diagram and decide which chains of ideas seem the most intriguing. Consider analyzing these ideas further by using one of the other prewriting strategies.

On the following page is an example of someone's use of clustering to explore the topic of culture shock.

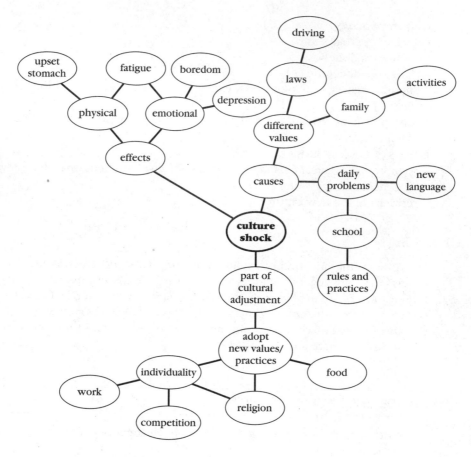

Cubing

Cubing is an invention technique that helps writers quickly view a topic from six perspectives. This activity involves drawing a cube around a topic and imagining that one is looking at it through the six sides. Each side receives a different label: *describe, analyze, compare, associate, apply,* and *argue.*

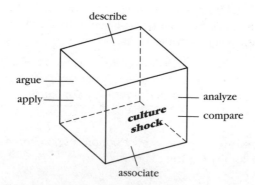

GUIDELINES FOR CUBING

When cubing, move quickly from one of the following perspectives to the next, writing down whatever comes to mind when you think about a topic. Don't stop until you've considered all six points of view.

1. *Description:* What does your topic look, sound, feel, taste, or smell like?

2. *Analysis:* How is it made? What parts can it be divided into? How do the parts relate to the whole?

3. *Comparison:* What is it similar to and different from?

4. *Association:* What does it remind you of? Does it relate to anything in your own experience?

5. *Application:* What can you do with it? How can you use it?

6. *Argument:* What arguments can you make for and against it?

Following is an example of someone's exploring the topic of culture shock from the perspective of association.

Culture shock reminds me of:

- a roller coaster ride
- an electric shock
- a transplanted flower
- a little child lost in a big city
- jumping into cold water
- taking an important examination

Using the Journalist's Questions

To view a topic from different perspectives, many writers find it helpful to ask the questions used by journalists when reporting an event:

- *Who* was involved?
- *What* happened and what were the results?
- *When* did it happen?
- *Why* did it happen?
- *How* did it happen?

Following is an example of someone's attempt to answer the question, Why do people experience culture shock?

- cut off from native country, family, friends, language, customs
- own values and beliefs brought into question

- cultural misunderstandings and misinterpretations
- stress of living in a new culture (daily problems: finances, housing, school, making friends)

Informal Outlining

Unlike freewriting, brainstorming, clustering, cubing, and using the journalist's questions, *outlining* is a more structured means of discovering ideas and relationships among them. An informal outline is a brief list of a writer's main points in the order in which they will appear. Usually the thesis statement (a sentence stating the central idea of the essay) and major supporting details for each point are also included. Many writers find informal outlines very helpful in clarifying and organizing their ideas.

Following is an informal outline of an essay on culture shock. (For a discussion of how to write an outline, see p. 251.)

Thesis: There are ways to minimize the effects of culture shock and to turn a potentially negative experience into a positive one.

1. Definition of culture shock
   - psychological disorientation due to living in a new culture
   - emotional symptoms (angry, homesick, frustrated, critical)
   - physical symptoms (upset stomach, diarrhea, too much or too little sleep)
2. Causes of culture shock
   - cut off from native culture, family, friends, language
   - exposure to different values, beliefs, customs (education, religion, gender roles, laws)
   - daily problems (finances, housing, school, making friends, speaking a new language)
3. Ways to minimize culture shock
   - learn about the new culture (before and after arrival)
   - improve language skills
   - make friends with people in the new culture
   - be open-minded, nonjudgmental, flexible, and good-humored
4. Conclusion
   - need to realize culture shock is a part of cultural adjustment
   - culture shock is a learning process (about oneself and others)

2. DRAFTING

In this stage of the writing process, you develop some of the ideas you discovered in the exploring and planning stage. When you write a first draft of an essay, you express your ideas in sentences and paragraphs without worrying too much about what is correct, appropriate, or relevant. Your aim in this stage is not to produce a perfect essay but to get down on paper, in rough form, your main ideas and supporting details, realizing that you will later revise them. As a result, your first, or rough, draft will often be full of mistakes (in grammar, spelling, punctuation, and mechanics) and include many ideas and details you will later change.

QUESTIONS TO CONSIDER BEFORE STARTING YOUR ESSAY

- Have I fully understood the assignment and the teacher's expectations?

- Who is my audience? What do my readers already know about my topic, and what might they want to know?

- What is my main purpose? For example, do I want to provide information or explain something? To persuade my readers to believe something or to take a certain course of action? To entertain?

Writing an Outline

To help draft your essay, consider writing an outline first (see p. 251). Many writers find outlines very useful in clarifying and organizing their ideas. Remember, however, that outlines are not carved in stone. They are a type of road map guiding writers to their destination. Once a writer has started the trip, he or she can follow the original route to the end, make detours along the way, or change directions altogether.

Writing a Thesis Statement

Whether or not you write an outline of your essay, try to formulate a *thesis statement* before starting your first draft. A thesis statement is a single sentence telling your readers the central idea of the essay and conveying your attitude and purpose. Writing this type of specific, or limiting, sentence can help you focus your ideas and organize your essay. (In college writing, students are often expected to include a thesis sentence early in their essay, usually at the end of the introduction; professional writers, however, frequently leave out such a direct statement of the main idea.) When drafting a thesis statement, be careful not just to present a general idea—for example, "Sociologists argue about the origins of gender differences." Make sure that you state your main idea and convey your point of view—for instance, "Although culture and biology both play a role in determining gender differences, the first factor is much more important."

QUESTIONS TO KEEP IN MIND WHILE DRAFTING YOUR ESSAY

- What is my thesis, or main idea?
- Do I state my thesis clearly and have a proper focus?
- What kinds of details will best support my ideas: examples, facts, statistics, reasons, anecdotes, quotations, definitions, and so on?
- Do I have enough specific details to back up my points?
- How can I best organize my ideas and supporting details in order to achieve my purpose? For example, do I want to describe something? To tell a story? To compare and contrast two things? To discuss causes and effects?

Structure of an Essay

Although the type of essay an author writes is determined by his or her subject, audience, and purpose (see the discussion in the glossary of *narrative, informative,* and *argumentative* essays), all essays consist of three major parts: an introduction, a body, and a conclusion.

ESSAY STRUCTURE

Introduction

One or two paragraphs that give a sense of the writer's topic and raise the reader's interest.

Body

The central part of the essay, in which the ideas supporting the thesis are developed. Each paragraph in the body explains, clarifies, or illustrates the thesis and either makes a new point or expands on a point already made.

Conclusion

One or two paragraphs that discuss the broader implications of the topic and bring the essay to a satisfying close.

The Introduction of the Essay

An effective introduction provides your readers with a general idea of your topic and captures their interest. Some writers include a thesis statement in the introduction; others prefer to omit this explicit statement and just to give a general sense of the topic or thesis (main idea). The most common type of introduction starts with a general statement about the topic, clarifies or limits the topic in one or more sentences, and then states the thesis of the essay in the final sentence. Other introductions begin with a specific detail or series of details and broaden toward a thesis statement. The particular type of introduction you write depends on your subject, audience, and purpose.

Following are two charts, one listing the strategies that many writers use to catch their readers' interest at the beginning of an essay and one listing things that should be avoided in an introduction.

INTRODUCTORY STRATEGIES

- Ask a provocative question that relates to your main idea.
- Use an engaging quotation.
- Make a controversial statement.
- Define (in your own words) an important term in the essay.
- Tell a brief story or anecdote relating to your topic. (This might involve a personal experience.)
- State a common belief and then declare a contrary view.
- Provide an unusual fact or statistic.
- Make an interesting analogy (a comparison between two things of a different kind or quality).

WHAT TO AVOID IN AN INTRODUCTION

- Don't blatantly announce your intent—for example, "In this essay, I will analyze. . . ." (Try to think of a more engaging way to convey your thesis and purpose.)
- Don't make an apologetic statement, such as "I am not an expert in this subject, but I will try my best to. . . ." (Don't apologize; this starts the essay out on a weak note.)
- Don't use a dictionary definition. (This device has become dull with overuse.)
- Don't make a promise that isn't fulfilled in the essay. (Unfulfilled promises are often annoying and confusing.)

The Body of the Essay

In the body, or central part, of the essay, the writer presents and develops his or her main points. Each of the body paragraphs explains, clarifies, or illustrates the thesis (main idea) in some way. Each body paragraph focuses on one main point: either a previously made point that the writer wants to explore further or a new point that supports the thesis. Most paragraphs in college writing consist of a *topic sentence*—a statement of the main idea of the paragraph—and details that support or explain the topic sentence. The topic sentence usually appears at the beginning of the paragraph but can also be in the middle or at the end. (Professional writers do not always include a topic sentence in their body paragraphs; some writers prefer to develop their ideas in a more indirect manner, implying, rather than explicitly stating, the main idea of the paragraph.)

The major characteristics of well-written paragraphs in an informative or argumentative essay are listed in the following chart.

CHARACTERISTICS OF BODY PARAGRAPHS

1. *Unity:* All of the sentences clearly relate to the main idea of the paragraph.

2. *Coherence:* All of the sentences are logically connected to each other. (For a list of devices that can help writers achieve coherence, see the entry for *transition* in the glossary.)

3. *Development:* Sufficient detail is provided to explain or support the main idea: examples, facts, statistics, reasons, anecdotes, definitions, quotations, and so on.

4. *Organization:* The ideas and supporting details in the paragraph are arranged in a clear and logical manner: *chronological order, spatial order, emphatic order,* and so on. (See the glossary for an explanation of these patterns, as well as the following rhetorical devices that can be used to organize paragraphs and whole essays: *description, narration, illustration, division, classification, comparison and contrast, cause and effect, process analysis,* and *definition.*)

The Conclusion of the Essay

The word *conclusion* has two meanings: (1) the end of something and (2) a deduction. When writing a conclusion to an essay, you need to think about both of these meanings. A good conclusion presents or reinforces your major deduction and also brings your essay to a logical end. Rather than simply repeating or restating your main points in the conclusion, it is usually more effective to discuss the broader implications of your topic. Try to leave your readers with one or two provocative thoughts to ponder rather than with a mere summary of your main points. Remember that your conclusion is the last thing your readers will see; think carefully about the impression you want to leave them with.

Following are two charts, one listing strategies that many writers use to end their essays and one listing things that should be avoided in a conclusion.

CONCLUDING STRATEGIES

- Review the main points of the essay. (This is more common in a long essay.)
- Discuss the broader implications of your topic.
- Make a prediction.
- Ask a provocative question.
- Use a quotation that reinforces your main point.
- Recommend a course of action.
- End with a brief anecdote that reflects your main point.
- Return to the beginning. (Refer back to an anecdote, quotation, question, analogy, and so on.)

WHAT TO AVOID IN A CONCLUSION

- Don't simply repeat or restate your main idea.
- Don't introduce a new idea that needs further development.
- Don't announce what you have done (for example, "In this essay I have tried to show . . .").
- Don't apologize (for instance, "I may not have considered every argument, but . . .").
- Don't end in an abrupt manner. (Your conclusion should flow smoothly and logically from the rest of the essay.)

---

3. REVISING

After composing the first draft of an essay, most experienced writers find that they need to revise it several times to sharpen their focus and to show more clearly how each of their main points supports the thesis. Revision means much more than correcting grammar, spelling, punctuation, and mechanics.

It involves a whole process of "re-vision"—rethinking and reshaping the content and structure of a draft to improve it at all levels: whole essay, paragraph, sentence, and word. To revise an essay, a writer *adds, deletes, rearranges,* and *rewords* material.

REVISION CHECKLIST

The following questions will help you evaluate and revise your essays:

Audience

- Who are my readers? Do they share certain characteristics, such as age, sex, ethnicity, occupation, educational background, or political beliefs?
- What do my readers already know about my topic, and what might they want to know?
- What are the interests, needs, and expectations of my readers?
- What attitude do I take toward my readers? Is it overly formal, informal, sarcastic, angry, confident, and so on?

Purpose

- Is my purpose clear—for example, to inform, persuade, or entertain?
- What do I want my audience to think or feel after reading the essay?
- Have I accomplished what I set out to do?

Clarity

- Is my thesis (main idea) clear?
- If I have a thesis statement, does it clearly convey my topic, focus, purpose, and attitude?
- Are all of my points and subpoints clear?
- Does each paragraph have a clearly stated or implied topic sentence?
- Should I add, delete, rearrange, or reword any material to make my ideas clearer?

Unity

- Is my essay clearly focused?
- If I have a thesis statement, is it specific enough?
- Do I include too many ideas in the essay?
- Do all of the sentences in each paragraph clearly relate to the main idea of the paragraph?

REVISION CHECKLIST *Continued*

- Do all of the paragraphs clearly support the thesis of the essay?
- Are there any digressions not related to my topic?

Coherence

- Are all of the sentences, paragraphs, and larger divisions of my essay logically connected?
- Are there smooth transitions, or connections, among the sentences in each paragraph?
- Are the connections among paragraphs clear?
- Do I use transitional words and phrases, pronouns, parallel structures, and repetition of key words to show relationships among ideas? (For a brief discussion of these transitional devices, see the entry for *transition* in the glossary.)

Development

- Do I support my thesis and main points with sufficient detail: examples, facts, statistics, reasons, anecdotes, quotations, definitions, and so on?
- Is this supporting detail convincing?
- Do I have a balance of generalizations and specific details?
- Does the introduction give my readers a sense of the topic and engage their interest?
- Does each body paragraph explain, clarify, or illustrate the thesis and make a new point or expand on a point already made?
- Does the conclusion explore the broader implications of my topic and bring the essay to a satisfying close?

Organization

- Do the individual paragraphs and the essay as a whole have a clear and logical pattern of organization? (See the entry for *organization* in the glossary.)
- Are all of my main points and subpoints in the best order?
- Do I need to rearrange any material within paragraphs to make my ideas clearer?
- Would the paragraphs be more effective if arranged in a different order?

Continued

REVISION CHECKLIST *Continued*

Tone

- Is the tone of the essay appropriate for my audience and purpose? Is it too formal, informal, critical, playful, optimistic, and so on?
- Is the tone consistent throughout the essay?
- If I do not maintain a consistent tone, is this intentional?

Title

- Do I have an effective title that states or hints at my topic and stimulates the interest of my readers?
- Is the title vague, obscure, or inappropriate?
- Does the title promise more than the essay delivers?

---

4. EDITING AND PROOFREADING

When you feel that the revised draft of your essay has suitable content, clarity, unity, coherence, development, and organization, you are ready for the final stage of the writing process: editing and proofreading. Editing involves looking closely at individual sentences for technical correctness (grammar, spelling, punctuation, mechanics) and effective structure and word choice. Proofreading involves reading the final draft of the essay for any typing errors.

Your point in editing the revised draft is not to produce a "perfect" essay but to make your meaning clearer and your language more forceful. Making mistakes is a natural part of learning how to write well. Yet even the most engaging essay will fall flat if your readers are continually distracted by incorrect grammar, misspelled words, misleading punctuation, and repetitious language.

The following questions will help you edit the revised draft of your essay.

EDITING CHECKLIST

Word Choice

- Do I use the most accurate and effective words to convey my meaning?
- Do I use concrete and specific words to make my writing vivid and clear?
- Do I avoid vague words like *aspect, factor,* and *interesting?*
- Do I avoid clichés (overused and stale expressions), such as *white as a ghost* and *better late than never?*

EDITING CHECKLIST *Continued*

- Am I careful not to overuse any words or expressions?
- Do I avoid unnecessary repetition (repetition that doesn't clarify or emphasize meaning) and wordiness?

Sentence Structure

- Is the sentence structure correct?
- Do I use adverb, adjective, and noun clauses correctly?
- Do I vary the sentence structure and length?
- Do I avoid long, rambling sentences (those with many coordinating and subordinating conjunctions) and too many short, choppy sentences?
- Is there a very long sentence that might be divided into two shorter ones? Are there two very short sentences that might be combined?

Grammar

- Is the grammar correct?
- Are there any problems with verb forms and tenses, subject-verb agreement, parts of speech (nouns, verbs, adjectives, adverbs, pronouns, articles, prepositions, conjunctions), or word order?

Usage

- *Spelling:* Do I misspell any words?
- *Punctuation:* Do I use periods, commas, semicolons, colons, quotation marks, apostrophes, and other punctuation correctly? Do I avoid sentence fragments, comma splices, and run-on sentences? (For a discussion of these terms, see the glossary.)
- *Mechanics:* Do I use capital letters, hyphens, italics, abbreviations, and paragraph indentation correctly?

Citation of Sources

- If I've taken ideas and information from other sources—through summary, paraphrase, or quotation—have I cited, or given credit to, these sources? (Be careful of *plagiarism*—the serious offense of presenting someone else's work as your own.)

Essay Format

- Have I followed the format requirements for the essay: proper margins, line spacing, page numbering, and so on?

APPENDIX B

OUTLINING

Title

Thesis statement (central idea):
  I. First main idea
     A. First supporting idea
        1. First detail (example, fact, reason, and so on)
        2. Second detail
           a. First supporting detail
           b. Second supporting detail
     B. Second supporting idea
        1. First detail
        2. Second detail
     C. Third supporting idea
 II. Second main idea
     A. First supporting idea
     B. Second supporting idea
III. Third main idea . . .

WHAT IS AN OUTLINE?

An outline is a graphic display of the main ideas and supporting details in a reading passage. An outline indicates the order of the ideas and details, their relative importance, and how they relate to each other and to the thesis (central idea) of the selection.

REASONS FOR OUTLINING

- Outlining helps you understand the main points and supporting details in a reading passage and how they relate to each other and to the thesis. Outlining also focuses your attention on the selection's organization and the author's purpose and emphasis.

- Outlines are an excellent study tool for examinations, because they help you comprehend and remember the most important information in class readings and lectures.

- Preparing an outline of your essays and research papers before you write them can help you clarify, organize, and support your ideas.

TYPES OF OUTLINES

There are two basic types of outlines: *informal* and *formal.*

- An informal outline is a brief list of the main points in an essay (or reading passage) in the order in which they appear. Usually the thesis statement—a sentence stating the central idea of the essay—and major supporting details are also included.

- A formal outline is considerably more detailed than an informal one. Following the pattern shown at the beginning of this appendix, a formal outline lists the main points and supporting details in an essay or reading passage. It indicates the order of the ideas and details, their relative importance, and how they relate to each other.

- Both informal and formal outlines can be written in full sentences (a *sentence outline*) or with single words or phrases (a *topic outline*). Both can be used to help write essays and to highlight the major ideas and supporting details in a reading passage.

GUIDELINES FOR OUTLINING ESSAYS

1. Use one or more of the exploring/planning strategies discussed on pp. 234–240 to generate a list of ideas and details relating to your topic.

2. Read through your list and look for patterns. Write down your main ideas and the major details supporting each one.

3. Write a sentence stating the thesis, or central point, of your essay. Place this at the beginning of the outline.

4. List the main ideas and supporting details in the order you think best develops your thesis.

Following are two sample outlines—informal and formal—of the article "Sex, Sighs, and Conversation: Why Men and Women Can't Communicate," by Deborah Tannen (pp. 43–45).

Informal Topic Outline

"Sex, Sighs, and Conversation: Why Women and Men Can't Communicate"

Thesis: Women and men use language differently, and this can cause frustration when they speak with each other.

1. Language differences for girls and boys
   - Girls create intimacy: play in small groups and tell secrets
   - Boys preserve status and independence: compete in large groups

2. Same differences for women and men (causing frustration)
   - Asking for directions
   - Discussing their day
   - Talking about problems
   - Talking at home and in public

3. Conclusions
   - Need to recognize language differences
   - Women and men blame each other less
   - Make small changes to improve relationships

Formal Sentence Outline

"Sex, Sighs, and Conversation: Why Men and Women Can't Communicate"

Thesis: Women and men use language differently, and this can cause frustration when they speak with each other.

I. Girls and boys use language differently.
   A. Girls create connections and intimacy.
      1. They play in pairs and small groups.
      2. They tell secrets to best friends.
   B. Boys preserve status and independence.
      1. They compete in large, hierarchical groups.
      2. They challenge others and display knowledge.
II. Language differences continue into adulthood and cause frustration.
   A. Women ask for directions and men don't.
      1. Women seek help in order to make connections.
      2. Men avoid help in order to maintain status and independence.
   B. Women discuss their day and men don't.
      1. Women talk about events to foster intimacy.
      2. Men say little due to an inexperience with intimacy.
   C. Women talk about their problems and men don't.
      1. Women explore problems in order to create connections and harmony.
      2. Men offer solutions and challenge others in order to preserve status.
   D. Women and men talk in different contexts.
      1. Women talk more at home in order to foster intimacy.

      2. Men talk more in public in order to maintain status.
         a. They answer questions first at meetings.
         b. They speak more on radio talk shows.
III. Women and men need to recognize cross-cultural differences in conversational styles.
    A. They will then blame each other less and feel less frustrated.
    B. They will then make small changes to improve their relationships.

APPENDIX C

SUMMARIZING

WHAT IS A SUMMARY?

A summary is a brief restatement, in your own words, of the main ideas in a reading passage. Depending on your purpose, when you write a summary, you will focus only on the main points in the selection or include several supporting details (examples, facts, reasons, and so on). Your main goal in summarizing a passage is to give your reader an accurate sense of the content and emphasis of the original.

REASONS FOR SUMMARIZING

- Writing a summary is an excellent way to make sure you fully understand a reading passage, because it requires you to restate ideas in your own words and to distinguish between main points and supporting details. Summarizing also focuses your attention on the *organization* of the passage and the author's *purpose* and *emphasis.* This helps you not only to comprehend the writer's ideas but to see their strengths and weaknesses.

- Along with outlines, summaries are a good study tool for examinations, because they help you understand and remember the most important information in textbooks and lectures.

- In addition to paraphrase and quotation, summary is a common way of incorporating sources into an essay, research paper, or oral report.

TYPES OF SUMMARIES

There are two basic types of summaries: *informative* summaries, which directly restate the main ideas in the original passage without mentioning the author, and *descriptive* summaries, which provide an overview of the main ideas in the selection and mention the author and title. (These latter summaries contain such statements as "The author states [argues, believes, implies] that . . ." and "The author begins [goes on to, concludes] . . . .")

CHARACTERISTICS OF A SUMMARY

A summary should be:

- *Concise:* You should include only one statement of the thesis (main idea), even if the author repeats it; review only the main points; and, if necessary, include several major supporting details.
- *Accurate:* You should include all of the main ideas, express them clearly, and reflect the author's emphasis.
- *Objective:* You should include only the author's ideas, not your own opinions, interpretations, and judgments.
- *Coherent:* You should have smooth transitions, or connections, between sentences.

GUIDELINES FOR SUMMARIZING

1. Reread the essay or article and decide on the main ideas (and supporting details) you want to include in the summary. Consider writing an outline to help separate the major and minor points of the passage.
2. Write a single sentence that explains the thesis, or main idea, of the whole reading. Use this as the first sentence of your summary.
3. Divide the reading into its major sections, each consisting of one or more paragraphs. Then write a one-sentence summary of the main idea in each section. (Depending on the length and complexity of the passage and whether or not you want to include supporting details, you might need more than one sentence for each section.)
4. Write the first draft of the summary by combining the thesis and section summaries. (You may rearrange the section summaries if you feel this better reflects the meaning of the original or combine two summaries that are related.)
5. Revise the summary as needed to make it clear, concise, and coherent and to reflect the author's emphasis.

Remember that when you write a summary, *you don't just copy statements from the original and put them together.* To summarize effectively, you need to *restate the author's ideas in your own words* and to *synthesize the material*—to combine information and group main ideas in a way that shows the relationships among them.

Following is a sample descriptive summary of the article "Sex, Sighs, and Conversation: Why Men and Women Can't Communicate," by Deborah Tannen (pp. 43–45). First read the article and then the summary.

[1]In her newspaper article "Sex, Sighs, and Conversation: Why Men and Women Can't Communicate," Deborah Tannen focuses on gender differences in the use of language and on the frustrations these differences cause when women and men converse with each other. — Thesis (¶2)

[2]She starts with an anecdote about a woman and man who are lost. [3]The woman wants to ask for directions and the man doesn't. — Summary of ¶1

[4]Tannen then outlines the major differences in the ways females and males use language, beginning in early childhood: girls learn to use language to share feelings with their female friends and create a sense of closeness, whereas boys learn to use language to establish their independence and compete with their male friends. — Summary of ¶s 3–4

[5]Tannen goes on to give a number of examples of the ways in which these different expectations about the functions of language continue into adulthood and cause problems. [6]Her examples involve conversations such as the one in the opening anecdote and the ways women use language to create intimacy and harmony and men to enhance their status and challenge others. — Summary of ¶s 5–11

[7]Tannen concludes her article by stressing the need for female and male partners to recognize that they often converse in different ways. [8]If women and men become aware of these cross-cultural differences, they will stop assuming that their own ways of speaking are correct and those of their partners are wrong and will make the small changes necessary to improve communication. — Summary of ¶s 12–15

Appendix D

PARAPHRASING

WHAT IS PARAPHRASING?

Paraphrasing a reading passage is similar to summarizing it: both involve restating someone else's ideas in your own words. But whereas a summary is a condensed, or shortened, version of the original, a paraphrase is a complete restatement, including all of the writer's main ideas and key supporting details. (In general, a paraphrase is as long as or longer than the original.) Your main goal in paraphrasing a passage is to give your reader an accurate sense of the meaning, tone, and emphasis of the original.

REASONS FOR PARAPHRASING

- Paraphrasing passages is an excellent way to make sure you fully understand them, because it requires you to read closely and restate the main ideas and supporting details in your own words.

- Paraphrasing key sections of readings can help you study for examinations, because translating another writer's language into your own helps you comprehend and remember what you have read.

- Paraphrasing and summarizing are essential for incorporating information from sources into your essays and research papers. Paraphrasing allows you to discuss an author's ideas without quoting every word and interrupting the flow of your writing.

CHARACTERISTICS OF A PARAPHRASE

A paraphrase should be:

- Faithful to the *meaning* and *emphasis* of the original passage. (Include all of the main ideas and key supporting details. Do not discuss your own opinions, interpretations, and evaluations.)

- Faithful to the *tone* of the original. (If the tone is ironic, nostalgic, enthusiastic, playful, and so on, this should be reflected in the paraphrase.)

- Largely *reworded.* (Use your own words as much as possible. Look for *synonyms* of words and phrases in the original. If you wish to retain key terms, place them in quotation marks.)

- Varied *grammatically.* (Whenever possible, change the word order and other grammatical elements. Also consider varying the sentence structure: you might make a longer sentence into a shorter one, a shorter one into a longer one, two sentences out of one, or one out of two.)

GUIDELINES FOR PARAPHRASING

1. First, reread the original passage several times to make sure you understand everything in it.

2. Then, without looking at the original, try to restate the general meaning. (If the passage is too long to remember, restate the meaning sentence by sentence or two sentences at a time.)

3. Next, reread the original passage one more time, making sure you have included all the important information in the same tone.

4. Finally, revise the paraphrase as needed. (For example, you might need to add transitional words and phrases within and between sentences to make your paraphrase flow smoothly.)

As an alternative, you may paraphrase a passage in the following manner:

1. Go through each sentence of the original passage word by word, substituting a synonym wherever possible. (Make sure each synonym can be used in the same context.)

2. Change the word order of each sentence.

3. Revise the paraphrase as needed.

Following is a sample paraphrase of a passage from Deborah Tannen's article "Sex, Sighs, and Conversation" (pp. 43–45).

ORIGINAL:

[1]"These divergent assumptions about the purpose of language persist into adulthood, where they lie in wait behind cross-gender conversations, ready to leap out and cause puzzlement or grief. [2]In the case of asking for directions, the same interchange is experienced differently by women and men. [3]From a woman's perspective, you ask for help, you get it, and you get to where you're going. [4]A fleeting connection is made with a stranger, which is fundamentally pleasant. [5]But a man is aware that by admitting ignorance and asking for information, he positions himself one-down to someone else. [6]Far from pleasant, this is humiliating. [7]So it makes sense for him to preserve his independence and self-esteem at the cost of a little extra travel time."

PARAPHRASE:

[1]These different expectations about the function of language continue into adulthood and are often an unexpected source of confusion and frustration when women and men talk to each other. [2]For example, women and men perceive the need to ask for directions differently. [3]Because women use language to make connections, they don't hesitate to ask for help. [4]In contrast, because men are concerned with maintaining status and independence, they are embarrassed to admit they don't know something. [5]As a result, they are reluctant to ask for directions, even if it means a longer trip.

Paraphrase		Original Passage
Sentence 1	=	Sentence 1
Sentence 2	=	Sentence 2
Sentence 3	=	Sentences 3 + 4
Sentence 4	=	Elements of Sentences 5, 6, + 7
Sentence 5	=	Elements of Sentences 5, 6, + 7

APPENDIX *E*

TRANSITIONAL WORDS AND PHRASES

An important feature of good writing is *coherence*. A coherent essay is one in which all of the parts—sentences, paragraphs, and longer divisions—are logically connected. One way to achieve coherence is through *transitional words and phrases,* for these help create smooth connections within and between sentences by showing relationships among ideas. (For other ways to achieve coherence, see the entry for *transition* in the glossary.)

Following is a list of the most common transitional words and phrases and their purpose.

Transitional Words and Phrases	Purpose
first, second, then, next, before, later, afterward, finally, eventually, in the meantime, while, during, often, soon, until, immediately	To indicate a time sequence
also, too, and, in addition, moreover, furthermore, besides, first of all, second, next, finally	To add an idea
for example, for instance, to illustrate, including, such as, in particular, specifically	To give an example or illustration

similarly, likewise, in the same manner, by the same token, at the same time, just as	To indicate comparison
but, yet, however, although, nevertheless, nonetheless, whereas, while, despite, in contrast, on the contrary, on the other hand, unlike	To indicate contrast
as a result, consequently, therefore, thus, hence, so, accordingly, because, since, for, due to	To indicate cause or effect
here, there, above, below, close by, far away, in front, in back, in the foreground, in the background, in the distance, adjacent to, opposite	To indicate place
indeed, of course, to be sure, certainly, obviously, clearly, without doubt, truly	To emphasize something
in other words, to put it another way, in simpler terms, in fact, that is, that is to say	To restate something
if, unless, even if, as long as, only if, whether or not, in case, in the event (that), provided (that), providing (that)	To indicate a condition
naturally, certainly, to be sure, admittedly, granted, of course, after all, and yet, whereas, even so, even though, although, at the same time, in spite of, despite, still	To indicate concession
in short, in brief, in conclusion, to conclude, in sum, to summarize, to sum up, on the whole, all in all, overall	To summarize or conclude

Appendix F

CONTEXT CLUES

"The average age at which babies begin walking is about 12 months, while 11 months is the average age for *cruising*. But ranges can vary so much that you shouldn't be concerned if your baby starts a little later or earlier. If your baby has already started cruising, you'll now notice a few variations being added to his activities. Once he feels reasonably comfortable *moving along a piece of furniture*, he will gradually hold on more loosely, sometimes forgetting to hold on at all." (From *First Year of Life*, by Robert L. Krakoff)

Cruising means to move along a piece of furniture.

WHAT ARE CONTEXT CLUES?

If you are reading a passage and come across a word or expression you are unfamiliar with, don't immediately reach for your dictionary. Often by looking at the *context* of the vocabulary item—the sentence and paragraph in which the word or expression appears—you can get a good sense of its general meaning.

Good readers often use *context clues* to figure out the meaning of an unknown vocabulary item. When you use context clues, you use the words you are familiar with in a passage and your own experience to make an educated guess about the meaning of an unfamiliar word or expression. You will not always be able to determine the meanings of unknown words (not every word has context clues), but most of the time you will, especially with some practice.

REASONS FOR USING CONTEXT CLUES

- Context clues help you figure out the general meaning of unfamiliar words and idioms, allowing you to continue reading without the interruption of using a dictionary. In college classes, you will be reading many long, complex essays and articles containing a number of unfamiliar words and expressions. Looking up in a dictionary every word you don't know takes far too much time and can actually hinder your reading comprehension.

• Guessing meaning from context helps improve your reading comprehension and speed. First, it develops your vocabulary. Most people remember a word better if they figure out the meaning for themselves rather than look it up in a dictionary. Second, using context clues helps you understand the logical connections within and between sentences. Making these connections (which you don't do as much if you use a dictionary) helps you infer meaning—an important reading skill.

MAJOR TYPES OF CONTEXT CLUES

There are four major types of context clues: (1) words with a similar meaning, (2) words used in contrast, (3) definitions (direct or indirect), and (4) general context.

Remember when using context clues to read the whole paragraph in which the unknown word or expression appears. You will often find the meaning of the vocabulary item later on in the paragraph. (See the example of *cruising* at the beginning of this appendix.)

Words with a Similar Meaning

• Try to find words similar in meaning to the one you don't know.

Example:

"Tuesday is always the worst day—it's the day the *drudgery,* boredom, and fatigue start all over again." (From "Confessions of a Working Stiff," by Patrick Fenton)

Drudgery means boring and fatiguing work.

• Look especially for *synonyms* (words with the same or nearly the same meaning), which writers often use to avoid repeating the same word.

Example:

"At the age of five, six, well past the time when most other children no longer easily notice the difference between sounds *uttered* at home and words *spoken* in public, I had a different experience." (From *Hunger of Memory,* by Richard Rodriguez)

Utter and *speak* are synonyms.

- Look for words and phrases signaling similarity, such as *likewise, similarly, by the same token,* and *in the same way.*

Example:

"Birdwhistell *maintains* that verbal communication represents less than 35% of the 'social meaning' of a situation, while more than 65% is expressed through nonverbal communication. *Similarly,* Albert Mehrabian *contends* that the total impact of a message is composed of a 7% verbal element, a 38% vocal element, and a 55% facial element." (From "Cultural Differences in Nonverbal Communication," by Peter S. Gardner)

Maintain and *contend* are synonyms.

Words Used in Contrast

- Look for words opposite in meaning to the one you don't know (these words are called *antonyms*).

Example:

"The child comes to school curious about other people, particularly other children, and the school teaches him to be *indifferent.*" (From "School Is Bad for Children," by John Holt)

Knowing the meaning of *curious* can help you figure out the meaning of *indifferent* (*curious* and *indifferent* are antonyms).

- Look for the word *not,* which signals a contrast.

Example:

"Generalizing about groups of people makes many of us nervous. We like to think of ourselves as unique individuals, *not* representatives of *stereotypes.*" (From "Sex, Sighs, and Conversation," by Deborah Tannen)

If you know what *unique* means, you can figure out the meaning of *stereotype* (a *stereotype* is a belief that does *not* take into account the uniqueness of individuals).

- Look for words and phrases showing contrast, such as *but, however, although, on the other hand, on the contrary, in contrast, nevertheless, whereas,* and *despite.*

Example:

"Barbara Gutek surveyed 1,200 men and women for a study on harassment. She asked her subjects whether they considered a sexual proposition *flat-*

tering. About 67 percent of the men said they would, while only 17 percent of the women agreed. *In contrast*, 63 percent of women would be insulted by a proposition, compared with 15 percent of men." (From "Striking a Nerve," by Barbara Kantrowitz)

If you know what *insulted* means, you can figure out the meaning of *flattering*. (The two words are antonyms. This is signaled by the phrase *in contrast*.)

- Look for adverbs with a negative meaning, such as *barely, merely, hardly, rarely, never,* and *only*.

Example:

"The *jejune* assignments that teachers give *rarely* lead to inspired student essays." (From "Makers and Users of Knowledge," by Peter S. Gardner)

If you know what *inspired* means, you can figure out the meaning of *jejune* (boring or uninspiring). The two words are antonyms. This is signaled by the adverb *rarely*.

- Look for words with the following negative prefixes: *un-, in-, im-, il-, ir-, non-, a-* and *dis-*.

Example:

"Sotopo *thrust* out his hand to grasp Adriaan by the hand, but the Dutch boy was frightened by the *unexpected* movement and drew away." (From *Nonverbal Communication: The Unspoken Dialogue,* by Judee Burgoon)

If you know what *unexpected* means, you can figure out the meaning of *thrust*—to push quickly (suddenly or unexpectedly) and forcibly.

Definitions of Words

When writers use an important term that may be unfamiliar to their readers, they will often define the term either *directly* or *indirectly*.

1. *Direct definitions*
   - Look for a formal definition.

Example:

"Each of us speaks a distinctive form of English which is not identical in every particular with the form spoken by anyone else; linguists call this individual variety of language an *idiolect.*" (From "The English Language in the Dictionary," by Frederick C. Mish)

   - Look for a definition or synonym signaled by commas and the word *or.*

Example:

"Cultural assimilation, *or* the melting-pot theory, has been a strong theme throughout the history of the United States." (From *Comprehensive Multicultural Education,* by Christine I. Bennett)

Cultural assimilation and the *melting-pot theory* have the same meaning.

- Look for a definition signaled by commas, parentheses, or dashes.

Examples:

COMMAS

"Alzheimer's disease, a progressive form of degenerative brain disease of unknown cause, affects an estimated 2 to 4 percent of people over age 65." (From *Human Sexuality,* by William H. Masters and Virginia E. Johnson)

PARENTHESES

"The disposition towards *ethnocentrism* (centeredness on one's own group) might well be the characteristic that most directly relates to intercultural communication." (From *Communication Between Cultures,* by Larry A. Samovar and Richard E. Porter)

DASHES

"Because the Incas preserved their mummies, it seems that they never felt the urge to represent their ancestors as gods in their art. Thus, the *huacas*—the mummies or the stones representing them—were not dedicated to particular gods." (From *World Religions,* by Geoffrey Parrinder)

2. *Indirect definitions*

- Look for examples that help define a word.

Example:

"While the *material aspects* of African cultures—technology of iron-working, wood carving, and weaving—died out or were greatly transformed, nonmaterial aspects survived." (From *Comprehensive Multicultural Education,* by Christine I. Bennett)

- Look especially for the phrases *for example, for instance, such as,* and *including,* which are used to introduce examples and elaborate details.

Example:

"Given *nucleation,* there are fewer role models from whom children can learn. There is less chance that a grandparent or elderly aunt, *for instance,* can tell stories about the important historical and mythical figures in a culture. Visits from relatives become a 'special occasion,' not a normal, everyday part of socialization." (From *Understanding Culture's Influence on Behavior,* by Richard Brislin)

From this example, you can guess that *nucleation* refers to families consisting of parents and children. These "nuclear families" contrast with "extended families" that consist of parents, children, and close relatives, such as grandparents and aunts.

General Context

Often you will not be able to find one of the first three types of context clues in a reading passage (words with a similar meaning, words used in contrast, or definitions). In this case, you will have to use your general understanding of the passage and your own experience to make an educated guess about the meaning of an unfamiliar word or expression. That is, you will need to use the meanings of the other words you are familiar with in the paragraph to limit the number of possible meanings of the unknown word or idiom. Using this technique, you will be able to figure out the general meaning of most unfamiliar vocabulary items.

Example:

"I was always hungry—oh, so hungry! The *scant* meals I could afford only sharpened my appetite for real food." (From "America and I," by Anzia Yezierska)

Knowing that the person speaking was very hungry because she didn't have money to buy enough food can help you guess the meaning of *scant* (small or insufficient).

Example:

"Why then can't they cultivate your fields and look after your goats while you make baskets for me? Not only this, they might gather for you the fibers and the colors in the bush and *lend you a hand* here and there in preparing the material you need for the baskets." (From "Assembly Line," by B. Traven)

From the context, you can guess that the idiom *to lend someone a hand* means to help a person.

Appendix G

EVALUATING A PIECE OF WRITING

In many college classes, you will be asked to *evaluate,* or *critique,* a writer's ideas. In order to judge the worth of what you read, it is helpful to bear the following questions in mind:

- What is the author's *purpose*—for example, to inform, persuade, or entertain?
- How well does the author *succeed* in this purpose?
- What *audience* does the author have in mind, and how does this help shape the content, organization, tone, and style of the writing? (See the entries for *tone* and *style* in the glossary.)
- Does the author state his or her ideas *clearly?*
- Does the author *organize* these ideas in an effective manner?
- Does the author provide sufficient *detail* to support his or her points—examples, facts, statistics, reasons, quotations, anecdotes, and so on?
- Is the information that the author presents *accurate* and *complete?*
- Does the author *distort* the information in any way or leave anything out?
- Does the author clearly separate *fact* from *opinion?*
- Does the author rely primarily on *logic* to make his or her points? Does the author appeal to the reader's *emotions?*
- Does the author take into account *different points of view* relating to the topic?

GLOSSARY

Adjective clause   A clause that modifies a preceding noun or pronoun; for example, "The man *who is sitting on the porch* is a friend of mine" (also called a *relative clause*). See **Clause.**

Adverb clause   A clause that modifies a verb, adjective, adverb, or whole sentence; for example, *"Although it was raining,* we still went for a walk." See **Clause.**

Analogy   A comparison between two things of a different kind or quality, such as a business and a football team. Writers often use analogies to explain something unfamiliar through something familiar. (Two common types of analogies are *similes* and *metaphors.*)

Analysis   A type of *critical thinking* involving the division of something into its parts and an explanation of their relationship to the whole.

Antonym   A word with a meaning opposite to that of another word; for example, *positive* is an antonym for *negative.*

Argumentative essay   An essay that tries to convince the reader to believe something or to take a certain course of action (also called a *persuasive essay*). Argument seeks to convince through logic, or reason, whereas persuasion more often relies on appeals to emotion. See **Informative essay** and **Narrative essay.**

Audience   The intended readers of a piece of writing. Keeping an audience in mind can help authors shape the content, organization, style, and tone of their writing.

Body   The central part of an essay in which the ideas supporting the *thesis* are developed. Each paragraph in the body explains, clarifies, or illustrates the thesis in some way.

Brainstorming   A *prewriting strategy* used to generate ideas and discover relationships among them. Brainstorming involves listing everything that comes to mind when one thinks about a subject.

Cause and effect   A common method of paragraph and essay organization involving an analysis of the reasons for or the results of an action, event, or situation.

Chronological order   A common pattern of paragraph organization involving the arrangement of events in a time sequence.

Clarity   A quality of good writing that is achieved when all of the points and subpoints in an essay are clearly and logically expressed.

Classification   A common method of paragraph and essay organization involving the arrangement of people, places, and things into categories according to common characteristics. (The first step in classification is usually *division.*)

Clause   A group of related words containing a subject and predicate. An *independent,* or *main, clause* can stand by itself as a complete sentence; for example, "*You have to study* if you want to pass the exam." A *dependent,* or *subordinate, clause* cannot stand by itself as a complete sentence; for example, "You have to study *if you want to pass the exam.*"

Cliché   An overused or stale expression, such as *white as a ghost* or *smooth as silk.* Good writers try to avoid such trite phrases and to express themselves in more original ways.

Clustering   A *prewriting strategy* used to generate ideas and discover relationships among them. Clustering provides a picture or map of the connections among ideas.

Coherence   A quality of good writing that is achieved when all of the sentences, paragraphs, and larger divisions of an essay are logically connected. See **Transition.**

Comma splice   An error that occurs when a writer uses only a comma to connect two independent clauses; for example, *The weather was very humid, this often made me feel quite weak.*

Comparison and contrast   A common method of paragraph and essay organization involving a discussion of the similarities and/or differences between two or more things.

Concession   An admission or acknowledgment that something is true, valid, or accurate.

Conclusion   One or two paragraphs at the end of an essay that discuss the broader implications of the topic and bring the composition to a satisfying close.

Conjunction   A word that connects words, phrases, or clauses, such as *and, or, but, when, until, if, because, although.* See **Coordinating conjunction** and **Subordinating conjunction.**

Connotation   The implied, or suggested, meaning of a word as opposed to its dictionary definition, or *denotation*. For example, the denotation of *home* is the place where one lives; however, the connotations of *home* are love, warmth, comfort, and security.

Content   The subject matter of a piece of writing.

Context   The part of a written or spoken statement that surrounds a word or passage and helps clarify its meaning.

Context clues   The hints provided by the *context* of a reading passage that allow one to determine the general meaning of an unfamiliar vocabulary item. (Context refers to the sentence and paragraph in which the unfamiliar vocabulary item appears.) The four major types of context clues are words with a similar meaning, words used in contrast, definitions (direct or indirect), and general context.

Coordinating conjunction   A conjunction that connects two or more grammatically equivalent structures. Coordinating conjunctions (*and, but, or, nor, for, so, yet*) are often used to create *parallel structure*.

Critical thinking   Looking beneath the surface of words to understand a writer's meaning and intention. Critical thinking involves *analysis, synthesis,* and *evaluation*.

Cubing   A *prewriting technique* that helps writers view a topic from six perspectives: description, analysis, comparison, association, application, and argument.

Definition   A common method of paragraph and essay organization involving an explanation of the meaning of a word or concept, often followed by one or more examples.

Denotation   The literal meaning of a word (the dictionary definition), as opposed to its *connotation,* or suggested, meaning.

Dependent clause   See **Clause.**

Description   A type of writing that tells how a person, place, or thing is perceived through the five senses (sight, hearing, touch, taste, and smell). Description is an important developmental strategy in fiction and nonfiction.

Development   A quality of good writing that is achieved when all of the main points in an essay are supported by sufficient detail, such as examples, facts, statistics, reasons, anecdotes, quotations, and definitions.

Division   A common method of paragraph and essay organization involving the separation of something into its parts. Division is usually the first step in the process of *classification*.

Drafting   The second stage of the writing process in which one gets one's ideas and supporting details down on paper in rough form. See **Writing process.**

Editing and proofreading The fourth stage of the writing process in which one checks for effective word choice and sentence structure, as well as correct grammar, spelling, punctuation, and mechanics. See **Writing process.**

Emphatic order A method of paragraph development used to emphasize the most important ideas, details, or examples. Common patterns of emphatic order include the arrangement of ideas from general to specific, from least important to most important, from simplest to most complex, and from most familiar to least familiar.

Essay A type of short, nonfiction composition based on a single topic and developing a thesis, or central idea. All essays have an *introduction, body,* and *conclusion. See* **Argumentative essay, Informative essay,** and **Narrative essay.**

Evaluation A type of *critical thinking* whereby one judges the significance or worth of something. Evaluating, or critiquing, a piece of writing involves analyzing such things as *content, organization, purpose, tone,* and *style.*

Example A particular fact, incident, or aspect of something that illustrates an idea or generalization. Examples, or *illustrations,* are the most common means of developing and clarifying ideas. See **Supporting details.**

Exploring and planning The first stage of the writing process in which one discovers, focuses, finds support for, and organizes ideas. See **Writing process.**

Exposition A type of writing whose purpose is to explain and inform. See **Informative essay.**

Fable A short story in which animals speak and act like human beings. The purpose of a fable is to teach a practical or moral lesson.

Figurative language Language characterized by *figures of speech* (non-literal language that evokes images, or mental pictures).

Figure of speech An imaginative comparison between two things that are essentially dissimilar. The most common figures of speech are *similes* and *metaphors.* Writers use figures of speech, or *figurative language,* to convey their ideas in a vivid manner.

Freewriting A prewriting strategy used to generate ideas. Freewriting involves writing nonstop for a certain amount of time without worrying about spelling, grammar, punctuation, and organization.

Genre A type of literary composition, such as an essay, short story, novel, poem, or play.

Idiom An expression whose meaning is different from the combined meanings of its individual words. Examples of idioms, or *idiomatic expressions,* are *to run into someone, to keep one's chin up,* and *to beat around the bush.*

Illustration An example that develops or clarifies an idea. See **Example.**

Image   A description of something using one or more of the senses (sight, hearing, taste, touch, and smell). *Figures of speech,* such as *similes* and *metaphors,* are common types of images, or *imagery.*

Independent clause   See **Clause.**

Inference   A conclusion arrived at by reasoning from evidence. To understand the unstated (inferred) meaning of a reading passage, one needs to look at the hints and suggestions a writer provides—that is, to "read between the lines."

Informal outlining   A *prewriting strategy* used to discover ideas and relationships among them. See **Outline.**

Informative essay   An essay that gives information and, when necessary, explains it (also called an *expository essay*). Informative essays use such patterns of organization as *classification, comparison and contrast, cause and effect*, and *definition.* See **Argumentative essay** and **Narrative essay.**

Introduction   One or two paragraphs at the beginning of an essay that give a sense of the writer's topic and raise the reader's interest.

Irony   The use of language to suggest something different from the literal meaning. *Verbal irony* (sarcasm) involves saying one thing but meaning the opposite. *Situational irony* involves a discrepancy between what is expected to happen and what actually happens or between what appears to be true and what is actually true.

Journalist's questions   A *prewriting strategy* used to view a topic from different perspectives. This technique involves asking the questions used by journalists when reporting an event: Who? What? When? Where? Why? How?

Mechanics   Conventions involving the use of capital letters, hyphens, italics, abbreviations, numbers, and paragraph indentation.

Metaphor   An implied comparison between two essentially dissimilar things; for example, *Life is a winding river.* A metaphor, like a *simile,* is a common *figure of speech.* Unlike a simile, a metaphor does not use the words *like* and *as* to make a comparison. (An example of a simile is *Life is like a winding river.*)

Narration   A type of writing that recounts events (tells a story), usually in a chronological sequence. Narration is an important developmental strategy in fiction and nonfiction. See **Narrative essay.**

Narrative essay   An essay that relates a writer's experience in narrative form and discusses the ways in which the experience is meaningful. In a narrative, or personal, essay, a writer shares an insight drawn from his or her own experience. See **Argumentative essay** and **Informative essay.**

Noun clause   A clause that functions as a subject, object, or complement; for example, "*Whoever is smoking* should stop."

Objective   Dealing with facts and conditions rather than with personal feelings and interpretations (the opposite of *subjective*).

Organization   The arrangement of ideas in a piece of writing. Common patterns of paragraph organization include *chronological order, spatial order,* and *emphatic order.* Patterns that can be used for both paragraph and essay organization include *description, narration, illustration, division, classification, comparison and contrast, cause and effect, process analysis,* and *definition.*

Outline   A graphic display of the main ideas and supporting details in a reading passage or intended essay. A *formal outline* indicates the order of the ideas and details, their relative importance, and how they relate to each other and to the thesis (central idea) of the selection. An *informal outline* is a brief list of a writer's main points in the order in which they will appear. Usually the *thesis statement* and major supporting details for each point are also included. Writers often use informal and formal outlines to help clarify and organize their ideas.

Paired conjunction   A pair of words that joins similar grammatical structures: *either . . . or, neither . . . nor, whether . . . or, both . . . and,* and *not only . . . but also.* Paired conjunctions (also called *correlative conjunctions*) help writers create *parallel structure.*

Paragraph   A group of sentences that develop a main idea. A well-written paragraph in an informative or persuasive essay has the following qualities: a clearly stated or implied *topic sentence, unity, coherence,* adequate *development,* and an appropriate pattern of *organization.*

Parallel structure   The balancing of similar grammatical forms within one or more sentences. Parallel structure is used to achieve *coherence* or to emphasize a point. Common parallel structures include words, phrases, and clauses joined by *coordinating conjunctions* and *paired conjunctions.* See **Transition.**

Paraphrase   A restatement, in one's own words, of the main ideas and key supporting details in a reading passage.

Part of speech   The class into which a word is grouped according to the function it performs in a sentence. The four major parts of speech are nouns, verbs, adjectives, and adverbs. (Other parts of speech are pronouns, articles, prepositions, and conjunctions.)

Persuasive essay   An essay that tries to convince the reader to believe something or to take a certain course of action (also called an *argumentative essay*). Persuasion relies both on appeals to reason and emotion.

Phrasal verb   A verb and preposition that together form a new vocabulary item—one that functions as an *idiom* (for example, *to call something off* and *to run into someone*). Phrasal verbs, or two-word verbs, are either *separable* (the noun may come either between the verb and preposition or after the preposition) or *nonseparable* (the noun must come after the preposition).

Plagiarism   Presenting someone else's words or ideas as one's own. To avoid plagiarism, it is important to cite, or mention, the source of the material one is using. (Plagiarism is a serious offense and can lead to course failure and even to expulsion from a university.)

Prefix   A group of letters attached to the beginning of a *word root* (the basic part of a word), such as *inter-* in *international*. In general, adding a prefix to a word root changes the meaning of the word. (A *suffix*, or group of letters attached to the end of a word root, usually changes the word's function, or *part of speech*.)

Prewriting strategies   Techniques that help writers discover, focus, find support for, and organize ideas. Common prewriting strategies include *freewriting, brainstorming, clustering, cubing*, using the *journalist's questions*, and *informal outlining*.

Process analysis   A method of paragraph and essay organization involving an explanation of how something works or how something is done.

Proofreading   The last stage of the writing process in which one checks the final draft of an essay for any typing errors. See **Writing process.**

Proverb   A brief popular saying that expresses a general truth; for example, *All that glitters isn't gold.*

Purpose   The goal or aim of a piece of writing (what a writer hopes to accomplish). The three most common purposes of writing are to *inform* (to provide the audience with information or to explain something), to *persuade* (to convince the audience to believe something or to take a certain course of action), and to *entertain* (to amuse the audience in some way). Keeping a purpose in mind can help authors shape the *content, organization, tone*, and *style* of their writing.

Revising   The third stage of the writing process in which one rethinks and rewrites drafts to improve the content, focus, and structure. See **Writing process.**

Rhetorical mode   The manner in which details and ideas are arranged in a piece of writing. The major rhetorical modes are *description, narration, illustration, division, classification, comparison and contrast, cause and effect, process analysis*, and *definition*.

Run-on sentence   An error that occurs when a writer doesn't use any punctuation or connecting word (*coordinating conjunction*) between two independent clauses; for example, *I saw that movie you told me about it was boring* (also called a *fused sentence*).

Sarcasm   Language whose purpose is to ridicule or criticize. Sarcasm is a type of *irony* in which what is said is the opposite of what is actually meant. (For example, if some people were supposed to help you with something and did not, you might show your displeasure by sarcastically thanking them for their help.)

Sentence fragment   A part of a sentence that is punctuated as if it were a complete sentence; for example, "He hadn't studied for the test. *Which was necessary if he wanted to get a good grade for the course.*"

Simile   An explicit comparison between two essentially dissimilar things using *like* or *as;* for example, *Life is like a roller coaster.* A simile, like a *metaphor,* is a common *figure of speech.* Unlike a metaphor, a simile is a direct comparison. (An example of a metaphor is *Life is a roller coaster*).

Spatial order   A common method of paragraph organization involving the description of objects according to their relationships in space, such as from near to far, left to right, foreground to background, and high to low.

Style   The individual manner in which a writer expresses his or her ideas. Style includes such aspects of writing as word choice, sentence structure, organization, tone, and the use of figurative language.

Subjective   Reflecting personal feelings and interpretations (the opposite of *objective*).

Subordinating conjunction   A conjunction that introduces a dependent clause and shows its relationship to the independent clause. (Some examples of subordinating conjunctions are *although, because, while, when, until, whereas, though,* and *providing.*)

Suffix   A group of letters attached to the end of a word root (the basic part of a word), such as *-ment* in *development.* In general, adding a suffix to a word root changes the function of the word, or its *part of speech.* (A *prefix,* or group of letters attached to the beginning of a word root, usually changes the meaning of the word.)

Summary   A brief restatement in one's own words of the main ideas in a reading passage. A summary should be concise, accurate, objective, and coherent.

Supporting details   The evidence that supports, or backs up, a writer's generalizations, such as examples, statistics, facts, reasons, anecdotes, quotations, and definitions. Without these concrete details, a writer's ideas remain abstract and unconvincing. Whenever possible, good writers try to show rather than simply tell their readers what they mean.

Synonym   A word that has the same or nearly the same meaning as another word; for example, *begin* is a synonym for *start.* (Synonyms can also be phrases, such as *on the whole* and *by and large.*)

Synthesis   A type of *critical thinking* involving the combination of ideas in a way that shows the relationships among them.

Thesis   The main idea or point of an essay. In informative and persuasive writing, the thesis is usually stated in the introduction.

Thesis statement   A sentence that states the central idea of an essay and conveys the writer's attitude and purpose. The thesis statement usually appears at the end of the introduction.

Tone   The attitude of a writer toward his or her subject and audience as reflected in the choice of words and details. The tone of a piece of writing can be angry, playful, serious, informal, distant, ironic, cynical, sentimental, humorous, and so on.

Topic sentence   The sentence that states the main idea of a paragraph. Although the topic sentence usually appears at the beginning of a paragraph, it can also be in the middle or at the end. Some paragraphs lack a clearly stated topic sentence, with the main idea being implied, or suggested, through details.

Transition   A word or phrase that logically connects sentences, paragraphs, and larger divisions of an essay. Smooth transitions help authors achieve *coherence* in their writing. Common transitional devices used to create connections within and between sentences include: (1) use of transitional words and phrases, such as *finally, moreover, for example, however,* and *as a result;* (2) repetition of a key word or phrase; (3) use of a pronoun to refer to a noun or other pronoun; and (4) use of *parallel structure.*

Unity   A quality of good writing that is achieved when all of the sentences and paragraphs in an essay support its thesis, or main idea.

Word choice   The words that a writer selects to express his or her ideas (also called *diction*). Whenever possible, experienced writers try to use concrete words to make their writing vivid and clear.

Word root   The basic part of a word to which a *prefix* and/or *suffix* is attached; for example, *graph* is the root of *autograph.*

Writing process   The process of writing an essay, involving four stages: (1) *exploring and planning,* (2) *drafting,* (3) *revising,* and (4) *editing and proofreading.*

Acknowledgments (continued from page iv)

Page 46, John Godfrey Saxe, "The Blind Men and the Elephant: A Hindu Fable" from the Preface to *Cultural Awareness Training Techniques* by Jan Gaston (Brattleboro, VT: Pro Lingua Associates, 1984). Reprinted with the permission of the publishers.

Page 53, Martin Luther King, Jr., "I Have a Dream." Copyright © 1963 by Martin Luther King, Jr., renewed 1991 by Coretta Scott King. Reprinted with the permission of The Heirs to the Estate of Martin Luther King, Jr., c/o Joan Daves Agency.

Page 65, Barbara Kantrowitz, et al., "Striking a Nerve," *Newsweek* (October 21, 1991). Copyright © 1991 by Newsweek, Inc. Reprinted with the permission of *Newsweek.*

Page 80, Jeanne Wakatsuki Houston and James D. Houston, "It Cannot Be Helped" from *Farewell to Mazanar.* Originally titled "Shikata Ga Nai." Copyright © 1973 by James D. Houston. Reprinted with the permission of Houghton Mifflin Company.

Page 89, Jonathan Kaufman, "Eleven Words That Cast the Power of Bigotry on Honeymoon Couple" from *The Boston Globe.* Reprinted with the permission of *The Boston Globe.*

Page 92, Maya Angelou, "Caged Bird" from *Shaker, Why Don't You Sing?* Copyright © 1983 by Maya Angelou. Reprinted with the permission of Random House, Inc., and Virago Press Ltd.

Page 98, Hamilton McCubbin and Barbara Blum Dahl, "Sex Roles" excerpted from *Marriage and Family: Individuals and Life Cycles.* Copyright © 1985 by John Wiley & Sons, Inc. Reprinted with the permission of Prentice-Hall, Inc., from the Macmillan college text.

Page 114, Susan Chira, "New Realities Fight Old Images of Mother," *The New York Times* (October 4, 1992). Copyright © 1992 by The New York Times Company. Reprinted with the permission of *The New York Times.*

Page 129, Noel Perrin, "The Androgynous Male," *The New York Times Magazine* (February 5, 1984). Copyright © 1984 by The New York Times Company. Reprinted with the permission of *The New York Times.*

Page 133, Charles Perrault, "Cinderella" from *Fairy Tales,* translated by Geoffrey Brereton. Copyright © 1957 by Geoffrey Brereton. Reprinted with the permission of Penguin Books Ltd.

Page 138, Carol Barkalow, "Women Have What It Takes," *Newsweek* (August 5, 1991). Reprinted by permission.

Page 140, Warren Farrell, "Men Have the Power—Why Would They Want to Change?" pages 3–8, Chapter 1, *Why Men Are the Way They Are: The Male-Female Dynamic* by Warren Farrell. Copyright © 1986 by McGraw-Hill, Inc. Reprinted by permission of the publisher.

Page 149, Ruth Sidel, excerpt from Chapter 1, "The New American Dreamers" from *On Her Own: Growing Up in the Shadow of the American Dream.* Copyright © 1990 by Ruth Sidel. Reprinted with the permission of Viking, a division of Penguin Books USA Inc.

Page 162, Patrick Fenton, "Confessions of a Working Stiff," *New York* (April, 1973). Copyright © 1973 by New York Magazine Company. Reprinted with the permission of the author, 21 Litchfield Avenue, Elmont, NY 11003.

Page 177, Tom Mashberg, "Worker Poll Shows Family, Fringes Gain Favor," *The Boston Globe* (September 3, 1993). Copyright © 1993 by Globe Newspaper Company. Reprinted with the permission of *The Boston Globe.*

Page 182, William E. Barrett, "Señor Payroll," *Autumn Southwest Review.* Copyright 1943 by Southern Methodist University Press. Reprinted with the permission of Harold Ober Associates Incorporated.

Page 185, Marge Piercy, "To Be of Use" from *Circles on the Water.* Copyright © 1982 by Marge Piercy. Reprinted with the permission of Alfred A. Knopf, Inc. and the Wallace Literary Agency.

Page 191, John Holt, "School Is Bad for Children," *The Saturday Evening Post* (February 8, 1969). Copyright © 1969 by The Saturday Evening Post Company. Reprinted with the permission of The Saturday Evening Post Society.

Page 202, Carol Simons, "They Get by with a Lot of Help from Their Kyoiku Mamas," *Smithsonian* (March 1987). Copyright © 1987 by Carol Simons. Reprinted with the permission of the author.

Page 217, Nicholas Gage, "The Teacher Who Changed My Life," *Parade* (December 17, 1989). Adapted from the book *A Place for Us.* Copyright © 1989 by Nicholas Gage. Reprinted with the permission of Houghton Mifflin Company.

Page 224, Kate Lombardi, "Reading, Writing, and Arithmetic and, Now, Right and Wrong," *The New York Times* (November 29, 1992), Westchester section. Copyright © 1992 by The New York Times Company. Reprinted with the permission of *The New York Times.*

Page 228, Harold Courlander, "Coyote and the Crying Song" from *People of the Short Blue Corn: Tales and Legends of the Hopi Indians* (New York: Harcourt, 1970). Copyright © 1970 by Harold Courlander. Reprinted with the permission of the author.

Illustration Credits

Page 25, Peter de Sève illustration from *In Health* (September/October 1990). Reprinted by permission of the illustrator.

Page 47, Deena R. Levine and Mara B. Adelman, figure "The Adjustment Process in a New Culture" from *Beyond Language: Cross-Cultural Communication, Second Edition.* Copyright © 1993 by Prentice-Hall, Inc. Adapted with the permission of the publishers.

Page 93, Jules Feiffer cartoon. Copyright © 1985 by Jules Feiffer. Reprinted with the permission of Universal Press Syndicate. All rights reserved.

Page 145, Cathy Guisewite cartoon. Copyright © 1986 by Universal Press Syndicate. Reprinted with permission. All rights reserved.

Page 186, P. Steiner cartoon from *The New Yorker* (July 2, 1990). Copyright © 1990 by The New Yorker Magazine, Inc. Reprinted with the permission of *The New Yorker.*

Page 230, PEANUTS® by Charles M. Schulz. Copyright © 1994 by United Features Syndicate. Reprinted by permission of United Features Syndicate, Inc.

INDEX

Accurate and effective words, 248
Addition
    transitional words and phrases,
        260
Adjective clause, 249, 269
Adverb clause, 249, 269
Althen, Gary, 4–14
"American Values and Assumptions"
    (Althen), 4–14
Analysis, 269
    in cubing, 239
"Androgynous Male, The" (Perrin),
    129–132
Angelou, Maya, 92–93
Antonyms, 269
    context clues, 264
Application
    in cubing, 239
Argument
    in cubing, 239
Argumentative (persuasive) essay, 15,
    269
Association
    in cubing, 239
Audience in writing, 57, 246, 269

Barkalow, Carol, 138–140
Barrett, William E., 182–185
"Blind Men and the Elephant: A
    Hindu Fable, The" (Saxe), 46–47

Body of an essay, 244
Brainstorming, 236–237. *See also*
    Exploring and planning an
    essay

"Caged Bird" (Angelou), 92–93
Cause and effect, 270
    pattern of organization, 244
    transitional words and phrases,
        261
Chira, Susan, 114–121
Chronological order, 270
    paragraph arrangement, 244
    transitional words and phrases,
        260
"Cinderella" (Perrault), 133–138
Citation of sources, 249
Clarity in writing, 246
Classification, 270
    pattern of organization, 244
Cliché
    avoiding, 248, 270
Clustering, 237–238. *See also* Explor-
    ing and planning an essay
Coherence in writing, 247
    paragraphs, 15, 244
    transitional words and phrases,
        260–261
    types of transitions, 277
Comma splice, 249, 270

Comparison and contrast, 270
    in cubing, 239
    pattern of organization, 244
    transitional words and phrases,
        261
Concession, 270
    transitional words and phrases,
        261
Conclusion
    of an essay, 244–245
    transitional words and phrases,
        261
Concrete words, 248. *See also* Sup-
    porting details
Condition
    transitional words and phrases,
        261
"Confessions of a Working Stiff" (Fen-
    ton), 162–168
Connotation, 157–158, 271
Context clues, 262–267
    definitions of words, 265–267
    general context, 267
    words used in contrast, 264–265
    words with a similar meaning,
        263–264
Coordinating conjunctions, 249, 271
Courlander, Harold, 228–230
"Coward, A" (Premchand), 34–41
"Coyote and the Crying Song," 228–
    230
Cubing, 238–239. *See also* Exploring
    and planning an essay
Cultural adjustment, 47–48
Culture shock, 47–48

Dahl, Barbara Blum, 98–105
Davis, Lisa, 24–27
Definition, 271
    as a context clue, 211–212, 265–
        267
    direct, 265–266
    indirect, 266–267
    pattern of organization, 244

Denotation, 157, 271
Description, 271
    in cubing, 239
    pattern of organization, 244
Development in writing, 247
    paragraphs, 15, 244, 247
Division, 271
    pattern of organization, 244
Drafting an essay, 240–245
    body, 244
    conclusion, 244–245
    introduction, 242–243
    questions to consider before start-
        ing an essay, 241
    questions to keep in mind while
        drafting an essay, 242
    writing an outline, 241
    writing a thesis statement, 241

Editing and proofreading an essay,
    248–249
    editing checklist, 248–249
"Eleven Words That Cast the Power
    of Bigotry on Honeymoon Couple"
    (Kaufman), 89–91
Emphasis
    transitional words and phrases,
        261
Emphatic order, 272
    paragraph arrangement, 244
Essay, 272
    argumentative (persuasive), 15,
        269
    body paragraphs, 244
    conclusion, 244–245
    drafting, 240–245
    editing and proofreading,
        248–249
    exploring and planning, 234–240
    informative (expository), 15, 273
    introduction, 242–243
    narrative, 273
    revising, 245–248
    structure, 242–245

Evaluation, 268, 272
  of writing, 268
Example, 272
  transitional words and phrases, 260
Exploring and planning an essay,
    234–240
  brainstorming, 236–237
  clustering, 237–238
  cubing, 238–239
  freewriting, 235–236
  informal outlining, 240
  using the journalist's questions,
    239–240

Farrell, Warren, 140–144
Feiffer, Jules, 93
Fenton, Patrick, 162–168
Figures of speech (figurative lan-
    guage), 154–155
  metaphor, 41–42, 61–62, 154–
    155, 169, 210
  simile, 41, 61, 154, 169, 174–175
Freewriting, 235–236. *See also* Ex-
  ploring and planning an essay

Gage, Nicholas, 217–221
Grammar problems, 249
Guisewite, Cathy, 145

Holt, John, 191–196
Houston, Jeanne Wakatsuki, and
  James D., 80–87

Idiom, 181
"I Have a Dream" (King), 53–56
Illustration, 272
  pattern of organization, 244
  transitional words and phrases,
    260
Image, 155, 273
Inference, 17, 58, 108, 156, 196–197
Informal outlining, 240. *See also* Ex-
  ploring and planning an essay; Out-
  lining

Informative (expository) essay, 15,
  273
Introduction of an essay, 242–243
Irony, 58, 273
"It Cannot Be Helped" (Houston),
  80–87

Journalist's questions, 239–240

Kantrowitz, Barbara, 65–73
Kaufman, Jonathan, 89–91
King, Martin Luther, Jr., 53–56

Lombardi, Kate Stone, 224–228

McCubbin, Hamilton, 98–105
Main ideas, 14
  in outlines, 250–251
  in paragraphs (topic sentences),
    15
  in summarizing, 254–255
  supported by details, 16
Mashberg, Tom, 177–181
Mechanics in writing, 249
"Men Have the Power—Why Would
  They Want to Change?" (Farrell),
  140–144
Metaphor, 154–155. *See also* Figures
  of speech
  examples of, 41–42, 61–62, 169,
    210

Narration, 273
  pattern of organization, 244
Narrative essay, 273
"New American Dreamers, The"
  (Sidel), 149–154
"New Realities Fight Old Images of
  Mother" (Chira), 114–121
Noun clause, 249, 269
Noun forms, 75–76

Objectivity in writing, 58, 74, 211.
  See also Subjectivity in writing

Organization
  of essays, 242–245
  of paragraphs, 15, 244, 247
Outlining, 250–253
  formal, 251–253
  informal, 240, 251–252
Overusing words and expressions, 249

Paragraphs, 15, 244
  body, 244
  coherence, 15, 244
  concluding, 244–245
  development, 15, 244
  introductory, 242–243
  organization, 15, 244
  topic sentence, 15, 244
  unity, 15, 244
Parallel structure, 247, 274
Paraphrasing, 257–259
  figures of speech, 41–43, 169–170
  sentences, 107–108, 123–124
Parts of speech, 132–133, 249
Perrault, Charles, 133–138
Perrin, Noel, 129–132
Phrasal verbs, 87
Piercy, Marge, 185–186
Place
  transitional words and phrases, 261
Plagiarism, 249, 275
Preconception, 20
Prefixes, 18–19, 109–111, 265
  clue to word meaning, 109–111, 265
  negative, 18–19, 265
Premchand, 34–41
Prewriting strategies, 234–240
Process analysis, 275
  pattern of organization, 244
Pronoun
  as transitional device, 247, 277
Proverbs, 21
Purpose in writing, 57, 246

"Reading, Writing, and Arithmetic and, Now, Right and Wrong" (Lombardi), 224–228
Repetition
  unnecessary, 249
Restatement
  in conclusion, 244
  transitional words and phrases, 261
Revising an essay, 245–248
  revision checklist, 246–248
Run-on sentence (fused sentence), 249, 275

Sarcasm, 58–59, 276
Saxe, John Godfrey, 46–47
"School Is Bad for Children" (Holt), 191–196
Schultz, Charles M., 230
"Señor Payroll" (Barrett), 182–185
Sentence fragment, 249, 276
Sentence length, 249
Sentence structure, 249
"Sex Roles" (McCubbin and Dahl), 98–105
"Sex, Sighs, and Conversation: Why Men and Women Can't Communicate" (Tannen), 43–45
Sidel, Ruth, 149–154
Simile, 154. *See also* Figures of speech
  examples of, 41, 61, 169, 174–175
Simons, Carol, 202–210
Spatial order, 276
  paragraph arrangement, 244
Specific words, 248. *See also* Supporting details
Steiner, P., 186
Stereotype, 20, 50, 63
"Striking a Nerve" (Kantrowitz), 65–73
Style, 64, 276
Subjectivity in writing, 58, 74, 211. *See also* Objectivity in writing

Subordinating conjunctions, 249, 276
Suffixes, 18, 76, 109–111
    changing verbs to nouns, 76
    clue to word meaning, 109–111
Summarizing, 254–256
    essays and articles, 254–256
    paragraphs, 106–107, 122–123
    transitional words and phrases,
        261
Supporting details, 16, 28–29, 210,
    276
Synonyms, 197–198, 276
    context clues, 263
    paraphrasing, 258
Synthesis, 48, 93, 145, 187, 231, 276

Tannen, Deborah, 43–45
"Teacher Who Changed My Life, The"
    (Gage), 217–221
Thesis statement, 241
"They Get by with a Lot of Help from
    Their Kyoiku Mamas" (Simons),
    202–210
Three-word verbs, 87
Time
    paragraph arrangement (chrono-
        logical order), 244
    transitional words and phrases,
        260
Title of an essay, 248
"To Be of Use" (Piercy), 185–186
Tone, 58–59, 74, 170, 211, 248
Topic sentence, 15, 244
Transition, 260–261, 277

transitional words and phrases,
    260–261
See also Coherence in writing
Two-word verbs, 87

Unity in writing, 246–247
    paragraphs, 15, 244, 246
Usage in writing, 249

Vague words
    avoiding, 248
Value judgment, 22
Verb forms, 75–76

"Where Do We Stand?" (Davis), 24–
    27
"Women Have What It Takes"
    (Barkalow), 138–140
Word choice, 248–249
Wordiness
    avoiding, 249
Word parts, 18–19, 109–111
    prefix, 18, 109
    root, 18, 109
    suffix, 18, 109
Word root
    clue to word meaning, 18, 109
"Worker Poll Shows Family, Fringes
    Gain Favor" (Mashberg), 177–181
Writing Process, 233–249
    drafting, 240–245
    editing and proofreading, 248–249
    exploring and planning, 234–240
    revising, 245–248